When History Is a Nightmare

When History Is a Nightmare

Lives and Memories of Ethnic Cleansing in Bosnia-Herzegovina

STEVAN M. WEINE

RUTGERS UNIVERSITY PRESS
New Brunswick, New Jersey, and London

Library of Congress Cataloging-in-Publication Data

Weine, Stevan M., 1961–
    When history is a nightmare : lives and memories of ethnic
cleansing in Bosnia-Herzegovina / by Stevan M. Weine.
        p.   cm.
    Includes bibliographical references and index.
    ISBN 0–8135–2675–2 (cloth : alk. paper).—ISBN 0–8135–2676–0
(pbk. : alk. paper)
    1. Post-traumatic stress disorder—Bosnia and Hercegovina.
2. Yugoslav War, 1991–1995—Bosnia and Hercegovina—Psychological
aspects.   3. Yugoslav War, 1991–1995—Bosnia and Hercegovina—
Atrocities.   4. Genocide—Bosnia and Herzegovina—Psychological
aspects.   5. Victims of state-sponsored terrorism—Mental health—
Bosnia and Hercegovina.   6. Yugoslav War, 1991–1995—Refugees—
Mental health. I. Title.
RC552.P67W45 1999
616.85'212—dc21   98–50650
                                                                                              CIP

British Cataloging-in-Publication data for this book is available from the British Library

Manufactured in the United States of America

To those Bosnian survivors who shared their stories in the hope of improving lives and history; to D. and K., elders who inspired and guided me on my life's journey, and children who inspire through their own quests for becoming; and to L., for her continued love and companionship

Contents

Epilogue   *223*

Preface

I'M OFTEN ASKED, "What led you to do all this work with Bosnians? Are you Bosnian?" When I answer that I am an American Jew, I'm then asked, "But does your family come from there?" No, my grandparents immigrated to the United States early in this century from several other places in Eastern Europe.

But there is a connection between my life and my work that comes alive when I am sitting with a Bosnian refugee. Sometimes my mind drifts and I feel as if my grandmother Kate—once an immigrant child full of dreams of life in a strange, new country—is sitting and talking with me. *Do not ever forget who you are*, she said to me one of the last times we were together. I was twenty-three, a medical student, and could not really know what she meant.

In listening to the Bosnians struggling over memories and identity, sometimes I feel I am listening to her. I expected that my work with Bosnians would be difficult; what I didn't anticipate was that it would engage this question and nurture a connection with memories that are so central to the history that has shaped my life and the life of my family. But that's another story.

For the past five years, my work as a psychiatrist has centered on clinical testimonial and research work with Bosnian survivors of ethnic cleansing. This work grew out of a personal commitment I made upon realizing that Serbian nationalists were committing the crime of genocide in Bosnia-Herzegovina.[1] Like many others, I felt morally outraged by this explosion of human cruelty, and by the unwillingness of governments to intervene to stop the horror. My work with Bosnians has been my response, my attempt to support these survivors and to oppose ethnic cleansing.

This book, which grew out of my work with Bosnians, reflects my different levels of involvement with survivors and witnesses to genocide in Bosnia-Herzegovina. Bosnia has been an important part of my professional work; it has also become a big part of my life. My family has developed close friendships with many Bosnian people. I have spent too much time away from home, traveling and working in Bosnia-Herzegovina. All this is inseparable from the call to advocacy work in support of Bosnians and in opposition to ethnic cleansing, to which so many Bosnians, internationals, and Americans have responded.[2] My life changed tremendously as a result of all these involvements. The experience has been simultaneously exciting, grueling, sickening, and inspiring.

This book is not written as an academic text based on my psychiatric research experience. The challenges of knowing this genocide are far too great to be contained within conventional psychiatric paradigms. Writing this text has been part of my search to find a new way of being professional in relation to mass political violence, its survivors and its witnesses—a way of being professional that takes into account both the moral engagement and the life involvement familiar to many who work with trauma survivors.[3] Also, like other scholars, I wanted to find a way to begin to understand the traumatization not just of individuals, but of a whole society and its culture.[4]

To this end I use stories and a biographical approach. The narrative voice and the biographical structure are capable of supporting a reality, a complexity, and a truth often lost in the more analytical forms of discourse common to my profession. My book includes stories told by survivors, promoters, and witnesses of ethnic cleansing. The intent is to give the reader direct access to actual voices, and to better show how ethnic cleansing has worked its way into people's lives and memories.

Being a psychiatrist helped to prepare me to listen to stories about lives darkened by the nightmare of ethnic cleansing. A psychiatrist's most valuable instrument is the open-ended interview conducted with intense curiosity; close, detailed listening; and high tolerance for complexities.[5] Over the years I have sought a way of talking with people about their lives that has moved away from psychoanalytic or diagnostic formulations to draw more upon historical, literary, anthropological, and biographical approaches—a way that encourages people to tell stories about who they are, and to reflect on the presence of history in their lives. In developing this approach I have been most grateful to Daniel Levinson, Ivan Pavkovic, Tvrtko Kulenovic, and Robert Jay Lifton for their insights.

Some of the stories in this text came from persons I saw in clinical work, some from persons I saw in a research capacity, some from acquaintances or interesting people I chanced to meet.[6] The resulting set of dialogues was strung together in the fabric of my life by a combination of curiosity, commitment, and chance. Several stories were gathered from secondary sources, including information about Bosnia-Herzegovina available via the mass media, the Internet, books, films, and other cultural documents.[7]

I had the good fortune of learning about the testimony approach of listening to survivors from the psychoanalyst and survivor Dori Laub and others who were involved with the Fortunoff Video Archive for Holocaust Testimonies at Yale University. Beginning in 1979, a group of psychotherapists and scholars started doing videotestimony interviews with Holocaust survivors. Dori Laub characterized the listener as "a companion in a journey onto an uncharted land, a journey the survivor cannot traverse or return from alone."[8] The kind of listening evident in the Holocaust testimony work—engaged but unobtrusive, nondirective but committed—seemed to me a good way to start to work with and learn from the survivors of ethnic cleansing in Bosnia-Herzegovina.

This way of listening to survivors became an object of study for the literary scholars Shoshana Felman, Lawrence Langer, and Geoffrey Hartman, who found themselves fascinated by the kind of communication found in the testimonies.[9] According to Hartman, listening facilitates a "welling-up of memories" (p. 145) that carry a unique knowing, whereby "the immediacy of these first-person accounts burns through the 'cold storage of history'" (p. 138). Like these and other scholars who make explorations in traumatic memory, I am searching for meanings that emerge indirectly. The approach is as literary as it is scientific; dialogic, not monologic.[10] It views the human landscape of Bosnia as a collage of many parts, many shades, and many realities. As an outsider looking in, I try to balance the need for recording the complexity and chaos with the demands of achieving clarity and interpretation.

Although this work has involved extensive travel in Bosnia-Herzegovina and Croatia, my journey into ethnic cleansing took place largely through talking with some of the many Bosnian refugees who resettled in the United States. The importance of this fact goes well beyond my own convenience. It is one marker of some crucial changes in our world that are central to this inquiry.

We often act as if these world events are far away, when in actuality survivors of ethnic cleansing are living right here beside us. By stepping outside the university clinic and going to meet with refugees in their homes or cafes, I came to realize that they are as near (or far) as I allow them to be. It is not only the mass media revolution and the information revolution that are changing our world; America is experiencing the largest immigration wave in its history. We can also see remarkable transformations in our society wrought by previous immigration waves, as our diversity continues to increase. Many immigrants come to the United States as refugees of political violence. Having become familiar with Bosnians and their culture, I now spot them on the beach, at the supermarket, waiting at stoplights, joined to the flow of American life.

Ethnic cleansing in Bosnia is a wake-up call from the nightmares history is now bringing home to us. Abroad, the fall of communism and the resurgence of nationalism in places like Yugoslavia, Rwanda, India, Pakistan, Russia, and China confronts the United States with new foreign policy challenges: how should we deal with the unexpected return of the nightmares of nationalism and genocide? At home, experiencing radical change due to the immigration of new peoples and the upward social mobility of existing minority populations, the United States must choose how to deal with the domestic challenges brought by diversity. This book prescribes no easy answers or quick remedies for these problems in Bosnia-Herzegovina and around the world; there are none. Still, I hope I can put forth here an understanding of and a sensibility about the importance of memories of collective traumatization that helps us better face our nightmares and make good our dreams.

Acknowledgments

THIS BOOK would not have come about without the mentoring I received, during my years at the Columbia University College of Physicians and Surgeons, from David Forrest and the late Jerry Maxmen, who helped me to find an interdisciplinary path into psychiatry. Also invaluable was the amazing Allen Ginsberg, who befriended and guided a young medical student wanting to learn about madness and poetry. At Yale University, I then had the extraordinary good fortune of seven years of mentorship from Daniel Levinson until his sudden death in 1994. I will never forget the supernatural extra brilliant intelligent kindness of his soul ("Footnote to 'Howl,'" Allen Ginsberg). I am also very grateful to have received needed support and guidance from Dori Laub, Mort Reiser, Donald Faulkner, Ira Levine, Marshal Edelson, Steve Bunney, Linda Schwartz, Helen Sayward, Ira Moses, and Dan Becker. There were invaluable conversations with Zlatko Dizdarevic, Richard Mollica, Alexandra Milenov, Steven Teich, Dolores Vojdvoda, and especially Karen Malpede and Robert Jay Lifton.

Many at the University of Illinois at Chicago have made this writing possible. I am most grateful to Boris Astrachan and Ivan Pavkovic. After Dan Levinson's legacy, it was impossible for me to believe that anyone could ever do what Ivan has actually done toward shaping and making real my dream for this work. My appreciation also goes to helpful colleagues including Joe Flaherty, Phillip Woolcott, Prakash Desai, Surinder Nand, and David Kopacz. A Faculty Fellowship at the UIC Institute for Humanities, with Linda Vavra and Gene Ruoff, gave me time to write and helped to connect me with an interdisciplinary community of scholars. The Illinois Department of Human Services, University of Illinois at Chicago, West Side Veterans Administration, Heartland Alliance, Chicago Health Outreach, Bosnian Refugee Center, Jerome Frankel Foundation, and Segal Family Foundation all helped to make the work possible.

So many Bosnian people let me into their lives and showed remarkable generosity toward me and my work. I am grateful in more ways than I can say to Emir Hodzic, Amer Smajkic, Zvezdana Djuric-Bijedic and Nebojsa Bijedic, Alma Dzubur, Tvrtko Kulenovic, Ismet Ceric, Slobodan Loga, Arif and Sabra Smajkic, Ibro Spahic, Azra and Enver Bijedic, Azra and Lutvo Dzubur, Ferida Durakovic, Aida Musanovic, Affin Ramic, Edin Numankadic, Kemal Hadzic, Sanjin Jukic, Obala Gallery, Senad Agic, and Zumra Kunosic. Tvrtko Kulenovic has helped in so many ways as a reader, translator, teacher, and collaborator.

The staff at Rutgers University Press have been consistently helpful and supportive. Doreen Valentine, Leslie Mitchner, Marilyn Campbell, and Evan P. Young all made special contributions. Yael Danieli and Jerrold Post helped greatly in bringing the book to fruition.

Grateful acknowledgment is made to Svjetlost for permission to reprint previously published material: *Mad Spear*, 1968; *Remembrance of the Century*, 1971; *Black Fairy Tale*, 1990. Parts of this book have drawn from articles I wrote in a number of journals and collected volumes. I would like to thank the following editors for their suggestions and support: Arif Tanovic at *Dijalog*; Michael T. Kaufman at *Transitions*; David Reiss at *Psychiatry*; Suzanne Poirier at *Literature and Medicine*; Bill Frelick at *World Refugee Survey*; Arnold Cooper at the *American Journal of Psychiatry*; David Kideckel and Joel Halpern, co-editors of *War in Former Yugoslavia: Culture and Conflict* (Penn State University Press); and Charles Strozier and Micheal Flynn, co-editors of *Genocide, War, and Human Survival* (Rowman and Littlefield).

Laura Frankel, Daniella and Kate Weine, David and Esther Weine, and Rhoda and Jerry Frankel deserve high praise for their incredible tolerance and loving support during several years of writing.

Above all I want to thank all the Bosnian survivors who met and spoke with me. I cannot give your names, but let it be said that this book could never have been written without you.

When History Is a Nightmare

Prologue

Survivors of ethnic cleansing often speak of their experience as a nightmare. They mean this in two senses: personally and historically. In this book I intend to deal primarily with the historical nightmares, and yet, since the two are essentially inseparable, I must also address the personal nightmares.[1]

The attempt to explain why ethnic cleansing occurred in Bosnia has become a central challenge for our time. This ethnic cleansing is seen as a signal event of momentous import, potentially resulting in global transformations in identity, nationality, and religion; it is unarguably the most horrific of all the extraordinary events that have shaken post-communist Europe.

There are two conventional explanations for what happened in Bosnia-Herzegovina. One is that it is basically a perpetuation of ancient ethnic hatreds. The Balkans, considered the most backward and primitive corner of Europe, are known for centuries of hatred and bloodshed. Their relative quiescence for the forty-five years after World War II was due to communist oppression. With the collapse of European communism, the true Balkan nature resurfaced, and the rivers ran red. The essential problem lies in the nature of Bosnia, if not all Balkan civilization; the region is seen as totally captive to historical memories of ethnic atrocities. There is no reason to believe that it will ever be any different; indeed, with the recent accumulation of more dead, the future is likely to be even worse.

The other common perception is that Bosnia was a utopian multi-ethnic society that suffered from sequential betrayals, first by its former fellow Yugoslavs and Bosnians, and then by its Western allies. The problem lies not in Bosnia per se but in the inability of others to respect it; in the Serbian and Croatian nationalists who raped an innocent Bosnia; and in the international community, especially the United Nations Protectorate Forces (mockingly called "Blue Helmets" by Sarajevans),[2] which stood by and did less than nothing to stop the killing. Before being victimized, Bosnia was a paragon of multi-ethnic living, having successfully reinvented itself after the terrible slaughters of World War II, not to mention many other prior historical legacies of violence, by effectively putting away the memories of ethnic atrocities. Bosnia today has been irreparably shattered by ethnic cleansing, by a world that is not good enough for it.

Neither explanation is satisfactory; both are at best only partial truths. They offer a unidimensional view of the social functions of memories of collective traumatization. Memories are either so present that they totally dominate, or so absent that they are totally irrelevant. Black or white.

Neither explanation takes adequate account of the processes through which a society and its individuals deal with historical memories. In order to have a better understanding of the nightmare of ethnic cleansing in Bosnia, I believe we must develop a more complex and nuanced view of the dilemmas of memories in the Bosnian experience, at both public and personal levels. We must therefore take a close and detailed look at some of the stories Bosnian people tell about themselves and their country. These narratives are by no means simple, straightforward, objective accounts of historical experience; rather, they are subjective, contingent constructions that are full of contradictions. The success of this inquiry very much depends upon the sense I am able to make of these complexities, and especially of the dilemmas of memory present in these narratives.

This inquiry comprises three primary claims: (1) A central component of the modern Bosnian experience has been the struggle to reconcile the historical experiences of living together with those of ethnic atrocities, and to use what understandings come of that struggle to define what it means to be Bosnian. (2) Cultural elites, including psychiatrists, manipulated historical and personal memories as an important part of the ethnic nationalist movement that culminated in ethnic cleansing. (3) The task of recovery from ethnic cleansing must involve cultural elites, again including psychiatrists, working with collective memories of traumatization so as to better define their place in Bosnian collective experience and to redefine Bosnian identity. My approach to these topics relies on a number of concepts articulated by several scholars in different corners of contemporary intellectual work on the significance of memory in shaping human life and history.

The sociologist Kai Erikson has described "collective traumas," by which he means traumas that not only affect individuals directly, but are "a blow to the basic tissues of social life that damages the bonds attaching people together and impairs the prevailing sense of community."[3] Robert Lifton's pioneering studies of the collective traumas of Holocaust and Hiroshima investigated psychohistorical dislocations, "the breakdown of social and institutional arrangements that ordinarily anchor human lives."[4] The central dilemma in the cold-war era catastrophes Lifton has studied was "the imagery of extinction of the human species versus the creation of a human future."[5]

In the past fifty years, Bosnia has survived the collective traumas of war and genocide twice: 1941 to 1945 and 1992 to 1996. There was also bloodshed before then. Genocide in Bosnia, however, was never the Holocaust in the sense that it has not been "eliminationist," à la Daniel Goldhagen.[6] After World War II, Bosnians experienced forty-five years of peace and relative prosperity in the Second Yugoslavia built by Tito, and settled into a way of life many have praised. The central threat in the Bosnian collective traumas of this century was not so much biological extinction, although there were indeed mass murders, but the shattering of a multi-ethnic way of life and its culture, and its replacement by the order of ethnic nationalism.

This raises another issue, concerning how nations deal with the tension between human diversity and national unity. The sociologist Edward Tiryakian has described this tension, and its interaction with religion, ethnicity, and race as a potent "cultural bundle" that can do both great harm and great good.[7] The historian Benedict Anderson characterized the nation as "an imagined political community,"[8] and Tiryakian described it as "the cognitive creation of literary and other cultural elites cum resistance leaders" (Tiryakian, 155). Communities are bound together not only by demographic factors, such as race, religion, ethnicity, and economics, but by something that lies in the culture people share, including the stories they tell one another about who they are as a nation.

Holocaust scholars, contemplating the persistence of a culture after mass traumatization, have spoken of a "collective memory."[9] This collective memory is a slippery concept, belonging more to humanists than to historians, more to "ritual memory" than to "historiography" (Hartman, 8). It is thought of as a "living deposit" (Hartman, 106), or after Walter Benjamin as "an uninterrupted or self-reparative process of handing down wisdom from generation to generation" (Hartman, 29). James Young, who studied Holocaust memorials, is correct to point out that this kind of memory is not "monolithic," but "textured" with "many layers and dimensions."[10] One of the most important layers has to do with the differences across generational boundaries. At issue here is not only the transmission of traumatic memories but also the transmission of the totality of culture upon which a people's survival depends.[11]

In order to understand how ethnic cleansing could occur in Bosnia, we must explore the collective memory associated with multi-ethnic living there. I cannot accept either of the assumptions I mentioned above—that Bosnia is a multi-ethnic utopia, or that it is a hellhole of ethnic hatreds. Given that one of the consequences of the destruction of Yugoslavia and the ethnic cleansing in Bosnia is the shattering of certain culturally anchored narratives, it should be possible to discover shades and facets of a collective experience that just a few years ago would have been presented as simply the way things were. In Part One of this book I explore stories about the experience of living together in Bosnia-Herzegovina, stories about ethnic cleansing, and stories about being a refugee. When individual Bosnians talk about these experiences, we learn about misery and destruction, but also about the imagery and knowing and moral crises that come of the effects of collective traumatization on people's lives and memories, which after all are the building blocks of history.[12]

The controversial political theorist Carl Schmitt's insights on "friends and enemies" suggest a way to understand the place of memories of collective traumatization in relation to the sense of communality in Bosnia-Herzegovina.[13] Schmitt writes that all human societies have a political dimension that can be reduced to the distinctions made between public "friend and enemy" (Schmitt, 26). Schmitt writes: "A people which exists in the political sphere cannot, despite entreating declarations to the contrary, escape from making this fateful distinction. If a part of the population declares that it no longer recognizes enemies, then, depending on the circumstance, it joins their side and aids them" (Schmitt, 51).

Schmitt assists us in seeing that there have been major problems concerning the place of memories in the mentalities and political culture of Bosnia during the Tito era, as well as in the subsequent crisis of trust in the post-Dayton Bosnian milieu. This can further our understanding of what made ethnic cleansing possible, and can also suggest ways of responding to the challenges of remembering in its aftermath.

However, I must confess that I have no desire to carry these claims as far as to psychologize the historical, social, cultural, and political phenomenon at hand. It does not make sense to me to deploy the language and concepts of psychoanalysis. Nor does it make sense to either reconceive these theories or create a new theoretical system.[14] I have not yet gained enough distance from the Bosnian experience to accommodate such a project, and it is not possible for me to impose that distance right now. I am aiming to create a different kind of experience and understanding for readers, one that sticks closer to the words and meanings in the stories of those whose lives are marked by the historical nightmare of ethnic cleansing.

After developing an understanding of the Bosnian landscape of memory, I look into the world of Serbian ethnic nationalism, to consider the place of memory in a nationalist movement. Part Two presents a series of three "case studies" (though not in the psychopathological sense) involving psychiatrists and psychiatric professionals who have been active in the Serbian nationalist movement. I certainly do not mean to declare (as does the Scientologists' Citizens Commission for Human Rights[15]) or even suggest that psychiatrists caused ethnic cleansing or that it could not have happened without them. I must confess that my choosing to examine them derives in part from my own curiosity, as a psychiatrist, about the practices and ethics of those who would be considered my colleagues. I do think the decision is justified; the role of psychiatrists in political violence and nationalism has been investigated by others, and the psychiatrists I will describe have in fact made important contributions to the Serbian nationalistic project and its ethnic cleansing.[16]

Armed with some understanding of the leadership, mentality, and narratives of nationalism that begot ethnic cleansing, we are better prepared to face the challenges of confronting the memories of ethnic cleansing in Part Three. Here I am again interested in possible psychiatric approaches, again partly for personal reasons, but also because of the work currently being done under the rubric of the international mental health and human rights movement.[17] In addition, I consider the activities of creative artists, who play a crucial role in representing, communicating, and humanizing the experiences of social traumatization. Finally, I look at community leaders in Bosnia and its Diaspora, who are playing a part in its awakening after ethnic cleansing, trying to confront the consequences of collective traumatization and to repair some of its vast and critical wounds.

Geoffrey Hartman said of Holocaust testimonies that "their real strength lies in recording the psychological and emotional milieu of the struggle for survival, not only then but also now."[18] I believe that through listening to individual survivors' testimonies, as well as the narratives produced by some cultural elites, leaders, and artists, we can develop a better understanding of the place of historical memory in the Bosnian experience. I want to believe that these same processes of inquiry can make a contribution toward a better future. If many survivors can give testimonies, and many others can receive, read, ponder and study them, and make art from them, it just may assist in a confrontation with the assault of trauma upon a collective memory that is perhaps one of the most endangered and essential elements of a better future.

Part I

Surviving Ethnic Cleansing

Introduction: Listening to History

If I had remained in my office at the psychiatric institute, they would never have come. To be able to work with Bosnian survivors I had to go outside and discover a whole new way of working, with much less professional distancing, and a greater sense of personal, social, and moral involvement. I had to cross some boundaries that are an intrinsic part of the psychiatric approach. But by doing so I came to know history in ways that would not have been possible had I observed the limits of my training.

One of the greatest rewards of this new venture has been the opportunity to work closely with Bosnian mental health workers in the United States. Refugees themselves, hired by the refugee service agency in Chicago with which I work, these people provide counseling, casework, and interpretation for other Bosnian refugees.[1] They are the bridge between American mental health professionals like me and the refugees we work with.

B. is one of these Bosnian mental health workers. Whenever there's a chance, the two of us like to slip off to a local cafe for some coffee and conversation. We talk about our work, or about the latest news from Bosnia. For the first few months of our relationship I learn very little about B.'s own story. I think it will just take some time. Afraid to make the mistake of pressuring him, I wait for signs that he is ready.

Something changes after I invite B. to join me in teaching a seminar on "Physician Witness to Genocide" to medical students at the University of Illinois at Chicago. He tells the students about his experiences living in Sarajevo during the siege. Hearing B.'s story for the first time, I see a side of him I have never seen before. Afterwards he seems shaken, unusually somber and quiet. I am not sure what to do. Is there a way for us to talk about all that he has been through, without him becoming the patient and me the doctor? We decide that he will tell me his story and I will listen to it and write it down. The story B. then tells me, of his life during the siege of Sarajevo, is not as extreme as many others I have heard, but it seems to bear some essence of the dilemmas of memory that are present in so many Bosnian peoples' lives.

Like many Sarajevans, B. prides himself on having been a part of that multi-ethnic cosmopolitan capital. He was a top student of the Academy and went on to study at the Medical Faculty. His family practiced Islam, B. says, *But we never practiced religion in a way that other people had to know. It was something we kept in our family and shared with our personal friends. From my childhood I had lots of friends. I never thought, is my friend Muslim, Serbian, or Croatian? It just depended on who was close to me. After doing my military service, when I established my identity and serious friendships, out of my five best friends, two were Muslims, one was Serbian, and two were Croatian.*[2] B. recalls that these identities were never evoked to characterize the person as something *other.* He would go to his Serb friends' house on Orthodox holidays to celebrate and drink slivovitz; they would join his family on Bajram.[3] That, he told me, is how he thought it always would be.

B. briefly mentions his grandfather, whom he had never met. Intrigued, I inquire further, and he tells me this was his mother's father, a merchant from Foča.[4] Then he tells me that this grandfather's head was severed on a bridge in Foča during World War II. A local Serb who had worked for him did it. The Chetniks had invaded their town. The grandfather had a chance to escape or hide, but chose to stay. The story goes that he hadn't done anything bad to anyone in his life, so why should he leave? *He stayed in his room. When the Chetniks came they took him to the bridge. His friend told him to jump in the river, and my grandfather said no. His friend jumped and survived, and my grandfather died on that bridge.*[5] The memory of that killing has been carried silently by the family for five decades. *My uncle knew the name of the guy who killed my grandfather, but they never spoke of it in front of me. I heard that he owns a restaurant somewhere in Austria. . . . My mother didn't like to speak about that.* B. then mentions in passing that his family often reminds him that he looks like his grandfather from Foča.

Fifty years later, in that same town, B.'s grandmother lost a son (B.'s uncle) to the Serb forces. A doctor in a town in Bosnia that had a Serbian majority, he was brutally murdered in July 1992. B. says of his grandmother, *And in fifty years she lost a husband and a son in two wars from the same people. Different persons with the same insignia, the same ideas, the same words on their lips when they knocked on her door.*

B. remained in Sarajevo for two years during the war, working as a surgeon.

Then suddenly he was presented with a chance to leave. Reluctantly, he took it. He had seen too many patients come back dead to the emergency room just days after he sutured them up. He had seen enough of war. He did not want to fight as a soldier. When the Americans offered to accept him as a refugee, he decided to go.

Compared to many other Bosnian refugees, B. had it easy. He was never in a concentration camp—although he will tell you that *Sarajevo is the biggest concentration camp in history*. He was not physically assaulted, raped, or injured. And when he got to America he landed on his feet, securing a good job within weeks.

At the time we first spoke, in 1995, B. was a refugee in America, a mental health worker serving other refugees, studying for exams that would let him complete his medical training in America. He expressed animosity toward Serbs: *It's very brutal for me. Behind the term "Serbian" stands a very strong genocidal policy and barbarian ideas. . . . For me that term Serbian is really something that evokes very dark colors and very dangerous things. Because of that I don't want to have contact with anything that bears the name "Serbian."* Yet B. maintains friendships with some Serbs from Bosnia—as long as they call themselves "Bosnian Orthodox," thus affirming their commitment to Bosnia as B. knew it, rather than to a Greater Serbia.

B. and I visit a Middle Eastern restaurant. B. tells me he doesn't like the way I use the words "multi-ethnic" and "multicultural." He prods me: do I know that by speaking those words I am buying into the idea that there are separate ethnic groups and separate cultures? Do I know that it wasn't that way in Bosnia when Bosnia was part of Yugoslavia? Do I know that it was only after the Serbian nationalists started making noise and spreading fear that people started thinking about those differences? The actual differences are trivial, argues B. It was aggression and politicians that made people see the world in terms of stark differences. To B., Bosnia was so committedly integrated that it preceded the very idea of multi-ethnic or multicultural.

He thinks I am inappropriately redescribing past reality according to present-day vocabulary. Perhaps he is right. Sometimes I believe so much in my own explanations that I don't notice when something different is right before my eyes. Still, I feel that what B. is saying doesn't make sense. It doesn't fit with my mental picture of Bosnia. Perhaps B. himself is doing the redescribing.

On the night the war first came to Sarajevo, when *the way it was* was suddenly shattered, B. did not believe it could be so. When the Serbs put up roadblocks in Sarajevo, B. sped his car around the checkpoints and got home safely from his girlfriend's place. *This could never happen here*, he thought. It was not a part of the reality of his life.

We thought, OK, we will respect the Serbian minority. We thought we will give democracy to everybody and live together like before. Like always. Now I see that it meant only the last forty years. But we didn't understand that it would mean only the last forty years. In my family we always knew who killed my grandfather in World War II, but we tried to push it to the back of our minds, to regard it like something that is history, and that will never happen again. We thought of that as the dark side of Yugoslavia and of World War II.

When we speak, three years into the ethnic cleansing, B. confesses that he should have known. His memory of the murder of his grandfather should have told him. I must say that we always had a sense that the Serbians know how to do barbaric crimes. Because of my grandfather. Because they cut off his head on the bridge in the middle of the town. He was one of the richest, and the guy who killed him was a poor Bosnian Orthodox he had supported all his life. And we had the sense that they knew how to do things that are very strange—not always of a clear mind. I did know that, but we didn't put that first.

B.'s story is a good example of the struggles over historical memory and identity that are so much a part of the Bosnian landscape. What concerns me at least as much as the particular factual details of his grandfather's killing is how B. constructs that memory to express his sense of his family in history. As I listen to B. tell the story of his grandfather, I think I am hearing the historical memory of the murder on the bridge being subtly revised and redeployed to tell a new story about Serbs in Bosnia today. This new story says that we knew all along that they were killers. But what about the story he grew up with, the one that says we lived together? How can you have it both ways?

And I wonder what story would B. have told me about his grandfather before ethnic cleansing. Would his grandfather's death on that bridge have carried the same sense of genocidal murder? Perhaps so—or perhaps it would have been more a story about my grandfather's death at the hands of a mad employee. By telling the story the way he does, B. is participating in the telling of a larger story, in which the recent Serbian nationalists' ethnic cleansing becomes the return of a genocidal nightmare from the distant past. B. is also distancing himself from the story taught to his generation in Yugoslavia, the story that downplayed those memories.

Seeing how B. struggled with historical memories in telling his story after ethnic cleansing makes me curious about how the memories of violent historical events have been reworked in the years preceding the ethnic cleansing, as well as how memories of the ethnic cleansing are being registered now in the individual and the collective memories of Bosnians. I have thus come to believe that central to ethnic cleansing, emanating from this catastrophe, are some very palpable dilemmas of memory. What are these dilemmas, and how can we understand them?

The recent bloodshed in Bosnia-Herzegovina is not simply the perpetuation of "ancient ethnic hatreds"; there have been prior atrocities, wars and genocides that are registered in people's memories. Yet for four decades—longer than the entire lifetime of young people like B.—the memories of ethnic killings during World War II and before had been vigilantly put away by Tito, replaced by the state-driven mentality of "Brotherhood and Unity."

B. is but one of millions of survivors from Bosnia and the former Yugoslavia caught between these two historical realities: ethnic atrocities and multiethnic communality. He has had radically discordant personal experiences of both peaceful coexistence and interethnic slaughter. He carries memories of both ways, each as real as the other. For Sarajevans, whose lives epitomized the state vision of living together, the contradiction presented by Serbian aggression is incredibly stark. You don't have to be from Sarajevo, however, to feel yourself being pulled in opposite directions by these two conflicting historical experiences.

Part One of this book explores the dilemmas of memory that are crucial to understanding different facets of the Bosnian historical experience: living together in multi-ethnic Bosnia in Yugoslavia (chapter 1), enduring ethnic cleansing (chapter 2), and living as a refugee after ethnic cleansing (chapter 3). Each chapter begins with a dialogue between me and a Bosnian survivor. These should be heard not as psychotherapy but as conversations between two people engaged in a type of exchange that is hard to name.

Chapter 1   We All Lived Together

One Survivor's Story—Merhamet

A good feeling comes when I walk down the long hall from the cramped offices of the Bosnian Mental Health Program to see E. Maybe it is the bright welcoming tone of his voice, or that he always offers a cup of hot coffee (even if it is an American brew rather than the strong Bosnian coffee I've come to love). E. is a thirty-something physician from Sarajevo, currently [ca. 1995] heading the Bosnian Refugee Center in Chicago.

E. tells me that he does not feel guilty for leaving Bosnia—he had already gone back to Sarajevo and given two years of service for his country while his family lived hand to mouth as refugees in Croatia. But when the opportunity came to do something for his family he chose to move to the United States. The job at the Bosnian Refugee Center is better than most others he can find (his refugee resettlement worker first told him to take a job as a janitor). When E. agrees to be the Center's director, he knows he is in for a real challenge. But he likes the idea that he will be doing something for the Bosnian people in America.

So far this work seems to suit him well. Still, there are many things he feels unsure about. He does not know what his life or his family's life will become. Nor does he know what will become of his country. And in the wake of the ethnic cleansing, he does not know how to make sense of his memories of living together with Bosnian Serbs and Bosnian Croats in the multi-ethnic communality that was Bosnia-Herzegovina. These are not merely abstract questions, nor only personal matters. As the Director of the Bosnian Refugee Center, he has to confront many new choices, and to guide the Bosnian community in deciding who will be included and who will be excluded. In his testimony he speaks of the dilemmas of memory on many survivors' minds, and the impact of these dilemmas on the choices they make.[1]

I remember Bosnia as a beautiful and peaceful country. We all lived together. Before the war, it was unnecessary to know if your neighbor was Serb, Croat, Muslim, or Jew. We looked only at what kind of person you were. We were all friends.

But now I think it is like a kind of earthquake. A huge catastrophe. After this war nothing will be the same. People will live, but I think they will not live together. They will not share the same bread like before. Maybe they will be neighbors, but I think the close relationship will not exist any more. Because the Bosnian people, especially the Muslim people, had a bad experience, partly as a result of our attitude.

"What exactly do you mean by 'our attitude'?"

We called that the "merhamet"—that you feel sorry for someone who has bad luck. Philanthropy. You like all people. You want to support everyone. If you can help, you help. You can even forgive bad things. You can find good in all religions. You will be good and decent to everyone.

"Merhamet" happens to be the name of the Bosnian Red Cross organization reputed to be charitable toward Muslims only, but E. uses it differently. To me it echoes the Titoist slogan of "Brotherhood and Unity." I ask E. how the two compare.

Only Bosnians believed in "Brotherhood and Unity" and agreed with that idea. I think that the politicians knew that, especially Tito. He repeated that slogan very often in Bosnia. When he gave speeches, he'd say, "You must uphold 'Brotherhood and Unity.'" And I think that the Bosnian Muslims were good followers of "Brotherhood and Unity." They believed in that, and they were big patriots in the former Yugoslavia. And I think that only Muslims and Macedonians tried to avoid any kind of conflict in the former Yugoslavia. They suggested that we all compromise. "For all"—that is one of the main sayings of merhamet. Personally, I believed in "Brotherhood and Unity," but now I don't believe in that. Because of merhamet I think the Bosnian Muslims forgot a very important thing—that it is not the first genocide against them. But people always forget. Bosnian Muslims learn the hard way.

What history have they forgotten, I wonder, and why have they forgotten it?

I think that we had an open heart for everyone. We worked together and we lived together. For example, my next door neighbor was a Serb. One night his mother knocked on my door. It was I think midnight and my wife opened the door. This woman was very upset. Her son had a sharp pain in his stomach. My wife, she is a doctor too, went into his apartment and examined him. Then she called me. I examined him, and we knew he had appendicitis. I recommended hospitalization and found a surgeon. The surgeon operated, it was a necessary operation. His appendix was almost ruptured, and the surgeon saved his life. Only one year after that, this same person stole my apartment.

Another example. I had neighbors above me. We'd always say, "How are you?

How are your kids?" When the war started, my neighbor shot at Muslim houses. I heard the shots and the empty shells fall on the floor above. And the very next morning he said to me, "Hi neighbor! Did you sleep well?" All night long he was shooting into houses to try to kill someone, and in the morning he asked me how did you sleep! Another neighbor, he said to me, after we heard the shelling in Sarajevo all day, and after we saw the picture on TV, he said, "Oh, the shelling is not necessary. It's enough if we stop the electricity, food, and water." And I looked carefully at that man. And I thought, with whom I am living? Who are they?

We had a powerful experience, we suffered so much because we believed in "Brotherhood and Unity" and we lived with merhamet in our hearts, and because of that we have been punished.

The primary target of the Serbian nationalists' genocide in Bosnia was the multi-ethnic way of life. Merhamet was a central part of that life. A Bosnian-language dictionary indicates that merhamet has multiple meanings: mercy, pardon, grace, alms, charity, kindness.[2] The sentence it quotes reads, "Do you have any merhamet in yourself?" Merhamet has been an important cultural value of Bosnia's multi-ethnic life, and a vital part of the worldview and collective memory of the Bosnian Muslims.

E. is the first person to really tell me what merhamet is all about. Our conversation gets me to thinking a lot about merhamet. While I have never before heard this term used in the way E. uses it, the values and attitude conveyed are a familiar element in many of the stories recorded by survivors. More than anything else I have read or heard, this merhamet brings out the essence of what Bosnian Muslim survivors are struggling with regarding memory and history.

Why then have Bosnians not said more about merhamet? Perhaps it is an attitude toward life that speaks for itself. Merhamet shows in the humanistic ways people deal with conflicts, frustrations, and disappointments. It need not be advertised. You don't talk about it, you live it. It is one of ways in which many Bosnian Muslims show a modesty that is hard not to admire.

Maybe it is also merhamet I see in the way some survivors seem to approach even the traumas and injustices of ethnic cleansing with a measure of acceptance. Life has brought this ethnic cleansing to them, and they will accept it. Not that they don't try to meet their own needs or to stand up for their rights. But somehow a good number of them manage not to get mired in bitterness and hatred. This sense greatly impressed me and many other Americans working with Bosnians, but we didn't know what to call it. Since my conversation with E., I have begun to think of this as part of what's meant by the attitude of merhamet. Perhaps there is still some merhamet left within them after all.

Surprisingly, merhamet is seldom named in the scholarly literature on Bosnia, although one can find traces of it in descriptions of Bosnian Muslims' sense of collective identity. For example, the anthropologist Tone Bringa writes:

"Bosnian Muslims conceptualize their common identity primarily through the knowledge that they share a particular moral environment."[3] Their social milieu was inclusive, not exclusive; heterogeneous, not homogeneous. Bosnian national identity was primarily dependent not upon ethnicity, but upon a multi-ethnic way of life. Making a commitment to preserve that way of life was something you did both for the common good and for the goodness of the self.

The historians Mark Pinson and Ivo Banac have outlined the historical basis of Bosnian Muslim identity. With no local religious authority (akin to the Serbian Orthodox Church), no historical period of dominance, and no epic myth of statehood, Bosnians based identity upon a "centuries-old common life, regardless of confession" as Tito said in 1940.[4] After World War II, Tito's government policy of "Brotherhood and Unity" provided the federal political context for Bosnian merhamet, the mentality of this way of life. This was further strengthened in the 1960s when Tito allowed the Bosnians to develop their sense of identity as unique from Croatians and Serbians.

Yet after ethnic cleansing many Bosnian Muslim survivors were not prepared or able to forget the recent traumas nor to forgive their perpetrators. When survivors bear hatred and fear that make it impossible to trust, this may be thought of as a disruption in merhamet. It leads one to wonder what the experience of living through ethnic cleansing will ultimately do to Bosnian Muslims' sense of merhamet. Their traumatic memories and trauma-induced feelings seem incompatible with merhamet and the way of life it promoted.

This belated introduction to merhamet has changed the way I approach the study of survivors of genocide in Bosnia. To understand the struggles of survivors and what is going to become of their lives and of their Bosnia, I now feel compelled to know what nationalism, genocide, and war have done to merhamet and what its future might be. But first I must consider the social and historical conditions that have nurtured merhamet, and examine its part in Bosnian Muslims' experience of living together in Bosnia-Herzegovina during Tito's Yugoslavia.

A Multi-ethnic Communality

Survivors recall that in both the cities and the countryside of Bosnia-Herzegovina, Muslims, Serbs, and Croats shared their lives with one another.[5]

We worked together. We slept together. Lived together. Ate together.

Our neighbors—we were like a family. Our flats were like one home. They had two kids. We lived together. We vacationed together. Spent holidays together. Overnight, they changed.

When we had Bajram, the entire street made baklava, and when we had Orthodox Easter all the street made colored eggs.

In Bosnia everybody lived together. Serbs, Muslims, Croats. Some places had more of one or the other. But in every place we lived together. Five thousand years together in the same place. Same country. Bosnia.

The experience of living together and the multi-ethnic attitude had a solid place in the stories, phrases, and words by which Bosnians told their histories. Bosnian Muslim survivors frequently use words like *mosaic, crossroads, interweaving,* and *many-colored carpet* to describe the multi-ethnic reality of their lives in Bosnia before ethnic cleansing.

The Slovenian poet Ales Debeljak has articulated the spirit behind the multi-ethnic experience of Yugoslavia in a metaphor that has brought tears to survivors' eyes:[6]

For me, popular slogans about "the celebration of diversity" were never mere philosophical speculation. As far back as I can recall, these differences were the crux of my experience of life at a crossroads of various cultures. When Westerners came to visit, I showed my pride in our federation's diversity with the kind of blissful matter-of-factness that a woodsman shows toward his pine forests, even though their luxuriance is the result of an even succession of dry and rainy days, not any special effort on his part. I considered the diversity of Yugoslav reality to be a fact of nature.

Listening to Bosnians speak of diversity in their lives in Yugoslavia, you realize that they are not reflecting an American sensibility. Diversity was a major feature of their daily reality, in an ethnic context very different from that of the United States.

Data from the 1991 census demonstrate what multi-ethnic communality looked like on the national map of Bosnia-Herzegovina at the historical moment just before genocide began.[7] In this census, participants could indicate if they were "Muslim Slavs," "Orthodox Serbs," "Catholic Croats," or "Yugoslavs." Of the 4,354,911 residents, Muslim Slavs were most numerous (44 percent), followed by Serbs (31 percent), Croats (17 percent), and Yugoslav and other (7 percent). Across the territory of Bosnia-Herzegovina, regions of Muslim, Serb, or Croat dominance tended to fall in isolated pockets rather than contiguous areas. This fact hindered such Western-led peace efforts as the failed Vance-Owen plan of 1993, which sought to engineer peace by dividing Bosnia-Herzegovina into three geographical regions of ethnic dominance. There was simply no clean way to cut it up.

Speaking about their multi-ethnic experience in Bosnia, many survivors give the impression that it worked so well and for so long because it was simply the natural order of civilization. A spirit like merhamet has an almost irresistible power to convince those living immersed in it that this is the only way life can be. Yet this multi-ethnic communality was not simply an ahistorical given. It had a basis in Yugoslav history.

Yugoslavia, which means "south Slavs," was born as a nation out of the ruins of World War I.[8] The collapsing Austro-Hungarian Empire had wanted the Serbs, the Croats, and the Slovenians to unite and form a government that would remain under their rule. When the empire folded, an independent Yugoslav state came into existence, at first called "The Kingdom of the Serbs, Croats, and Slovenes" (Malcolm, 169). Bosnia and its Muslim population jockeyed for their place in this new state, and by the 1920s Bosnia was being defined as one of its regional entities. Violent ethnic clashes culminated in 1929 with King Alexander changing the state's name to Yugoslavia and partitioning the land into nine banovines, which broke up the territorial integrity of the clashing regions. The 1930s saw continued struggles between ethnic groups trying to defend their interests, and brokering efforts by the central government and its leaders to keep Yugoslavia together. The nationality questions were by no means resolved when Yugoslavia was invaded and quickly defeated by the Nazis in 1941.

Despite its minimal tactical significance in the overall German war plan, Yugoslavia in World War II was a bloodbath.[9] More than one million Yugoslavs were killed, mostly by other Yugoslavs. The Germans established the "Independent State of Croatia" with a Nazi puppet government called the Ustasha. The Ustasha joined in the Nazis' genocide against the Jews, and even more enthusiastically committed genocide against the Serbs. More than 100,000 Serbs, Jews, and Croats were murdered in Ustasha concentration camps like Jasenovac. Two resistance groups emerged: the Communist Partisans, led by Tito; and the Serbian Royalist Chetniks, led by Draza Mihailovic. When the Germans were defeated, Tito and the Partisans controlled the new government, and the communist Second Yugoslavia was born.

Tito's Yugoslavia comprised six republics (Slovenia, Croatia, Bosnia-Herzegovina, Serbia, Montenegro, and Macedonia) and two autonomous regions (Kosovo and Vojvodina). At first, the government acknowledged five official national groups—Slovenians, Croatians, Serbians, Macedonians, and Montenegrans. A predominant goal of the communist government's national policy was to strike a balance among the different national groups and to maintain power over all of them. Under Tito's rule, gains and losses in political representation were vigilantly calibrated so that no one group was disproportionately rewarded or punished.

Muslims had to wait decades before they were given the same constitutional standing as Croats and Serbs in Bosnia-Herzegovina. After World War II, Bosnia-Herzegovina was considered a "mixed" region and Muslims were not even identified as a national group. In the 1948 census, Muslims could identify themselves as "Muslim Serbs," "Muslim Croats," or "Muslims, nationally undeclared" (Malcolm, 197–198). The First Party Congress stated that the Muslims "have not yet decided on their national identity" (p. 197), and assumed that they would eventually merge with either Croats or Serbs. In the 1953 census, Muslims could declare themselves "Yugoslav, nationally undeclared" (p. 198).

Not until 1961 were the Muslims officially recognized as a distinct ethnic group; that year the census called them "Muslims in the ethnic sense" (p. 198). As his policies of internationalism flourished in the 1960s, however, Tito began to see the advantages of acknowledging and supporting the Bosnian Muslim community. Their status changed significantly in 1963, with the inclusion in the new Bosnian constitution of the statement "Serbs, Croats, and Muslims allied in the past by a common life" (p. 198). The census form in 1971 was the first to speak of "Muslim, in the sense of a nation" (p. 199).

Though the 1963 constitution gave Muslims equal status with Serbs and Croats, some important distinctions remained. The majority of Bosnian Muslims lived in urban areas, where ethnic mixing was highest. Their collective identity was organized around the experience of living together with other ethnic groups, whereas Bosnian Serbs more often lived in rural areas where there was less mixing. Furthermore, Catholics and Orthodox living in Bosnia could consider themselves Bosnians, but also Croats and Serbs, thus affirming their ties to a rival republic and ethnic identity. But Bosnian Muslims had no Muslim republic with which to ally themselves. Croatians had a Catholic Church in Croatia, and Serbs an Orthodox Church in Serbia, but the Muslim clerical authority was much further away, in Turkey. Of the two million Bosnian Muslims reported in 1985, only 17 percent were identified as religious (p. 222). Merhamet, not Muslim nationalism, characterized their worldview. The social forces of communist ideology, urbanization, multi-ethnic living, Islam, and Western consumerism and popular culture had shaped and nurtured this predominantly secular culture.

For Bosnian Muslims, this merhamet was the only lifeline. Without a cultural tradition or a government providing support for organizing around Muslim nationalism, their very existence as a people depended upon the acceptance and well-being of the multi-ethnic liberal vision. Bosnian Muslims' merhamet only worked if the Serbs and the Croats, the Bosnian Serbs and the Bosnian Croats also supported a multi-ethnic paradigm. Not until too late did Bosnians see that without Tito's special efforts their multi-ethnic communality would break down. Until then multi-ethnicity and merhamet had seemed invincible.

Intermarriage

Of all the cultural institutions in the Bosnian multi-ethnic communality, the practice of intermarriage was the most salient. A census report from the 1980s found that 30 percent of marriages in Bosnia were across ethnic lines.[10]

The intermarriages I encountered firsthand fit perfectly in the multi-ethnic milieu of Yugoslavia, but in an ethnically partitioned Bosnia or a Diaspora they stood in stark isolation. One woman from Sarajevo tells me:

They say we have a mixed marriage. What does this "mixed" mean? I'll tell you what it means. It means that one is human and one is animal. That is what it means to them now. It never was that way before.

She speaks out of a deep bitterness. She could have been either Muslim, Serb, or Croat and felt largely the same. The world that had once favored her marriage has somehow changed so profoundly that what had been accepted and even treasured only a few years ago has suddenly been rendered vestigial and taboo.

The topic of intermarriage can be a metaphor for the tragic breakup of Yugoslavia, in gut-wrenching portraits of the disintegration of multi-ethnic Bosnian families.[11] But one risk in telling stories of the dominance of so-called "blood ties" is that these stories may not accurately reflect the way intermarriage was part of a socially and culturally determined way of life, supported by a collective memory of tolerance and coexistence. More than that, musing on the inevitability of the demise of intermarriages, considering it roughly akin to some evolutionary biological process, does not show the hope, struggle, or possibility of somehow reconstituting the way of life that has been shattered.

Historically, intermarriage was one of the basic sociocultural structures that served as a backbone for multi-ethnic communality in Bosnia-Herzegovina and the former Yugoslavia (along with essential economic, educational, social, and political structures). It was a cultural jewel that its citizens were proud of. It was a special product of a special cultural commitment, and it offered men, women, and children a unique family life.

The psychologist Inger Agger, who studied intermarriage in Bosnia during and after ethnic cleansing, wrote: "Only when the marriage crosses some potentially dangerous boundary does it gain this special connotation of being 'mixed,' as, for example, when the marriage crosses the boundaries between religions, races or ethnic groups in a special social and political context."[12] In Bosnia, this can mean a marriage between Serb and Croat, Serb and Muslim, or Croat and Muslim. Before ethnic cleansing, intermarriage was not considered "mixed," because the people were not considered to be other. After ethnic cleansing, intermarriage is "mixed marriage," and intermarried couples are in a compromised position. Even in Chicago, the tendency is for different groups of refugees from Bosnia and ex-Yugoslavia to stay with their own. A Muslim woman married to a Serb man, for example, will meet with much frustration and resistance in the exile communities. Existence becomes even more problematic for their children, who go to school and meet children of other refugees who aren't from one of these so-called "mixed marriages."

When sitting with a *mixed couple*, as they are half-pejoratively called, I find myself watching more closely what is said, especially when we are all together. If we are in a group, and someone says something about Serbs, I start to feel uncomfortable, and look their way. Sometimes I notice them looking into each other's eyes. It's like a way of checking in to see if things are all right, a way of staying connected. The Bosnian Muslim spouse holds back. But when the Bosnian Orthodox spouse leaves the room, the Bosnian Muslim spouse will change the subject back to politics and speak more openly and passionately. Even then, though, there seems to be a hesitance to go too far—a conscious choice to put the commitment to the secular, multi-ethnic relationships that are a part of your life clearly above your investment in a particular ethnic national experience. Listening in on these conversations, it is as if one can actually hear the faint tones of merhamet trying to be heard above the din of ethnic nationalism.

Survivors who are in "mixed marriages" find themselves in the best and the worst of positions (with the characteristic dark Bosnian sense of humor, they will say "mixed up" marriages). Their life as a couple still embodies the principle of multi-ethnic communality in Bosnia-Herzegovina. Yet without that same multi-ethnic communality to support them, they are isolated in their commitment and often besieged by others who are threatened by the idea of intermarriage. Divorced from this social context, it is incredibly hard for these couples to maintain their loving commitment to each other; so much of their world urges them to view their partner as less than human. Already, many mixed marriages have ended tragically. How many will last? Making a mixed marriage work will require extraordinary strength and determination to stick with love in spite of the opinion of one's community.

Surely something important is reflected in one survivor's statement about the joy that they found in a multi-ethnic way of life and the difficulty they've had in accepting a mono-ethnic paradigm. Such affirmations of merhamet and refusals to abandon it should not be overlooked. Mixed marriages may be the most important bearers of the seed of merhamet in the new Bosnia—if they survive at all.

And what of their children? The stakes could not be any higher than they are for Bosnian children of intermarriages. Their fates will be enormously impacted by the fate of Bosnian multiethnic living. They are in the most difficult position of all, having to choose between mother and father, one to hate and one to love.

Often I ask myself what I am now. The only answer I find is that I am a Yugoslav and I will always be a Yugoslav.

Youngsters are forced to come up with answers that are really no answer at all. The Second Yugoslavia is dead. And Bosnia-Herzegovina cannot be what it once was. Is there a way these young people's refusal to identify with a particular ethnic group can have any validity or consequence? The young may be the only ones brash enough to actually say it, or fluid enough to actually change their identity. The fate of the living memories of multi-ethnicity and merhamet depends in large part on the younger generation, vulnerable yet powerful, as a bridge to the future.

Sarajevo

Regarding brotherhood, etc., many people said that was only fiction. That it didn't exist in Yugoslavia. I can't accept that because Sarajevo was something special. Our spirit was absolutely different. We knew and we had always known that all of us are the same. I never thought, when listening to someone's name, which religion or which nationality is he? It just wasn't important. When somebody says that Yugoslavia was artificial and that brotherhood was artificial, I cannot accept that. Sarajevo was a real city with fraternity, equality, and liberty.

"It was living proof," I commented.

Our lives were proof, really.

Sarajevo was far and away the clearest embodiment of multi-ethnic communality in all of Bosnia. Founded 550 years ago, the city lies in a river valley encircled by tall mountains. Its unique geographical position was a central determinant in how the city existed for many, many years as a trade and cultural center, and in how it was nearly annihilated in the three-plus years of siege.

It was this geography that had given shape to the unique life and spirit of Sarajevo, a place described by the Sarajevan writer Dzevad Karahasan as "enclosed and isolated from the world, so to speak, cut off from everything external and turned wholly toward itself."[13] Sarajevo consisted of a central downtown area called the Bascarsija, encircled by residential quarters called mahalas on the surrounding hillsides and valleys. The spirit of the city was unabashedly pluralistic, with each ethnic group coexisting equally with the others.

Sarajevans cherished and lavishly described those images or moments in their city life when all the parts were in perfect balance. Their Sarajevo was "a city in which temples of all faiths of the book can be seen in one glance" (p. 5).

Karahasan describes the Hotel Europa as the city's physical and semantic center (p. 89). Poised precisely on the line where the Turkish and the Austro-Hungarian city spaces met, the Hotel Europa "belongs to one and to the other, at the same time, while remaining beyond both" (p. 89).

The kind of mutual belonging embodied in the Hotel Europa is a paradigm for the way self and other, coming from different collective groups, could uniquely enter into one another in pluralistic Sarajevo. "The hotel belongs to the Turkish quarter in the same way that the image of ourselves in the gaze of another belongs to us; it is an image that speaks equally about the Other and about ourselves" (p. 90).

Living in pluralistic Sarajevo was about having the daily experience of car-rying within you images of yourself in the eyes of the other person, as centrally as images of yourself in your own eyes. Each was given an affirmative place in the self.[14] This unique cognitive sense also describes the kind of self merhamet made possible for all Bosnian Muslims, but especially Sarajevans. With the physi-cal reality of their city so completely embodying the delicate balancing of the Bosnian multi-ethnic communality, and their lives so thoroughly committed to living together, Bosnian Muslims' conception of self was unusually open to be-ing defined by its relation to other ethnic groups. Merhamet meant that the self of the Bosnian Muslim, like the Hotel Europa, belonged not to one camp, de-fined by excluding the other, but to an inclusive collective.

Survivors from Sarajevo give gushing confessions of the love they had for their city. One Sarajevan told me this story.

I am like other people from Sarajevo. All of us think "I love Sarajevo more than anyone." That is how it is with me. I like my city more than anyone from Sarajevo, and I will give you one example. I escaped from the army three times just to come to one small hill to see Sarajevo. I didn't come down to see my parents or my sister, I just wished to see my city, my town, and after that I came back. It wasn't important what happened with me. I just wished to see my city.

Some Sarajevans took it upon themselves to talk to the outside world about their unique way of life and the threat to its existence, in the hope that they might save Sarajevo. On February 27, 1993, as the siege of his city persisted, Karahasan left Sarajevo for the West. He wrote to a friend:

> I believed at first, like other Sarajevans, that the "free world" would not
> permit an unwarranted slaughter of us civilians; later on I believed, like
> other Sarajevans, that the world permits the slaughter of civilians only
> because it does not yet understand and does not yet know what is
> happening in our old country. I pleaded that the idea there are "three
> sides in the conflict" is wrong because it overlooks the most numerous
> "fourth side"—the Bosnian population, which prefers integration,
> tolerance, and a Bosnian multicultural community. (p. 106)

Reading Karahasan's text, or listening directly to Sarajevans, one senses how hard it is for the person who has experienced merhamet to explain it convinc-ingly or defend it to the skeptical outsider. It is perhaps as difficult as trying to explain to another what love is. Most Bosnians discovered how much easier it was for outsiders to believe the stories of ancient ethnic hatreds and violence being offered by the Serbian nationalists than to see it their way—that there was a fourth side, a multi-ethnic society where merhamet flourished.

Yet in some ways the historical view of merhamet, romantically expressed by Karahasan, has an exaggerated quality in common with that of its opposite, ancient ethnic hatreds. In a way, both are partial truths: the description of merhamet tends to push aside the troubling memories of World War II; the stories of ancient ethnic hatreds more blatantly deny the historical tradition of multi-ethnic coexistence. Perhaps this exaggerated quality is part of what has made it hard for some outsiders to accept the Bosnians' view of multi-ethnic communality. To the outsider, it just didn't seem like the whole truth. And in fact it was not.

When Sarajevans talk about their city, they express that special kind of elitism common to inhabitants of the modern metropolis—a belief not only that they stand at the pinnacle of social and cultural development but also that they are safe there. Sometimes the city dweller forgets that the city exists in a state, and that the culture and the norms of city life are not necessarily equally cherished by those who live outside the city. Sarajevans used to say "I am going to Bosnia" before leaving their city. This statement echoes a sentiment often expressed by New Yorkers—Woody Allen once said that he lived not in America, but on an island off its coast.[15] The city dweller can also have the illusion that the way of life is as rooted, as solid, and as permanent as the buildings, streets, and bridges. But a way of life is as rooted in memories (or their disappearance) as it is in concrete and steel.

We Are Europeans!

An old man crawls out of the rubble of a building like a rat and asks a United Nations soldier, "Don't they understand we're Europeans?"

Bosnian Muslims protested before, during, and after ethnic cleansing that "We are Europeans!" It was both a claim made to others and a way of identifying themselves to themselves. After all, nobody wants their identity to be redescribed. As the lights went out, the walls came down, and it got harder and harder to live, to breathe, and to see oneself as one had in the past, it was completely understandable to hear Bosnian Muslims asserting their European identity. It was, after all, who they thought they were.

They spoke, in part, believing that they could persuade the European Allies to come and save them from genocide. Bosnian Muslims had been put in the miserable position of having little more than declarations to use in their defense. Still, their statement was not based only on sentiment. The Bush administration, trying to distance itself from Bosnia on the eve of the 1992 presidential elections, had claimed that Bosnia was a "European problem."[16] In obeying the Western governments and giving over their arms to the United Nations troops, the Bosnians had staked their future on the Allies' proposition that Europeans would solve this problem together. But that was not what happened.

When Bosnian Muslims proclaimed themselves Europeans to the West, it was to correct a widely held cultural misperception that all Muslims were fundamentalists, zealots Americans had learned to demonize in the wake of the 1981 Iranian hostage crisis, the downing of Pan Am flight 103 over Lockerbie, Scotland, and the bombing of the World Trade Center in 1993, to name only a few incidents. Like many Westerners, the Bosnian Muslims led largely secular lives, observing the traditions of their religion several times a year, on special holidays, when they joined with others in prayer. For many, religion was less a matter of ritual practice, and more detectable in the traces it leaves upon the spirit, in cultural values, and in a special feeling of familiarity and connectedness with others.

By identifying with Europe, Bosnians were defending themselves against a generalized anti-Islamic sentiment in the West but also against the barrage of propaganda spread by Serbian nationalists—propaganda riddled with hysterical cries of "Jihad," "Mujahedeen," "Allah Uagbar," and images of the crescent, the sickle, and the Kur'an.

Bosnians also protested that many Westerners hold a highly biased view of the Balkan peoples as savage and primitive. Sometimes when first meeting Bosnians, I have been teased: "What, you think that we are some kind of animals, beasts? That we did not have a civilized life, that we did not eat with forks and spoons?" Bosnians have come to expect that what outsiders know of them is the assassination of the Archduke Francis Ferdinand, which gave rise to World War I, the disintegration of Yugoslavia, the war between Croatia and Serbia, and ethnic cleansing. However, this was not their sense of themselves.

Younger Bosnians, including B., were not possessed by memories of war, but of good times and youthful ventures throughout Europe, as reported by the poet Ales Debeljak:

> Most of all we wanted to know in what European town Oscar Peterson would be playing next summer and when John Fowles's newest book would hit the bookstores in nearby Trieste, Vienna, or Munich, if not Ljubljana. We traveled widely and unhindered, both within Yugoslavia and abroad. We made pilgrimages to jazz and rock concerts as far afield as Moers, Florence, and Montreux. We believed that mass culture gave us more in common with youth in London than with our parents.[17]

Another young person spoke of how he learned he was a European when he traveled to the Islamic world. He noticed that he dressed, and ate, and thought differently. Bosnian Muslims also drew a connection between their cultural values and those of the liberal democracies of the West. Was it because they saw commonalties in the enjoyment of private life, that they perceived themselves as embodying the same basic political and cultural values? In any case, they fully expected the West to recognize this truth, and unite with them in common defense of shared values. These turned out to be false assumptions. In the Westerner's mind, the dream of a multi-ethnic way of life—a living manifestation of the collective memory of merhamet—was too easily overshadowed by countervailing historical nightmares of communism, ethnic nationalism, war, and atrocity. Yet for Bosnians, particularly the younger generations, the sense that they all lived together was accompanied by the belief that they had miraculously vanquished the nightmares of World War II. This one liberal aspect of their lives deflected their attention away from the harsher aspects of their far from liberal democratic political system.

Bosnian Muslims also seemed unaware of what claiming their European identity meant for Bosnian Serbs. The Bosnian Serb, more rural and more oriented toward the Orthodox cultures of the East, associated European identity with the Nazis, the Italian Fascists, and the Croatian Ustasha. To them, expressing an allegiance to Europe hearkened back to the suppressed collective memories of World War II and Serbian suffering in general. It was not reassurance, but provocation, and to them, justification for taking extreme measures.

The identification with Europeans was completely predictable, and yet, sadly, it became absolutely paradoxical. Had this Europe they clung to really existed in the way that they imagined, then surely it would have done something consequential to save them. And when no European governments came forth it was no longer possible to say "We are Europeans!" in the same way. Indeed, for many Bosnians there would no longer be that sense of pride in this continental identity. How could there be when other Europeans took away their weapons and allowed them to be helplessly slaughtered right in front of their eyes?

But to let go of being European is to open oneself up to yet another deprivation. For when there is no larger collective with which you can align then you do not know who you are, and you as a member of a people have lost your shape. This is something no human can endure.[18]

How ironic that at the end of the twentieth century, which has so demonized Islam, a group of Muslims would be trying to awaken the moral imagination of Europe and the West. The sting to Westerners of the irony of this claim is not lost on many Bosnians. Sometimes they seem to be saying: "Even from this far corner of Europe, we are a better representation of what it means to be civilized Europeans than you. Shame on you, Europe and America, for betraying your commitments to freedom and diversity."

In May 1993, when the Western allies decided not to defend Bosnia with military force, President Alija Izetbegovic said: "If the international community is not ready to defend the principles which it itself has proclaimed as its foundations, let it say so openly, both to the people of Bosnia and the people of the world. Let it proclaim a new code of behavior in which force will be the first and the last argument."[19]

Statements such as these, made in a posture of justifiable outrage, voice positions that may change over time. Or perhaps not. To which larger constellation of values the new Bosnia will belong remains to be seen. So does the question of how Bosnian Muslims will apply this new code of force to Bosnian Serbs, Bosnian Croats, and other ethnic and religious minorities within Bosnia-Herzegovina's redrawn borders.

Another Survivor's Story: Responsibility

The only ones who are not responsible for what happened are children and animals. Every one else is responsible. Really.[20]

I spoke with several Bosnian Serbs and Serbs during the war (not counting those who remained committed to the Bosnian government side). Each time I tried, I found that it was impossible to have more than a few words with them. *Sarajevo is not under siege. It is occupied and we are defending it. Muslims are taking Serbian land....* They were much too far from acknowledging that ethnic cleansing was happening. Being that I was not willing to relinquish my own partiality, there was never enough common ground for us to even continue a conversation. But N., a Bosnian Serb, was different.

N. lived in Sarajevo and believed in multi-ethnic Bosnia. Not unlike many Bosnian Muslims, N. puts most of the blame on the Serbian nationalists. But she does not see the problem as coming exclusively from the aggression of the outsider. Being a Bosnian Serb, she feels that she can see things Bosnian Muslims can not.

I will tell you a story that you will probably not hear from anyone else. I don't have a chance to tell these things to any Bosnian people because they do not understand. Maybe you as an American can listen to these things and understand.

Her mother's father, a Serb, was killed by a Croat, the best man at his wedding, in World War II. Her father's father fought with the Serbs against Ustasha and was killed. When she was a child her mother told her what befell both of her grandfathers. N. remembers that she was told *in a factual, not emotional manner. My mother never taught me to hate Croats.*

N. always loved Yugoslavia, and she thought that Tito did an excellent job of holding the country together. He kept Stalin and the Soviet Union at bay, and quelled conflicts among the different ethnic groups. In our meeting, she spots Noel Malcolm's *Bosnia* and glances at a few paragraphs that criticize Tito for being a Stalinist in the postwar years. She says it is absolutely not true.

He was a human being. He was not perfect. He made mistakes. But he did an excellent job and for fifty years there was peace and we had a great life.

N. warns me not to belittle what Tito accomplished for Yugoslavia, as so many others have. She is sick of hearing Tito attacked by other Bosnians.

N. speaks disparagingly of Bosnian Muslim survivors who now knock Tito and the Communist Party. She herself had been a member of the Party. *But only in the gymnasium.* Her teachers told her she had to join the Party because she was a good student. *I was young. I didn't know about those things. After a few years I didn't join again.* She is critical of Bosnian Muslims who were in the Party, who for years enjoyed its benefits, who now point their fingers and say that it let them down.

But who was the Party? The Party was them. For many years they enjoyed things. That's OK. But then they destroyed it.

"How did 'they' destroy it?"

For me it all ended at the time of the elections. You could vote for the three nationalistic parties or for the Communist party. And what they all did, is that each of them voted for Izetbegovic, Karadzic, and the HDZ. Each of them didn't just vote for one. They put a mark next to all three. So they put them in power. They are responsible. They will not tell you that. They all wanted to destroy the Democratic Party. To put in place the nationalistic parties. They were all together in that. One friend told me, "Today they will be united against Democratic Party, but then they will have to kill each other." He was right.

As far as N. is concerned, "they," meaning all Bosnians, had betrayed their responsibility to care for their multi-ethnic and democratic way of life. The state system they had was not perfect, but it kept the peace and enabled the majority of people in Bosnia, and the former Yugoslavia, to have good lives. N. feels that it is too easy for the Bosnian Muslims, so victimized by Serbian and Croatian nationalists, not to look at what they themselves could have done to keep the multi-ethnic society alive.

It is understandable that N. points out the contradictions and the small betrayals of multi-ethnic living by Bosnian Muslims, given that she herself has at times been the target of their animosity. However, I for one do not believe that these shortcomings meant there was something the Bosnian Muslims could have done as late as 1992 to prevent the ethnic cleansing.

What N.'s story does suggest is how totally unprepared all Bosnians had been to respond to the threat to multi-ethnic society posed by the nationalists, in part as a consequence of what communist rule had done to their system of values. As long as Tito persecuted and oppressed any expressions of ethnic nationalism, controlled the civic dialogue, and shaped the public memory, multi-ethnic living was safe. However, families did not forget about the deaths of their loved ones in World War II, and this became the seed of a potent collective memory. The Communists believed too much in the power of the government to contain and control memory, and too little in the power of the family as a wellspring of memory.

Beginning after Tito's death, and accelerating in subsequent years, the political sea changed in a way that made it impossible not to hear about historical memories of suffering. Nationalistic intellectuals and political leaders picked up where the state's historians left off, and the public was saturated with memories of the past, of World War II and earlier, and of previous association with ethnic nationalist grievances and aspirations. N.'s story caused me to consider what other kinds of experiences or involvements people could draw upon in their lives that would shape their relationship to historical memories. She speaks about how this worked in her life.

I guess I was one of the lucky ones. Because my parents never taught me to hate. Then because I married a Muslim man. And especially because I had Sarajevo. Sarajevo was unlike any other place in Bosnia. In Sarajevo we were all together. It was something that we all came to love.

Being a cosmopolitan urbanite in Sarajevo was important, but N. could see that it took more than merely cherishing Sarajevo to keep Bosnian multi-ethnic living alive. Being in a mixed marriage was her primary way of making a multi-ethnic commitment a part of her life. But marriages like hers were never made as political statements. It was simply a way of life.

N. cannot say what more it would have taken to protect multi-ethnic communality and merhamet. But it seems that something was missing in the vast social space between the family and the state, one of the gravest flaws of communist societies. Memories of World War II and the tensions between ethnic groups were talked about in the family, and were discussed by political leaders, but elsewhere in a person's social existence any meaningful dialogue on ethnic nationalism had been effectively silenced by communism. Had Yugoslavia and the Bosnian Muslims' future been mortgaged on this enforced public silence of the historical memories of World War II and the dangers of ethnic nationalism?

The Silence of Yugoslavia

When you talk with Bosnians about the lives they once had in Yugoslavia, you mostly hear glowing confessions of their deep love for both Yugoslavia and Bosnia-Herzegovina.

I was born in a lovely and happy country, Yugoslavia.

We had excellent lives in an excellent country.

I had everything you need for a life. I loved the place. I was born there and I would die there.

Sometimes it sounds odd to hear survivors of ethnic cleansing reminisce so glowingly about the Yugoslavia where they lived together, given the slaughter that came afterward. And yet, if Yugoslavia was a truly wonderful place to live, how then did it collapse? There is no single answer to this question. However, I believe that one important part of the answer concerns how Tito dealt with the historical memories of World War II.

The Tito regime organized its collective identity around the historical event of the Partisans' victory, which it unambiguously named the People's Liberation War. The official narrative of this war claims that it was a war of liberation against the German fascists and a revolutionary class war. But the historical evidence indicates that it was a civil war that had been provoked, aided, and abetted by the Nazis, and to a lesser extent by the Italians under Mussolini. The predominant historical view of the postwar era, however, kept the focus primarily on the dangers of fascism, not ethnic conflicts.

Decades later, in 1972, Tito belatedly confirmed what many had long suspected when he said, "It was well and true a civil war, but we did not want to admit it at the time, because it would have been detrimental to our cause."[21] Tito's totalitarian rule had deployed communist ideology and governmental structures to unite the conflicting ethnic groups within Yugoslavia. History was reinvented with the communist revolution and its struggle against fascism and the bourgeoisie occupying historical ground zero. Other memories or interpretations were forbidden.

To Tito and the other leaders of the second Yugoslavia, the project of rebuilding one nation out of many peoples who had just inflicted unimaginable atrocities on one another necessitated the establishment of an especially strong narrative that would erase memories of ethnic atrocities and tell a very different story about the war. Beginning in 1941, a history was written that explicitly served the construction of the Second Yugoslavia as a new communist state. War, killings, and the deaths of the bourgeoisie and the fascists were thought of as necessary means to the communist end. To continue to speak of Ustasha or Chetniks in other than the most negative terms would only fan the flames of ethnic nationalism. Bosnian Muslim survivors report that the generation that grew up after World War II was encouraged not to indulge in these private memories. There was no history other than that of the Communist State, the best guarantor of peace. Tito was its leader and the protector of the Yugoslav ideal. He had set the nation on a course that promised to move it away from its dark past, and into a bright future. For four decades, Tito and the state tolerated no divergence from the official narrative. The state's ability to bring the embattled ethnic groups together into a new Yugoslavia was seen as one of its most important achievements. Yet as in other communist societies, this also destroyed public ethics, in particular concerning ethnic diversity. A moral understanding of the threat of ethnic nationalism as a public enemy never developed in Tito's Yugoslavia.[22]

With so many Bosnians having died in World War II, it is no exaggeration to say that each and every Bosnian family suffered the loss of at least one loved one. A great many of the Bosnian Muslim survivors we spoke with reported that they lost a father or a grandfather. Many died fighting for the Partisans, the Chetniks, the Ustasha, or another group; others died as civilians in a concentration camp, in their homes, or on their city streets, like B.'s grandfather. Again and again, I am struck by survivors' hesitancy to speak about these deaths. Clearly, this is not something they were used to talking about with anyone from outside their families, if at all. Within families, some things were said, but more was left unsaid. In public discourse, the only war deaths that could be discussed were those who were on the side of the Partisans, and the story had to fit the state's heroic narrative of communist nation building. Juxtaposed to the official narrative, which was monotonously reiterated again and again at all levels in society, was a troubling silence. The younger generation of Bosnians grew up in this silence.

Sometimes after listening to survivors speak nostalgically and idealistically of the years of peace they enjoyed in the former Yugoslavia, I try to challenge them on their investment in that state and its narrative. But I can find no compelling argument against them. These survivors of ethnic cleansing do not want to hear me raise questions about Tito. Before Tito there was war, and after Tito there was war. His supreme achievement was that he kept the peace for forty-five years. It was Tito's policy of "Brotherhood and Unity" that made merhamet possible in Bosnia. As N. said, how can you argue against forty-five years of living together in peace? One Sarajevan took this one step further: *If Tito was a God for us, then your American God is the dollar. What would happen if someone took all your money away?*

Of course, challenging their narrative memories of Yugoslavia put these survivors of ethnic cleansing in a serious bind. How could you ask those who had suffered under the nationalistic visions of Milosevic, Karadzic, and Tudjman to be critical of the multi-ethnic vision of Tito? Yet it was the survivors themselves who provided me with clues to this silence and to the trouble it gave them. On the one hand they would say resoundingly and positively, "We had a great life in our country." Yet there was also a definite awareness that there was a dark side to Yugoslavia. Precisely what constituted this dark side, however, was kept secret and locked away. For almost the entire lifetime of these survivors, there had been practically no public discourse on the dark side of the state. While their parents' generations might not have made it a focus, neither could they make it disappear from their families, even with their children growing up in an era of peace.

Interestingly, the younger generations, in their attempts at youthful divergence from the communist establishment and its official narrative, seemed shadowed by that same darkness. But rather than rewrite the story of Yugoslavia and World War II, they took a more individualistic, existential view. Debeljak wrote:

"Instead of socialism and its spectacular burial, we focused on the scars, nicks, creases, and grimaces on the faces of individuals. We felt our way around the depths of the human soul in the agonized silence during a wake, when the reign of death begins to relent but hasn't yet vanished altogether and the soul can so easily stray amid the shadows of paranoia and anxiety."[23]

It was the time of rock and roll, not preoccupation with national and ethnic topics. Nobody paid attention to those things.

The older generation of the League of Communists did not spawn a younger generation that held fast to the party ideology and culture. The younger generations' struggles for meaning in their lives did not serve to transform the socialist state's culture or its historical narrative in a way that meaningfully changed its official silencing of war memories. Instead, it seemed as if the state and its narrative were becoming less and less relevant to ever growing segments of the population, for whom the call of private life far outweighed any preoccupation with political thinking.

Many survivors, and many outside commentators, speak of nationalism as if it were a virus that came and infected the beatific Bosnian political corpus. I have come to see it differently. The silence of Yugoslavia's memories, and the social void that was opening around that silence, became the space that would give birth to the nightmare of nationalism that erupted after Tito's death and the decline of the socialist system of Yugoslavia. Extending this medical metaphor, if nationalism were a virus, then the host had long been seriously immunocompromised. Yugoslav Communism had never allowed the development of personal meaning nor a civil ethics nor any other structures for preserving and passing on historical memories that could have provided some resistance to ethnic nationalism.

The absence of a coherent and believable historical record of World War II among Bosnians represents the lack of one such structure.

My parents lived through World War II, but in my family we never discussed that.

In World War II, some members of my family were killed by Chetniks. My mother would sometimes mention it, but then she would change her mind and say, "I don't want you kids to have bad memories. It is better to forget it all. You all see that we have to live together."

This absence is really quite remarkable. It suggests that Yugoslavia, including Bosnia-Herzegovina, was a country widely loved by its citizens (those that had not fled or been crushed by communist oppression) but also profoundly misunderstood by them. The ethnic wars that blighted Yugoslavia during World War II were never adequately processed, individually or collectively. Tito bought peace by force and compulsory silence. It was a wonderful life, but in retrospect it seems seriously flawed, even doomed. There was a great hole at the center of merhamet. Memories could be forcibly expunged from the social and political life of Yugoslavs for forty years, but they could never be extinguished. The nightmare of history could not be erased. So when the leader who managed that system died, and the system that maintained the silence crumbled, then the gaps in the narrative became more apparent to all, and open to the manipulations of a few communist officials who wished to retain power in the new circumstances. Given the absence of any credible narrative of the historical realities of World War II, let alone the present-day realities, it then became feasible to re-elicit the memories and to rewrite the narrative. The fact that the state narrative had clearly favored the victors, the Partisans, and denigrated the Ustasha and the Chetniks, also made practically inevitable the belated and bloody redressing of these memories by Croatian and Serbian nationalists.

The historian Stevan Pavlowitch, a Serbian émigré, wrote about the downside of Tito's iron grasp on historical memories of World War II: "Such a dogmatic approach was indeed successful, but it succeeded in dividing the Yugoslavs. It turned them away from all that could emphasize the historic importance and the moral value of the partisans' resistance. By changing debates into trials, it inflamed passions instead of soothing them."[24]

Whatever attempts there had been to rewrite the narrative of World War II in a way supportive of multi-ethnic Yugoslavia came too little, too late. For example, Pavlowitch reviews a number of texts offering a new look at World War II that were published at the beginning of the dialogue that followed Tito's death. These texts seemed less intent on providing a historical understanding that would be supportive of the idea of the Yugoslav nation, and more concerned with using the past to serve nationalistic ambitions that would shatter the Yugoslav ideal. These nationalistic sentiments came from the same strain that would later culminate in the nationalistic Memorandum of the Serbian Academy of Arts and Sciences.

Pavlowitch's book, *The Improbable Survivor: Yugoslavia and Its Problems, 1918–1988*, with its now ironic title, addresses that moment in time just before war came. The historian offered a prescription for the serious problems that were then ailing Yugoslavia:

> If the Yugoslavs are to continue living together in a united country, and
> if that country is not to become again the proverbial powder keg that
> starts off European crises, it is essential that they should be able to
> participate fully in the development of their community. They must be
> able to appreciate its deeper advantages, to reflect on what put them on
> the path to unification before the First World War, and what made them
> kill each other and yet remain united during and after the Second
> World War. They must be able to express their different ways of

thinking otherwise than by hurling themselves into sectarian impasses. (p. 156)

In other words, Yugoslavs would have to recontextualize the experience of living together by setting it in relation to certain historical, social, and moral realities that had been silenced. Unless "Brotherhood and Unity" could be put to this test and thus strengthened, it would be shed as just another vestigial cultural artifact. Without "Brotherhood and Unity," and without cultural values shared among all the different groups in Bosnia, Serbia, and Croatia, the Bosnian Muslims' merhamet could not possibly stand alone.

Some former Yugoslavs have offered prescriptions of their own for how to redress the problems of historical memories. Many of these are more examples of than solutions for the problems that confronted the Yugoslavs. For example, the Croatian writer Slavenka Drakulic characterized the Yugoslav life of her generation in her "Afterword" to Karahasan's book on Sarajevo: "The experience of our postwar generation was not war, but forgetting that it had happened, not hatred, but tolerance, not conflict, but coexistence."[25]

Drakulic compares Karahasan to Primo Levi. Both spoke from a dark place, insisting that we remember the genocide and stand warned about its repetition. But the problem was that the work of remembering had been left until the crisis was already upon them.

Instead of doing the hard work of remembering, the Yugoslav postwar generation had been working hard at forgetting. They had extended the cultural silencing of memories of World War II begun by their elders. By the time the defenders of a multi-ethnic way of life took this matter up, it was impossible to catch up with the ethnic nationalists, who had long since rewritten those memories in stories that energetically supported their fervent claims to power.

Where were the Primo Levis of World War II in Yugoslavia? Those few brave souls who dared to speak out plainly against the silencing of genocidal memories? Those leaders who could not only spark a collective remembering but also enhance their moral commitment to preserving a multi-ethnic life? One way or another, Tito and his communist society had silenced them. One survivor says it all:

While the others were preparing for war, we still believed in a dream.

| Chapter 2 | Living Through Ethnic Cleansing |

A Survivor's Nightmare

H. is a middle-aged man from Prijedor who spoke of his odyssey in the Omarska concentration camp in testimony psychotherapy.[1] His story is like those of many men from towns or villages throughout Bosnia-Herzegovina who were taken from their families and forced into concentration camps. H.'s story is narrative evidence of ethnic cleansing and how it crushed lives and memories. But the telling of the story is itself an event in which memories are transformed, portending change for H. as a survivor, and perhaps for others. Three of us sit on folding metal chairs in the drab meeting room at the Bosnian Refugee Center: H., the Bosnian mental health worker D., and me.

H. says his troubles began on June 20, 1992, when Serb forces came into the factory where he had worked for years and fired all the Muslims. The next morning they went to Muslim homes, rounded up the men, and brought them to a concentration camp on the grounds of an old manor called Omarska.

I was one of the first people brought to Omarska. After ten days there were 20,000 prisoners. They put us in a big yard. There were 70 percent Muslim, 20 percent Croat, and 10 percent Serb. The guards shot anyone who tried to leave and sometimes shot for no apparent reason.

After three days the "investigations" began. I was in them twenty-five times and only one time did I leave on my own legs. In the investigations they always beat us. Guilty or not guilty.

Ethnic cleansing killed scores, but most people hit by this wave of violence and forced removal were actually left alive. Whereas the truth of the genocide against the Jews is most often signified by the number murdered—6 million— the truth of ethnic cleansing is perhaps best conveyed through the stories and statistics of its displaced living. It has been said that you cannot interview the Holocaust dead, but you can talk with some of the millions of living Bosnians who bore witness to the myriad truths of this ethnic cleansing: the unpreparedness and shock at the end of living together; the harsh immediate and lasting marks left by terror; the collective trauma done to the sense of merhamet.[2]

For the first ten days they didn't give us any food. Then they fed us once a day at 6:00. They gave us three minutes to come from our building to the kitchen. Some of us were more than fifty meters away, and we had no chance to reach the kitchen. Those who came had three minutes to eat. Those who did not had no food. The guards formed a line that we had to run through to get to the kitchen. As we ran they beat us with guns, wheels, and tools.

After eleven days I asked them to let me go to the washroom just to wash my face. When I got there I didn't see that two men from Kožarac also came inside along with some soldiers from special units. The soldiers started to beat them. When they saw me they took me to a place with a big sink and started to beat me. They told me to lick the floor of this washroom for 20,000 people which was dirty with urine and sewage. They broke my ribs. I vomited for one month. I vomited blood.

Sometimes they put us in a 4 x 4 meter room—700 people. They told us to lie down and they closed the windows and the doors. It was summer. We lay like sardines in a can. Those on top were in the best position. Every morning some on the bottom were dead. Every morning a guard came with a list and called people's names. Those they brought out never came back.

One day they came at 3 a.m. and they brought out 174 people. I was with them. They lined us up behind a building they called the White House. Ten soldiers came with automatic weapons and they started to shoot us. Only three of us survived.

The worst event was when I watched one young man as they castrated him. Right now I can hear his cry and his prayers to be killed. And every night it wakes me. He was a nice young man. His executioner was his friend from school. He cut his body and he licked his blood. He asked him just to kill and to stop all that suffering. All day and all night we heard his prayers and his crying until he died. This is something that I cannot forget. It gives me nightmares and makes sleep almost impossible. I can't remember the people who were the executioners. For me all of them in those uniforms were the same. I can't remember who was who.

At the end of our first meeting, H. said, *I am all tears. When I speak about that even though my eyes are open I see all those images in front of me.*

THE SECOND MEETING begins tentatively, with H. saying, *It is difficult to talk about anything when all the days were similar.* So we review the last meeting's testimony with him and ask some questions to restart the dialogue.

Here in my neighborhood there is a man who was with me in the camp. He was a prisoner, like me, but he had the duty to beat us in order to save his own skin. And he did that very well. He wasn't alone. I know many examples of people like him.

They had to do that just to survive. But I preferred it when he beat me. I always stayed on my feet. He didn't beat as hard as the others. I remember also one other man. He was a Muslim. He was very violent. He killed many, many prisoners. Finally we prisoners killed him by our own hands.

"You were there when that happened?"

Yes, I was there. They moved him from our camp but then after some time they brought him back. And they pushed him inside in a crowd of prisoners because they knew what would happen. All of us participated in that. One thousand people. And nobody could say "I killed him" because all of us did. I didn't directly participate in the killing. But I was in the same room. I do not feel guilty. I wished to be in that group—the execution group—and I wished to participate in killing him. But I was really very weak.

I have to say something about the first prisoner who beat us and any other person who had to do the same job he did. Some people came to my house in Chicago to ask me to sign a note condemning him. I didn't do that because I do not think he is guilty. He helped many people. He didn't beat us like the Serbs did. He saved many, many lives. He needed to do that to save his own life.

Our region had very rich soil, and we had many farm animals. Day after day the Serbs brought our animals, and Muslim butchers had to slaughter them and put them in freezer trucks. Every day for two and a half months freezer trucks took that meat somewhere. Almost everything went into Serbia. The Serbs passed through our region especially to find gold and money. If someone wished to take all your property, he came and asked you to sign a paper that was something like a will, and you left him everything that you had—car, truck, house, and everything inside. And for that he gave you a piece of bread. But if he went to your house and couldn't find everything you signed over to him, then he would kill your family and come back into the camp and kill you.

I want to tell you something else. We had a special platoon. About a hundred prisoners had the duty of taking the bodies of murdered people, putting them in trucks, and bringing them to a special place with pits to dispose of them. They knew where they put all the Muslim bodies. One day before our camp was closed, before the Red Cross came, the soldiers killed all of them. Serbs killed all one hundred Muslims just to wipe out all witnesses. I was not in that group because I was too weak and too thin.

As the second meeting ends, H. says he is feeling better, but that he is still being terrorized by a nightmare. A man is screaming but H. cannot see his face. He does not know what this is. Someone he has seen before? Something he did wrong? The dream, which comes every night, is torturing him.

We BEGIN the third meeting by reminding H. that we last talked about the man in his dream. H. sits silently, looking puzzled as a few minutes pass. Then suddenly brightening, he speaks.

Now I remember who is that guy from my dreams! I remember his name. He was the financial manager in my factory. Every night he told me to say hello to his wife and children. His name is Vahid.

He is overjoyed that he has finally remembered.

But I still can't remember his face.

He was a very educated person. A master of economics. But his behavior was so modest, so normal, and he was friendly and helpful with all the people in our factory. When the war started, he was brought with us to the concentration camp. Because he was a very important person, they beat him a lot. But he continued to help people. If the Serbs wanted to beat somebody, he actually changed places with that person, and they beat Vahid instead. When we ran for food, he helped the weak and sick people. If somebody didn't run, Vahid gave him food and brought him through the kitchen. And because of that, they beat him even more. Finally they killed him because he was like a celebrity in the concentration camp.

H. looks for a moment as if he is back in the camp. Absolute terror and grief. Then a striking change.

"What's coming up now?"

I am so happy because I remember him. Now I am sweating a lot and I hear his voice and his words three days before they killed him, when he told me, "I am next, and please, if you survive go to my home and say hello to my wife and my children."

H. can now see the face of the man in his dream.

Third night, two o'clock in the morning the guard came and he brought a list with names of people. We were in a big garage. It was 1,300 people. And he read the names. At the end was Vahid. When Vahid stood to go he told us maybe we would see him tomorrow. Early in the morning we saw ten bodies lying near the garbage containers. A yellow truck came, picked them up, and took them away.

I don't know how somebody can survive all that torture, such crimes. I remember one man, my neighbor, they cut his skull with a tool and we saw his brain. It was absolutely open. When he moved, his brain moved. And that man survived.

Did I mention about machine oil? I was in a garage with ten other people. There was a long channel full of motor oil and dust. One guard who watched us would always tell me, "Go take your meal!" He gave me a plastic cup of motor oil that I had to drink. Every day, for thirty days, until they moved him to some other concentration camp. I got dysentery and terrible diarrhea. One year later, whenever I inhaled or exhaled very deeply I smelled oil. I have no mucosa in my gut and I have very strong acid. When I am nervous, acid comes into my mouth like water, my mouth is full of acid.

He speaks again of Vahid.

That night the guards came to take people. When they spoke his name, the whole garage fell silent. We were shocked and very sad. We didn't cry because we had no tears, but we did something else. We started to sing without words. In that way we gave him our best wishes and best regards. We really were very sad when we saw his body the next morning. He was our leader before and during the war.

"What did you sing?"

It wasn't song. Not a real song. It was something like humming, and it was a sign of sadness and a sign of rage. They came in the garage and they beat us for hours and hours. The garage was so full of people that they had no place to pass, so they stepped on our bodies. And we had achieved our goal, because they were angry. We sang because we wished to see the Serbs angry. We were sad, but also because it was the only way to show them how much we loved that person.

And I also want to mention Vahid's nephew. When he came to the camp, he went crazy. I remember one night the camp was really full of people, and they put us in that big kitchen. Maybe four hundred people were in the kitchen, and at one point that young man, he stood up and he said, "Wake up, people. In the name of Allah, why do we permit them to do this with us?" At that moment some guards came and shot him. But they didn't kill just him. They killed the ten people around him too. I thought he was brave. But now I think he was crazy, because a brave person tries to save his own life.

We did not have enough room to move our bodies. Everyone stood in his place and moved his body back and forth. We sang from our guts. When they came into the garage, and they started to beat us, the more they beat, the stronger and stronger we sang. It was a special feeling. Our voices were very weak because we were hungry. When we spoke it was almost like you couldn't hear, very very quiet. But for me any sound was so strong.

There was little way to show what you felt, because you did not have the right to talk, to use words. If you used words they killed you. If you showed only signs, like an animal, the guard doesn't know what you feel. He can only beat you. He doesn't kill you.

We promised each other when we were in the camp that we would keep in touch and that anyone who knew what happened to another would inform his family. There were two times when I had to tell another prisoner's family that he had been killed. We didn't want to mislead the families. We promised we would tell the truth.

H. concludes the third session: *I am so happy because I recognized the man from my dreams, and maybe now I will stop. Maybe now he will not come in my dreams.*

H. thinks Vahid's family might be in Germany, but he has been unable to locate them.

H.'s testimony invites and repels at the same time. It is a nightmare one does not wish to enter—but a nightmare that compels in part because it contains a struggle to remain generous and decent when others have intended for you only humiliation, suffering, and death. Is there any way out of the nightmare? The survivor wants to know, and waits.

Warning Signs of Things to Come

Bosnian Muslim people, with their strong experiences of living together under the Yugoslav system of "Brotherhood and Unity" and within the cultural milieu of merhamet in Bosnia-Herzegovina, saw clear signs of impending troubles, but resisted interpreting them as signifying the approach of anything resembling ethnic cleansing.

We could smell the war in the air. But we kept hoping, lying to ourselves.

We were lulled by the old system into believing in the stability of our multi-ethnic life.

Until the very day ethnic cleansing abruptly smashed into their homes with the fist pounding on the door or the exploding grenade, most refused to believe that anything like it would ever happen in Bosnia-Herzegovina. Yes, they had watched the slow deterioration in the economic, social, and political fabric of Yugoslav society throughout the late 1980s, and the political crisis in the early 1990s. Yes, they had voted in the referendum of 1992 in which the Bosnian people chose to secede from Yugoslavia and become an independent country.[3] And yes, they even saw the war between the Serbs and the Croats and the terrible prolonged battle of Vukovar on TV.

We all felt that the war in Croatia was happening far far away from us.

I felt as if I was reading a novel about those things.

Despite all the evidence of worrisome political changes happening all around them, Bosnians did not believe that their lives were on the brink of an abyss. Instead of preparing to defend themselves in April 1992, Sarajevans held a massive peace rally.[4]

I remember how everybody went to Sarajevo for the peace rallies. They were holding huge photographs of Tito, hoping that he was going to save them from bloodshed. They could not believe that Yugoslavia, Tito's Yugoslavia, could fall apart, and that there would be a war. Muslims particularly could not believe it. The idea of Yugoslavia was deeply rooted in their being; they all shared the idea that I told you about, the idea of Bosnia as home to all of its people.

We also attended the peace rallies. We were at the big rally in front of the Bosnian Parliament, when a Serb sniper killed some of the demonstrators. The atmosphere at the rally gave us the feeling that everyone was against the war, and that we would be able to stop it, because there were so many of us. Of course, it only lulled us further.

Some survivors speak of the moment when they finally realized just how far the nationalists were willing to go in pursuit of their vision. Some report that it dawned on them when the nationalist parties won in the 1992 elections.

Suddenly everybody was talking politics. It was no longer football and basketball, but which party will win, and who will take which part of the country.

Everything started during that election when the nationalist party won. Then people started to separate into two different types: those who think about living together and being together, and those who talk about separation and different religions and nationalities.

When the political leaders of SDS said they had a plan to divide people and create an ethnically pure society, I was really surprised. How can they do that? How can they divide people in one city, in one building?

Some survivors report that even when directly confronted with material evidence of an impending crisis, they found it impossible to believe.

Several times, across from my apartment building, I'd see a big truck, and I'd think, Oh my God, what's this big truck doing there? I had binoculars, so I could see what was in the back. It was flour, sugar, and oil and the people came with personal cars and trucks, and they took the flour and everything they needed for the house. And I told my wife, "Can you imagine people bought 300 kg of flour? What's the reason?" And my neighbors bought the same, and I thought, maybe if they are buying I have to buy something. I bought a few cans.

I remember there was a huge military transport with buses, trucks, and army vehicles heading through Gacko. It lasted two or three days. They were carrying heavy weapons and ammunition. They no longer looked like the Yugoslav army, although that's what they called themselves. The vehicles were marked with Serbian nationalist symbols, slogans like "God protect Serbia" and such. The soldiers, those reserve people, did not look anything like Yugoslav army soldiers used to look. They were middle-aged, plump, with long beards—they looked like Chetniks. They were no longer displaying the Yugoslav flag; they had a Serbian nationalist flag. At that point it would have been easy for us to come to the conclusion that there would be no place for us in Gacko in times to come, but at the time nobody thought about it that way.

Some people were saying that the Serbian doctors at our medical center were taking away materials. Some citizens had noticed them taking away their stuff in their cars during the night. I didn't want to believe that. If I accepted that, then I would have to accept that the overall system of values was going to collapse. It was much better for me not to believe.

Yet even actually seeing their Serbian neighbors making strange preparations was not enough to convince many Bosnians of impending disaster. Why not?

In the days before the ethnic cleansing, instead of gathering supplies and arms, sending their children abroad, or leaving the country, a great many individual citizens were engaged in personally reaffirming their commitment to multi-ethnic Bosnia, both to themselves and to the people around them. The Bosnian government was taking pains to show the Bosnian Serb leaders that they had absolutely no desire for war and that they were fully committed to multi-ethnic coexistence. The Bosnian government was actively trying to show that the nationalists' propaganda was not true. To go any other way would only have encouraged aggression further. To affirm their commitment to multi-ethnic living at least gave peace a chance. Or so it seemed.

There was an initiative to take our children to safety. The new school director told us not to do that. Some Serbs were thinking that we would take the children out in order to feel more free to attack the Serbs. Unbelievable! So it was they who felt threatened by us. The school director told us that if we did not bring our children back within seven days, the Serbs would consider it proof of their suspicions about us. So we brought the children back. We did not want to give them reason to attack us.

So preoccupied with showing the other side they had not changed, Bosnians did not notice that the other side already had.

In spring 1992, more survivors reported calamitous changes coming suddenly to schools, businesses, and hospitals. Still some resisted.

When the war started, the chief of the department, a Serbian doctor, said that we would continue to work in the hospital, treat all people, not take sides whatever happened.

It rapidly became impossible for them to brush off these changes, or even to speak out on their commitment to multi-ethnic coexistence.

After the war began in Croatia, it seemed like the teachers were trying to disparage our abilities. I had been at the top of my class. Then I started getting Bs. One teacher in particular, the history teacher, was the most nationalistic. At first there was small talk, little comments, and then it escalated until it was propaganda. My friends and I took it as a joke. We laughed about it. It was crazy. We would be sitting in the classroom raising our eyebrows and joking about the teacher. Then it seemed to become more serious. I remember one Serb girl in our class. She was also a good student. All of a sudden, the professor began speaking to her as if they were having private conversations. Like no one else was there. She was a nationalist. She put up symbols of the Serb cross in different places. We were surprised, because she had been very friendly. All of a sudden the teacher was having a discussion with her about the need to get rid of the Muslims.

When the student became tense and guarded in our interview, I asked him how he felt. He said that was when he knew: *It was not a joke anymore.* He could see that his friends and his teachers had really changed.

An adult survivor speaks of what happened at his place of work. *At work there were constant provocations, people would play around with weapons, but I put*

*up with it thinking that it would pass. I heard them saying that all Croats and Mus-
lims were going to be slaughtered, killed, but I never believed that would actually happen. They often asked me if I was a little "Ustasha," and they gave me that nickname.
All of this was more or less normal for me until they came to my place. First they told
me that they would set all my things on fire, that it all had to burn because it was
Muslim, and after all of these provocations they took me to jail. At the (police station) they hit me and yelled at me and looked for a Serbian flag, to nail it on my head.
They even said they would carve it on my forehead.*

Bosnians realized very quickly that the changes were not limited to just a
few organizations they might be able to do without, to a few extremists, or to a
few gestures. This was really a major fracturing of their nation's way of living
together.

*When the war started I saw that what had been only an idea had become the
reality. It began as an idea. But it became something more. Suddenly the only thing
that mattered was your nationality. Not who you are. Not how much you are a man
or not a man. Only what nationality you are.*

*Until yesterday you had been a person. You had your life and family. All of a
sudden you walk around a city in which you feel strange, reading signs with messages
like "Muslims and dogs cannot go into buses." It really makes you believe that you
are not an individual human being. You feel like an animal.*

Many were dragged down to the local police station and beaten by the new
Serb authorities, who would say:

*"What do you Muslims want? We are going to drive you out like the Jews in
World War II, and those of you that resist, we're going to kick you in the ass." That
was when I realized what was happening. Until then I thought it was a joke. Because
we all lived together so well.*

Some Sarajevans speak with envy about one group that from early on took
it all very seriously, anticipated what was to come, and got out. That was the
Jews.[5] One Jewish doctor, a woman, told her Muslim colleague some months
before the fighting broke out in Sarajevo that there would be war. He teased
her about her "Jewish suspiciousness." In 1993 she called him in Sarajevo from
her new home in Western Europe to say, "See, wasn't I right?" Another doctor
says that the Jewish experience of surviving the Holocaust taught them how to
protect themselves, whereas the Bosnian Muslims never learned any such lessons from their history.

What Bosnians had learned added to their self-deception, their downplaying
the threat of nationalism. Although the signs were right in front of them, they
did not believe that ethnic nationalist violence was about to happen. Even after all that has transpired, one survivor reports feeling that *We were really cheated.*
Cheated in the sense that the others were trying to pull something on them,

being themselves on the surface even as they were putting their nationalist plan into action. He still does not want to accept that these people he knew were transformed into something other. He is giving them the benefit of the doubt, hoping that they will soon stop this and return to being the friendly neighbors they once were.

By the time most Bosnians recognized what had changed, it was already far too late. They were a nation of defenseless civilians facing a well-laid military plan for murder, terror, and forced removal. They never had a chance.

Betrayal

A businesswoman's former employee, who was a Bosnian Serb, set her house afire and made her stand and watch with him.

"Well, boss—everything you had burned." I told him, "I will make it again one day, and you will not get any better." He had red eyes. It frightened me. I dropped the conversation. I tried to disappear in the crowd.

Again and again survivors give accounts of people being betrayed by neighbors, family members, best friends, business partners, teachers, doctors. Not enemies or strangers, but people who were a part of the fabric of their lives.

Again and again survivors report that they never dreamed that these familiar people could turn on them. What they all report is that even five minutes before it happened, they did not believe that it was actually possible for their neighbors to become killers. Were the transformations indeed that rapid, or is it that Bosnian Muslims were unable to recognize or understand the changes before them? Someday it will be important to actually study the perpetrators and understand more about what they did and why they did it, questions that have only recently been comprehensively addressed in connection with the Holocaust.[6] Now we can begin by exploring these friendly relationships that turned deadly, images of which emerge from listening to Bosnian survivors. The reports of betrayal do not all sound the same.

Many betrayals are described as acts of greed.

After seven days in detention, my best friend came. We had to give him everything we had. He took us to our house and burned it down and made us watch it. He said, "I know you have money and jewelry. Give me everything."

There are innumerable stories of people who had their possessions or their home taken away by someone who knew what they had, saw a chance to take it, and made speedy use of that chance. These cases seem motivated more by personal gain than by politics. People could settle an old score or get something they wanted for themselves. The marks of destruction that Serb forces left in Muslim flats show that they always looked for hidden money and jewels, much like the Nazis did to the Jews. However, they didn't stop there; they took everything—toilets, doors, molding, the kitchen sink. Then, more often than not, they burned the building down.

Some betrayals are described as a personal abandonment.

Suddenly they did not know you on the street and would turn their heads away not to recognize you. They pretended as if they had never seen us in their lives.

Many of our friends were Bosnian Orthodox. In April the Serbian army occupied Banja Luka. The Bosnian Orthodox agreed with Serbian politics. Our good friends changed their behavior. They left us. All our friends, our neighbors. They did nothing for us. One neighbor and close friend was a secretary in the Republic of Serbia government. She could have helped us. Her husband was in the police. They turned their back on us. My colleague at the institute—a colleague of twenty years—dismissed me from my job. Now he is the boss in the institute. I thought he was a good person. He left me and my family without money.

Friends or coworkers or neighbors, people to whom you would ordinarily turn in time of need, would not help as you were being turned out. Their allegiance to you had been superseded or negated. They regarded you as if you didn't exist anymore. On the other hand, many survivors report that Bosnian Serbs did in fact come to the aid of Bosnian Muslims, and some paid for that with their lives.

The drunk soldier recognized our neighbor, who was his superior, and he let go of my uncle. Our neighbor brought both men home. My father was seventy at the time, and my uncle was sixty. That man who saved my uncle was a Chetnik officer, and he probably did many things that would qualify him for the War Crimes Tribunal. But he was our neighbor for many years. And as a neighbor, he rushed to help our family. He is a criminal, and yet I am grateful to him.

The doctor wrote on a piece of paper that my husband needed urgent surgery, and stamped that paper, adding the request for immediate transportation to Sarajevo because of surgical emergency. I went to the Red Cross and told them how we had to leave immediately. Then they arranged the transportation to the barricades with the UNPROFOR. When I was leaving, the doctor told me: "Don't tell anybody because my life will be in danger, but all the Muslims that remain here are meant to be shot dead." I just froze.

The kind of betrayal mentioned least often by survivors is the betrayal overtly marked by ideology. Even when survivors demanded political explanations from their perpetrators, the Serbs often did not provide them:

The next morning my mother saw a close friend of the family, someone who had been to our house for dinner. She went across the field to him. He was now a Serb commando in military uniform. She asked him, "Why is this happening?" and she pleaded with him to make it stop. He said, "Shut up, and get in the bus."

Survivors' stories indicate that the betrayers did not make much attempt to justify their behavior in ideological or political terms. Nor, for that matter, did survivors understand events that way. Neither of these facts is surprising, because after all, most citizens of the former Yugoslavia were not politically minded.

Despite widespread agreement among Bosnians about the important role of nationalist ideology in driving the social changes that culminated in ethnic cleansing, it is striking that a dominant image of the war which they and others present is that of "neighbor killing neighbor." According to this decidedly non-political view, ideology was merely a cover for a litany of human moral weaknesses. There is as yet no way of knowing for certain how people were led to betray or why they chose to do so. This matter is still intensely debated regarding the Holocaust, about which much more information has been gathered over the past fifty years.[7]

This image of betrayers that survivors tend to create, of confused, culpable, terrified, greedy and sadistic human beings, does ring more true than an image of ideologically driven robots. In any case, the formula for ethnic cleansing did not require that all perpetrators talk the talk, as long as they were willing to walk the walk. It was via the blunt fact of their occurrence, and not how they were explained, that betrayals delivered their destructive blow to the way things were. By precipitating betrayals the nationalists were able to implode the institutions of friendship, collegiality, community, and even family that were at the center of the multi-ethnic life.

These betrayals leave the survivor with an extraordinarily difficult psychological burden that one naturally seeks to push away. Some survivors keep accounts of personal betrayals hidden by telling a story that is manifestly more about politics. A forty-five-year-old man tells his story to the interviewers for more than two hours, always referring to the perpetrators as the "Chetniks." The interviewers believe, incorrectly, that the assailants were all strangers belonging to warring hordes who came from far away to kill and destroy. At the same time, the survivor's wife is telling her interviewers that she and her husband had actually been attacked by people whose dinner guests they had been the week before. This is the survivor's (and the interviewers') attempt to avoid acknowledging the magnitude of the personal betrayal.

I experience an acute realization of the awful burden left by betrayals when visiting a Bosnian family in their home late one night with my wife. They want to show us the photo albums their aunt in Bosnia miraculously saved and mailed to them. It is late and we want to go home to sleep, but once the books are opened we simply have to stay. Sipping Bosnian coffee, we leaf through the heavy books looking at snapshots and portraits of the family life that war had put far behind them—birthday parties, excursions to the country, holidays, concerts, graduations, friendly gatherings. Then E. interrupts the pleasant reliving of the family's past: *Those are the people that betrayed us. They are living in our apartment!* He can never forgive them. Nor can he tear their pictures out of the album. They were in too many photos and are too much a part of the survivors' lives for their haunting presence to simply be erased. They used to celebrate all their kids' birthday parties together before those connections were burned.

Ethnic Cleansing

Massive brute military aggression from without was required to abruptly shatter the way things were. During the summer of 1992, in towns and villages across Bosnia, the military operation of ethnic cleansing began by laying siege to the places where Bosnian Muslim civilians lived. These sieges were calculated military and paramilitary terrorist operations, not the spontaneous eruptions of "ethnic hatred" the perpetrators and apologists would ludicrously propose. They involved attacks from nonlocals such as the JNA (Yugoslav National Army), Bosnian Serb forces, and irregular Serbian paramilitary units such as those belonging to the infamous terrorists Arkan and Seselj.[8]

Bosnians were shocked to see that the JNA, which they referred to as "our army," was now directly attacking them. How could this be? Being attacked by their own army, which they supported with their taxes and depended on to protect them, made absolutely no sense at all to the survivors.

We all thought that the army was going to save us. I am bitterly disappointed because of the role that the army had in this war. When the first tensions occurred, I thought that they were going to put an end to it. But, they took the other side. And it was our Yugoslav army, which we trusted and believed in.

The military was aided by paramilitary units such as the Chetniks, the infamous Serbian nationalist fighters from World War II.

It was common to see army vehicles in the city with soldiers wearing Chetnik insignia, who were often drunk and who used to shoot in the air. They looked to me like real Chetniks, which I had seen before only in films about Word War II.

Military and paramilitary units like Arkan's came from Belgrade and committed atrocities, expelled families from their homes, and looted their property.

A number of Bosnians later learned that in their towns and villages, many Serbs had secretly gathered to lay the plans and prepare themselves for this day. Then all the strange preparations they had overlooked suddenly made sense. It must have made perfect sense to the architects and managers of the ethnic cleansing. Typically, they would launch the first shells or fire the first shots, immediately militarizing the situation. They would then arm the local Serbs and involve them in killing, terrorizing, and looting their own town. It added up to an insurmountable force that easily had its way with defenseless Bosnian civilians.

They destroyed the mosque. Then the Chetniks came in cars and talked over a loudspeaker: "Get out of your houses. Assemble in the square." They talked about the rules of the game: "You are second-class citizens. No work, no pension. Kids can't go to school." We were treated as if we were illiterate. One old woman asked them, "Why did you destroy our mosque?" They said, "Well, you have to get used to the idea of praying to our God." They wanted to destroy our identity. They treated us like cattle.

> I arrived at "Keraterm" on June 14th. I was captured in the village Sivci after the Chetniks entered, encircled, and bombed the village. The villages were given away. Those of us who were up there from other villages attempted to organize the Sivci villagers but did not succeed. They [Chetniks] told us repeatedly to come down and continue with our lives and nothing was going to happen to anyone. As we came down, they surrounded and captured us and started to kill us. As they brought people out of a house they would kill them. Whoever was taken behind a house would be killed immediately.[9]

Most sieges were of limited duration. Their aim was to create chaos, militarize the town, and expel the Muslims and the Croats. This was feasible in the small villages and small cities of Eastern Bosnia, which were "cleansed" in a matter of days. Even in a larger city like Banja Luka, where the cleansing would literally take years, the Serb forces used much the same methodology, publicly slaughtering some Muslims in order to frighten the others into leaving.

The imported criminals were committing the atrocities, but it was the local Serbs, our former neighbors, who were pointing their fingers and telling them what to do. Serbian people were completely influenced by their propaganda, which said that we were a threat to them and that we had planned to do what they were doing to us. It was mass hysteria and a mass movement for all non-Serbs. Later they were hunting for individuals from their lists. Any Serb could find a Muslim, put him in a car, drive him away, and kill him, because of some old misunderstanding, or for no reason at all.

When the Serb forces engaged in ethnic cleansing took a city street, some citizens were immediately slaughtered, as if to scare the others into doing as they were ordered. The Serbs announced their plans over the local radio and via loudspeakers. They ordered citizens to leave their homes. But first they wanted to know where the Muslims' money and belongings were, and they wanted these signed over to them.

Sometimes they took someone's child and said they would kill him or her if they did not get a set amount of German Marks.

They started to burn down all the Muslim properties. Even those with white flags (those who recognized the Serbian Republic). They said this was the part of the city where the terrorists came from, therefore it had to be burned altogether. They said, "You have to leave." They took all our documents and threw them in a big basket and burnt them all. We were nobody now.

The terror was approaching us from without. It started in the villages, then there were murders in the outskirts of the city. It was getting closer and closer to the center with the aim of scaring the inhabitants who did not want to leave their homes, who were hoping that things were going to be over one day. The Serbs were showing us the opposite, trying to teach us that we had no business being in our own city and the best thing for us would be to leave everything and go out.

We were told that if our family was in our house tomorrow after twelve o'clock, we would be killed. We thought it would be better not to hide, but to go peacefully. So we were taken away to a camp on a vehicle. There we saw so many corpses in the fields. The first dead person I saw was covered with flies. The stench was terrible. My mother, sister, and I had to spend the night hiding in a field. I slept in a ditch next to many dead bodies. I am sure that some of them were bodies of people I knew. I could not sleep, I just lay there asking how it could be happening.

The events were taking place with unbelievable speed. We had no time to think. No one could dream about massacres, concentration camps, and genocide. It all took place in less than a month. Obviously everything was prepared ahead of time.

The atrocities included rape perpetrated by the Serb forces from outside, but also by local men and boys. Cvijetn Maksinovic, a twenty-two-year-old Bosnian Serb prisoner of war, said that rapes were committed, "all to scare the people off, to make them run from Brcko and make it clear to them there was no return for them."[10] Rapes were committed in the victims' homes, in public, and in "rape camps."[11]

The men were told to leave their families and to gather in some designated public place. Deportations were massive operations that were systematically planned and implemented, though with plenty of room for local variation. Means of transportation had been made available, usually buses, but sometimes trucks or trains.

Then they moved us in four buses to a jail in the town of Nova Gradiska. Along the way there were many control points manned by Serb policemen. Each time we passed one of those points, the Serbs would ask that some of us be handed over to be slaughtered. But our Serb guards on the bus didn't allow them to take any of us. When we asked the Serb policemen on the bus about our destiny, they replied that everything depended on the situation at the battlefront. If they—the Serbs—were in need of men to exchange for their own prisoners, then they would let us live; if they didn't have prisoners that they wanted to free in an exchange, they would kill us.

The worst drives led to the concentration camp.

The drive to Omarska was horrible. They taunted me and hit me
sometimes, and told me that I would never again return to Prijedor, and
that they wanted an ethnically clean Greater Serbia. They drove me
through Kožarac . At every one of their checkpoints they stopped and
took me out with the intention of shooting me right on the spot. They
told me to take a good look at Kožarac, which no longer existed and
never again would. I could only see destroyed and burned houses. They
told me that this was no longer Kožarac, that it was now Radmilovo.[12]

Once the process of genocidal destruction was set into motion, it spread
like a brush fire. Ethnic cleansing was so successful in terrorizing the population and getting them to relinquish their homes that Bosnian Muslims started
"cleansing" themselves. By then a change was observed:

In the beginning things were simple. The authorities wanted the people
out, and the people wanted to stay. Now, the authorities want them out,
and the people want to go. They're saying that they just want to get out.
People are coming to us and saying don't stop the ethnic cleansing.
People are wasting the last of their money to bribe themselves out of
Serb-controlled areas. It's called self-cleansing.[13]

Ethnic cleansing was working. Bosnians were getting the idea that they could
no longer live together.

After the adult men were deported to concentration camps, many of their
wives and children were thrown out of their homes and left to flee across the
countryside. They traveled on foot through forests, over mountains, and across
rivers. They slept in fields, barns, or with relatives or friends. They were in search
of a safe haven and their missing loved ones.

*There is no way to explain how fearful and stressful that was. Not knowing what
was going to happen to us was the hardest part.*

Death could come night or day.

A woman recalled paying all her money to a Serb man who agreed to drive
her and her children to the Croatian border where they could cross. She told
him that she didn't trust him. *"What do you think I'll do?" "You know the stories.
Serbs are doing very bad things to our women." "Those who are doing that are villagers. City people don't do that. We city people didn't start this war and don't want it
that way. We had to join to be loyal."*
For the lucky ones, the journey through Bosnia ended at the Croatian border, where they put their lives in the hands of war profiteers and tried to bribe
their way across to safety.

They stopped us at two checkpoints on the bridge. The soldiers said, "100 DM each. Who does not give will not pass." It was better with the Croats. They said, "Welcome to life again."

Concentration Camps

Merely mentioning the term "concentration camp" conjures up death images of the Nazi concentration camps of World War II. Most of us have had the grim images of Auschwitz burned into our memories—so much so that even to speak the words "concentration camp" in the Bosnian context establishes a strong connection between ethnic cleansing and the Holocaust. Many were quick to draw this parallel; many others strongly resisted it.

It is wrong simply to equate Serbian concentration camps with Nazi concentration camps. An Auschwitz, for example, was a highly systematized death factory that took years to evolve and was the pinnacle of the Nazis' final solution—the final stop in the Nazi death machine, where Jews were brought to be killed en masse. When Bosnians speak of concentration camps, they primarily mean detention facilities where civilians were brought against their will, held in harsh conditions, and subjected to starvation, illness, forced labor, atrocities, and death. In comparison with their Nazi counterparts, Serbian concentration camps were hastily and sloppily set up. Omarska and Manjaca came closest to being death camps, but none ever evolved to the degree of sophistication or mechanization of death that was Auschwitz. This is not to minimize the mass killings and rapes that certainly did take place in those camps, and the other horrific traumas and suffering that detainees were subject to; it is just that the Serbs were not so systematic about it.

Concentration camps in Bosnia were set up in commandeered existing large public spaces, such as sports stadiums, schools, prisons, farms, mines, or warehouses.[14] They were not on sites specially constructed for the purpose, a fact that had dire consequences for the health of the detainees.

They put us on something like a farm. Nothing special. It was terrible. They spoke very bad words. It happened at midnight and they told us "be ready for your last trip."

The locations were not at all prepared to handle such problems as sewage, water, or food.

For me, I had one quarter of a loaf of bread every month. I remember one day they made some beans and they threw out the beans into some channel near the camp. We ran to that channel and we took those beans with our hands. We took soil and grasses and everything. It didn't look like beans, but we were very hungry. And we didn't think about it. We knew it was beans.

Because the detainees were starving, it is no surprise that they thought and dreamed constantly about food and drink.

We weren't afraid of dying. One glass of water was more important than life. I remember one old professor from Stolac who shared a bed with me, and he told me, "It will be much easier for me to die if I am full. Just tell me to eat. After that they can kill me."

Because these camps were essentially regional centers that received persons deported from the surrounding region, many of the detainees not only knew one another but they also knew many of the camp guards and soldiers. This offered some advantages, such as special favors from friends, but also set up the possibility for harsh betrayals.

The camp guards knew, or at least alleged to know, what was happening with the families and loved ones of the detainees. They used this knowledge as power over the detainees.

Besides all that torture, one day they told us they had started to kill our families. They told my neighbor that they had killed part of his family. Then we saw the trucks with our families being transported. Our nightmares came again. We began to cry.

Sometimes the detainees' families would come to the camp and try to visit with their loved one, or attempt to bargain with the guards. The right bribe could win the detainees special treatment or even release. One woman paid her own brother-in-law, a camp guard, a huge amount of money to secure the release of her husband. The guard took the money, but did nothing.

Sometimes acquaintances took on a lethal dimension in the camps.

One survivor recalled that the worst thing that could happen to someone in the camp was when a new contingent of Serbian troops arrived every fifteen days to relieve the older guards. An acquaintance from one's hometown might be among the newcomers. That acquaintance would murder you because he didn't want a living witness to remain. The survivor grew a beard so as not to be recognized.

One Bosnian journalist who survived a camp said that he was absolutely certain that an international journalist had saved his life by doing a story on him that made the international press and caught the attention of political leaders.

> Foreign journalists arrived and began to film us. They caught me first, next to the barbed wire, and I began to talk when one of the guards standing behind said: "Record the names of all those talking so we can kill them." I hardly said anything, except that I was hungry and exhausted. I was not allowed to say much. Everyone who said more to the journalists and had their names recorded was taken by the Serbs that night—to be killed.[15]

Visits from foreign journalists, human rights observers, or health care workers would also lead to deadly acts of reprisal. One survivor tells about one night in the camp after a Red Cross visit.

They took out ten men and had them lie on the ground, and then they stood on some blocks about a meter and a half high and jumped off and landed on their chests. They broke their chests and killed the men that way. That was the hardest for me, seeing their ribs broken, sticking out through their skin, seeing them rolled over, no skin on their back, just black.

Some reports from journalists had a positive effect. After Roy Gutman, the first Western journalist to break the story of the camps, published his reports in *New York Newsday*, some camps were shut down.[16]

These camps did not exhibit any of the highly systematized or medicalized selection process seen in Nazi camps. The fate of the detainees in a concentration camp depended (but only to a limited extent) on how the Serbs viewed him.

One survivor reported, "There were three categories of prisoners in Omarska: 1. a group determined for execution; 2. a group determined for exchange; 3. a group that Serbs considered to be useless."[17]

We still have much more to learn about camp life, but what I know from survivors' stories indicates that the fate of the survivors depended a great deal on chance and impulse.

In some of the camps there were apparently efforts to ritualize the atrocities. One survivor spoke of the *ethical behavior* within the camps. The Manjaca commandant proclaimed that it was unethical to kill after 9 p.m., so the nightly ritual of executions took place between 8:45 and 9:00, with a trumpet blast at 9:00—following ancient custom—to mark its ending.

Camp life was more disorganized than not, impulsive and chaotic. From survivor reports the perpetrators appear to have been not so much systematic as relentless in their committing of atrocities and killings. It seems the guards would dream up sadistic fantasies and make the detainees enact them, with deadly consequences.

One survivor describes how they would take two men and make them beat each other. *It was horrible to watch. Hundreds of times one would hit the other, the other would hit back. They were true beasts. Then after hours they would beat the two people to death with their rifle butts.*

Judging from survivor accounts, interrogations seemed to be motivated not by any serious desire to obtain information but by the sadistic wish to torture some and terrorize all.

During interrogation they asked me about guns. The accusations were ridiculous: we had no guns nor any list of names of Serbs we intended to execute!

"Each night the Serbs called some of us out for interrogation. Sometimes we heard screaming. The Serbs sadistically joked with some of our men: they forced a few boys to kiss one another and after that they beat them, asking: 'What are you doing? Are you homosexuals?'"[18]

Beatings and torture were a constant theme in camp life. Some appeared to do it for sport.

I used to work in many Serb houses because I was a carpenter. I did a very good job. I remember one person came one weekend and brought me some biscuits. But I also saw that man beating another. We were always afraid of certain people. We called them weekend soldiers. They were the worst. They were people who worked in Switzerland, France, Germany. They came to camp on the weekend. They killed as much as they wanted to and they left.

Others were apparently motivated by greed.

When they decided to empty the other camp, they called us and said to sign indicating that we would leave them all our property, and only under that condition could we leave Prijedor. They took all my money. What else did I have to do before I could leave? I had to pay my telephone bills and electric power for next month and to buy a bus ticket to Croatia.

Some of the worst traumas involved watching others suffer and die and being helpless to intervene.

I spent fifty-six days in this camp. Every night I listened to the people crying and moaning, begging and pleading for their torturers to stop, trying to convince them of their innocence. They were guilty on only one charge: for being Croatian or Muslim.

The worst thing was watching old people who died because they were sick. Nobody helped them. They needed only fresh air. Maybe they could survive. And I remember two old men, who went seven days without food, and finally they died.

You hear a voice moaning and you ask where is that cat from. The others say, "That is not a cat. It's a man." And you see him, sitting twisted, crying in a voice that does not have anything human about it. You hear his wailing for an hour or so, then it wanes. They cut the testicles off the poor fellow.

Because the boundaries that encircled the camps were not so sharp, life within the camps could be influenced by other outsiders, including foreign journalists.

They only increased the quantity of food when they knew that television crews would be visiting and filming. That food would be distributed, and they would say: "This is the amount distributed every day." We only had that amount when foreigners came to tape us.

The mass rape of women also went on at the camps. Women were held in concentration camps like Omarska, and serially raped by the guards. In Serb-occupied areas such as Grbavica or Vogosce, women were taken from their homes to a flat or school that was set up like a brothel for Serb forces. There Serb troops would wantonly abuse the women, before killing them or sending them back to their families.

Ethnic cleansing gave us camps as improvisational structures, like Omarska or Manjaca, but also camps that were stark transformations of existing civil structures, such as the United Nations' "safe havens."[19] Sarajevans stretched the term "concentration camp" to describe the conditions of their city under siege. Zlatko Dizdarevic wrote: "The story of the camps began, unfolded, and is drawing to an end right here in Sarajevo, the biggest concentration camp the world has ever seen, and it is unlikely the world will ever witness one of its size again."[20]

Sarajevo, like Zepa, Tuzla, Srebrenica, Gorazde, and Bihac, was declared a "safe haven" by the United Nations. According to the plan, the United Nations forces would protect a city's inhabitants from aggression in order to prevent a refugee crisis from erupting. A major motivating principle was to prevent mass movements of refugees before they began. The United Nations troops disarmed Bosnian locals and discouraged them from defending themselves. The safe haven was to be a zone of civility within a war zone, enforced by UNPROFOR. Instead UNPROFOR wound up assuming full responsibility for the civilians' defense. Yet the United Nations Protection Forces were poorly armed and had no clear mandate to protect the inhabitants—only to allow humanitarian aid to get through. The Serbs, brazen and unfazed by the U.N.'s halfhearted resistance to their ethnic cleansing, turned the safe havens into killing centers for the defenseless citizens living there. No more outrageous example can be found than what happened in Srebrenica in July 1995, when the Serbs overran the U.N. forces and "cleansed" the town, killing as many as 20,000 men and boys.[21] Many survivors call the safe havens concentration camps and view the United Nations as their guards.

Bosnians and those who knew Yugoslavia were stunned to see how remarkably possible were these stark transformations. According to Robert Lifton, it is in part the historical advent of the Holocaust that has opened the door for these kinds of transformations to occur.[22] It is thus understandable that reflections on surviving and witnessing the Serbian nationalists' ethnic cleansing so often associate it with the Holocaust.

Survivors themselves often draw connections between their genocide experience and that of the Jews.

I remember all the pictures from the second war, where I watched Jewish people suffering in fascist concentration camps—but I think all this now is more than what Jewish people survived.

A survivor likens the camp he was in to Dachau, and the Chetniks to the SS and the Gestapo. He recalls telling them that they were much worse. The SS had two S's on their emblem, but the Chetniks had four; they were doing a twice *better* job.

Survivors like these are probably referring less to the Holocaust specifically than to the killing field that was Bosnia during World War II. Memories of those killings, long silenced, were re-emerging in response to the new genocide.

Bosnians were specifically drawn to the image of the Holocaust, because it was supposed to have taught the world "Never again." When the world did not act on that manifesto, many survivors of ethnic cleansing found themselves vehemently disagreeing with those outsiders who observed differences between this genocide and the Holocaust, and who therefore said that ethnic cleansing was not genocide.

> It does not matter what one calls those camps. They may be called concentration camps, holding centers, prison camps, isolation premises, etc. The point is that after the ethnic cleansing of their hometowns, people have been exterminated in those camps for their religious, racial, and national identity in the most atrocious manner: through starvation, without a just trial, and without a detention order. This is genocide. This is what Nuremberg sought to condemn, the Holocaust that everybody said must not be repeated anywhere, at any time. The Holocaust was made possible because people kept quiet, because evidence was kept in someone's drawer, and because the false humanists gave ambiguous comments.[23]

Once again, there is a group of survivors compelled to tell their stories, and driven to say, "Never again!," agonizing over whether their message will be heard.

Urbicide

The siege of Sarajevo, a city that was home to 500,000 people, lasted more than three years, visiting unimaginable destruction on this cosmopolitan center.[24] Several years ago, I was surprised to find myself in a disagreement with a Bosnian doctor who had remained in Sarajevo throughout the siege. Isn't the siege of Sarajevo a part of the ethnic cleansing of Bosnia-Herzegovina? This doctor emphatically insisted that the siege in Sarajevo is absolutely not ethnic cleansing as it has come to be practiced in other places in Bosnia.

In Sarajevo, the siege is a war. Those who decided to leave left because they didn't want to fight in the army, or because they wanted to live in a better place.

For this doctor, it is a matter of Sarajevan pride on behalf of those who stayed and endured the siege. The ethnic cleansing that swept through Eastern Bosnia left you no choice but to leave or die. But you could stay, resist, and survive the siege of Sarajevo. Many did. It is an insult to this doctor, and to all Sarajevans who resisted the siege by the very act of their staying there, to believe otherwise.

Yet the accounts from Sarajevo testify to how unbearable life was for its citizens, defenseless against the torrent of bullets and shells from the enstrangling Serb forces on the hills above.

One sunny day I was on my balcony and suddenly a shell hit the park and killed one little girl instantly. I cannot describe to you the screaming of the kids but I can still hear it now. One boy was wounded in his leg, the other child lost his arm. It was screams and blood all over. As a rule, a second shell would hit the same place after a couple of minutes to kill the people who ran to help the wounded. It was their strategy and we knew it. But we did not think about it. All the adults ran downstairs to help the kids. Fortunately, that time they forgot the second shell.

When I came to that crossing, the sniper started firing and we could not move. So we had to lie down on the ground in order to be protected by the concrete wall. We spent two hours there, and every time we attempted to move, the guy on the other side would shoot. He did not let us move. My face was completely black from fear. It is so difficult to describe that feeling of fear and humiliation. As if you are looking straight into the face of death.

I just stood there hopelessly, watching what was happening, and feeling miserable about myself for not being able to help. I could hear screams of women and I knew that some families were trapped on the upper floors and they could not be rescued. You could look at it but you could not help. I felt such pain when this was happening.

The worst and saddest thing is to wake up in the morning and start thinking how and whether it was possible at all, to get water, flour, firewood. And then the same happens the next day and the day after that, months, years. That is the definite destruction of an individual.

Many retired people who could no longer stand life as it was under the siege were killing themselves by jumping through the windows. Many times I heard the screams as I was walking in the street, and later learned that one more person was not able to stand this situation any more.

I felt like a bird in a cage.

The perpetrators of ethnic cleansing targeted not only people but also their human physical environment. We have all seen the images of bombed-out buildings in Sarajevo and the destroyed bridge in Mostar. Seeing those pictures in the newspapers and on television brought to my mind images of destruction from World War II: the total ruin of Dresden, Hiroshima, or Leningrad.

When I first learned about those places in high school, I never imagined them as places where people lived. They were some nonhuman wasteland presided over by soldiers from one army or another. When I saw the photos of destruction from Dubrovnik, Vukovar, and Sarajevo, I initially thought of them the same way—as just places of dead buildings.

Traveling through Bosnia-Herzegovina during and after the war, I saw—literally—the bigger picture. There are destroyed buildings next to living buildings on one city street. Little girls sitting on the stoop of their house, which has been shelled and almost totally ruined. Men and women working the garden next to their ruined home. Clotheslines filled with clean laundry alongside little more than a pile of bricks. The city of Sarajevo itself, even after nearly four years of siege, is seriously wounded, but stubbornly alive.[25]

When survivors from Sarajevo talk about the siege's destruction, they talk about the destruction of individual lives, but also the damage done to apartment buildings, roads, offices, trams, parks, mosques and churches, hospitals, museums, restaurants, and theaters, all willfully and intentionally destroyed by the shelling. But by far the single greatest act of physical destruction, in Sarajevans' minds, happened in the summer of 1992, when Serb forces destroyed the National Library of Bosnia-Herzegovina. Enes Kujunkzic, Director of the National and University Library of Bosnia-Herzegovina, summed it up:

Not only are people destroyed, but the cultural heritage of the people is being wiped out.[26]

For the European city dweller, the physical bearers of that cultural heritage are just as central to their daily lives as a home. Europeans inhabit a physical space where buildings and structure are much greater embodiments of history, culture, community, and spirituality than even the American urbanite can claim to know. Because they have such a deep and elaborated relationship to buildings and monuments, they experience destruction of their human physical environment differently. Destruction of the European's city brings about a level of trauma and loss that goes well beyond the functional roles of the roads they drive on and the buildings they work and live in. It can obliterate the survivors' place in the historical evolution of the life of their society. It can shatter the soul of the people.

This fact was not lost on the Serb forces, who appeared to go out of their way to destroy structures that had special significance for the Bosnian people. In Banja Luka alone, sixteen mosques were destroyed.

They destroyed all our religious places. Our mosque. Our cemetery. The old bridge in Mostar. They destroyed our history.

The intentional destruction of buildings and monuments of cultural and historical significance led Bosnian architects to become outspoken witnesses to the "war destruction of building heritage."[27] These architects have published journals and held photographic exhibits internationally that have functioned as "specific testimony of a barbarian attempt to destroy a CITY."

The architects have coined a new vocabulary to name this kind of destruction to a city. They call it "unprecedented urbicide." They say that "Sarajevo today is a town of necropolis, namely, a town-necropolis."[28]

"Sarajevo has been transforming from a town of the living into the town of the dead! . . . It could become a kind of a really negative symbol: even the burial

mound of civilization (or at least what the world of today means by civilization)—
something sad and terrible, like Hiroshima for example" (*Wararchitecture*, 22).

We do not seem to have the psychological language or concepts to describe
adequately how the destruction of a city traumatizes its inhabitants. From survivors we hear that "Each new day brings new wounds to our town. Places of
our childhood, memories, houses and streets of our youth are being destroyed.
Each new shell is a new scar" (*Wararchitecture*, 85)

Destruction of the physicality of the city, an essential part of the fabric of
the lives of its citizens, damages the integrity of the self. Merhamet, for example,
vitally nourished by the self's relationship to its physical/cultural environment,
can lose a substantial part of its vigor amidst the ruins of destroyed mosques and
bridges. One Sarajevan youth's poem expresses the pain of being surrounded by
images of rubble and ruin.

> "I bend my head down walking through the streets
> 'cos I don't want to keep in mind
> the horrifying architecture of ruins
> as the last image before I go away.
> Will my city ever be urban again?" (*Wararchitecture*, 90)

This is the question that stood behind many a Sarajevan's decision to stay
or to go. Sarajevans who are staying say that Sarajevo is still enough of what it
was for them. Sarajevans who have left say that the Sarajevo they knew no longer
exists. It is true that their exodus was not so forced as that of the villagers pushed
at riflepoint onto a bus, but in a way it was just as inevitable. The aggressors
had destroyed their urban life.

The siege precipitated tremendous changes in Sarajevo's population. Between 1992 and 1996 more than half the population of the city emigrated. Displaced persons from its suburbs and from throughout Bosnia took over the
abandoned apartments and overflowed into refugee centers. Many Sarajevan
Serbs and Croats and "mixed persons," feeling less at home in the new milieu
in Sarajevo, also chose to leave.

*Our world fell apart from all sides. From the outside, where our countrymen were
shooting at us. From the inside, where the city fabric was being destroyed. It was no
longer the city we knew.*

How Did I Get Through?

There are those who say that they don't have a clue about how they came out
alive. So many survivors in Bosnia and in exile were so caught up in meeting
basic survival needs that they have not yet found the space or the will to approach the questions of how or why they survived. Some survivors speak of a

moment when they had to do something clever, even if it went against their character or their honor.

In order to survive it was necessary to tell lies.

"I think I saved myself by my persistent claim that I have no brothers or children."[29]

Other survivors attribute their survival to a strange sense of invulnerability.

I knew I couldn't die. I wouldn't let them kill me. Strange powers stirred within me. Each night there was shelling. I never thought the bullet might come my way. I convinced myself that I would live.

Some report that this emergence of a personal will to survive came out of their desire to live to tell the truth of what was done to them. A young man was asked if he was afraid of death.

You don't think about that. Because you think that it's important that somebody survives. Somebody.

Other survivors tell stories that contain an extraordinary moment, when in the midst of atrocity they suddenly find the strength to somehow publicly mark both the historical truth of the crimes being committed against them and some affirmative essence that they thought worth surviving for. These are desperate moments, when there is nothing the survivor can do, and at the same time it is absolutely essential that something, anything be done. Curiously, a number of these moments involve singing.

We would get together and sing the old songs, but it was completely different, because you were always aware that at that very moment somebody was getting killed or rotting in the trenches. It was a completely different kind of singing. We sang because we were, I guess, hopeless.

A woman decides to sing aloud on the street of her occupied town, when Muslims are forbidden to even speak to one another. *I just felt like it. I sang, "Bosnia, if they take you from me. . . . " That was my way to rebel. To express my anger. At that moment I didn't care at all if they killed me or not.*

A man who survived a camp tells of an evening when the detainees spontaneously broke into songs about Bosnia until the guards threatened them and told them to quit. *It was our way of protest.*

I am reminded by this of the supper club scene in *Casablanca,* when the group of Allies shout down the party of German officers. There is a kind of heroism in the singing of a patriotic song. I picture that woman proudly marching down a street she once knew. If only for a few minutes, she owns that street. Once again, she belongs to her city, and it belongs to her.

H.'s story of the men's "humming" in the concentration camp elicits a different response. When Vahid is taken away to be killed, there are no words to say what needs to be said. I feel that I need to hear it myself, so I ask H. if he can make that sound again. He raises himself up from his chair, body straight and taut, arms by his side. He rocks slightly back and forth, and a rough bass-like vibration comes from deep in his chest. It is a kind of mourner's Kaddish stripped bare. It is all they can then give to their friend who has given them so much. Of course it isn't enough, but it is something.

It leaves me speechless. Psychiatrists have a bias toward those who can talk about their experiences. And so with survivors, we often ask them to tell us everything, and how they thought about it, and how they felt about it, and what it all meant. For those survivors of ethnic cleansing whose experiences of atrocity remain so largely unarticulated, any chance to tell and be heard can be a way to get parts of the self back and to discover truths.

And yet there are times when it seems that it is those survivors who say nothing at all about how or why they survived who come closest to revealing a truth of ethnic cleansing. A genocide such as ethnic cleansing cared not at all for the individual. It was a grim and overpowering attempt by one group to destroy another group's way of life. In that sense, the individual victims did not choose their fate.[30] Some had only the slightest opportunity to make a few small choices. For most Bosnians, their fate was chosen for them. To think otherwise is a delusion.

And yet, when those who lived through ethnic cleansing find it possible to tell, to sing, to imagine, to joke, or to hope about their traumatic past, then it is also time to start thinking about the Bosnian future. Those who lived through ethnic cleansing and who carry the memory are the repositories of the history that will be written on ethnic cleansing, and the future life that will emerge from its ruins.

I said to myself, "Whatever my destiny, whatever God decides—will happen. You can kill me, but you can not break my spirit." Yes, there were people without scruples, but on the other hand, there were people who shared and gave, as if they were transformed by this experience.

Instead of humiliation and helplessness, I started feeling superior to those criminals whose bestiality toward innocent, unarmed people was shameful. Something in me helped me preserve my dignity, helped me remain human.

Chapter 3

The Experience of the Bosnian Refugees

J., November 1994

I first meet J. in Queens when she joins a group I co-lead for recently arrived Bosnian refugees. At the end of the third meeting she announces that she will not come again—as a forty-two-year-old single mother with three children, she does not have the time. A few months later, when the playwright Karen Malpede tells me about the incredible eyes of a woman she met at a Bosnia rally near the U.N., I know it is J.[1] Not long after that, our families gather together for dinner. J. wants to tell me more than we can manage that night, so we arrange to meet again.

I cannot forget what she told the group about her husband's death in 1992 while he was defending Bihac. After learning that he died, she grieved with her brother and his family, and especially her young niece Azra. Looking into Azra's eyes made her feel as close to whole as was possible in those dark times. Three days later, she heard a huge crash outside where the children are playing. A shell had killed Azra and splattered her body over the street. J. cleaned up the remains. Not long afterward J. found a way out of Bihac and came to America with her children.

The experiences of ethnic cleansing J. endured were by then familiar to me, since I had been talking to many refugees. The experiences of these survivors living in exile, linked but not identical to the experiences of survivors in Bosnia itself, are now an undeniable part of the Bosnian experience.[2] What I find so compelling in them is the struggle that comes of the refusal to surrender to the shattering of their lives and memories by genocide. It is something one can actually see in J.'s eyes.

We meet a few weeks later, at a time when Bihac appears about to fall. We abandon our plan to do a testimony of her trauma story and just start talking.

I'm thinking an awful lot, but the first thing I have to say is that I have nothing to say. Especially for the last week. I feel like I have been sentenced to death and that I don't deserve the punishment because I have done nothing wrong.

"What have the last few days been like?"

First I want you to know that I had a desire to know the truth of what was happening over there, but at the same time I wanted to know that what was happening wasn't true. It was when I became aware of the truth and what was happening. I have a lot of family there. What I was thinking was that I want my brother and my sister-in-law to kill the children and themselves so that they should not be allowed to fall into the hands of the Serbs. Because I don't want them to be faced with the horror and fear of death. At first I even had a fever and then I remembered that my brother kept a gun. I would like to talk about those children who are like my own children and who are now in this situation.

"What children are you thinking about?"

My sister's children. And my brother-in-law's children and my brother's children. I remember their eyes and I see them.

"Their eyes?"

When they were happy and when they were crying when they were growing up. I feel that nobody has the right to sentence anybody to death. I feel that we Bosnians have sentenced ourselves to death. I feel guilty.

"I don't understand what you mean."

What I can't understand is how anyone can think of their next-door neighbors as their future enemies! That's not how we felt and we certainly weren't prepared. We lived together, ate together, drank together, sat and talked the way we are talking here now.

Before all those friendships ruptured and brought death into all their lives, J. did not think there could ever be such troubles. Now, she sees enemies everywhere, and mounts desperate defenses. Her mind turns back to the children.

I feel about these children as if they were my own. And I have almost come to the point where I want them to be saved more than I want my brother and my sister-in-law to be saved. I am acting as if I were to decide who is going to stay alive and who is going to die.

"It's understandable to me why you are focusing on the children and their eyes."

I don't remember them the way they looked the last time I saw them. I saw them when they were growing up. My sister's son had unusual eyes that always looked teary, even when he was not crying. I spoke with him twenty days ago and he said to me very simply, "I'm now grown up. I'm already six years old." They all have different colored eyes which are very expressive and carry a strong hope for life. What I am most afraid of is that he will die. No, what I am even more afraid of is the hours waiting to be killed and watching their parents or relatives being killed and beaten. Serbs are not just killing people. They are massacring.

"No one's eyes, but especially a young person's eyes, should have to see those things. Do you still see her eyes?"

Yes, I still see Azra's eyes. I think that she had very special large dark brown eyes. I always drew a lot of strength from the children's eyes. They don't have evil. They are hopeful.

You asked why I haven't talked about this. The answer is I really don't have anyone to talk with about this. My feeling is that I don't even want to talk with people who I know will not be able to understand.

"One thing I hear from you is how extraordinarily difficult it is to try to be in two places at once—to try to be here and in Bosnia."

Of course the consequence is I can't concentrate on studying at all. Sometimes I have to disconnect my phone, which means that I am disconnecting myself from the world. Then I hear some news and it's back. . . . Why do I think about saving them when no one can be saved? If God gave me the chance I would save the children. How can anyone think of people who are still alive as if they were already dead? I saw a man who was killed by Chetniks, and saw from his wounds that he was tortured. I am afraid that that will happen to the children. I wish they could die in a more humane way.

I am thinking that evacuation is the way. But it doesn't look like anybody is doing anything about it. Bihac is surrounded. Someone has to force the Serbs to open the way for people to get out. When the Serbs are full of victory and glory and happiness they just can't pass up the chance to kill. It's not possible for them to behave otherwise. They are just going to remain in the city and gradually reduce the population, and then whatever is left will be theirs. They are very powerful. Look at their faces. [J. holds up that day's *New York Times* with the front page photo of triumphant Serb soldiers on top of their tank.] *Remember, they are executioners!*

"What they are doing is evil. . . . Once you have known evil and what evil can do, there is no erasing that from your mind. . . . There is no assurance that it won't again happen. Still, I picture you going through your day trying to have a life here, and I wonder, what could you say or do that might allow you to get some distance from those kinds of disturbing images?"

When I look at Ermina, my four-year-old starting to play and explore, I feel that I don't need to make any special effort to distance myself. When I first left Bosnia and I was living in Zagreb, I didn't want to live at all and I didn't care for the children. My husband's uncle suggested that I give one of my sons to the United Arab Emirates. It shook me. I didn't answer him then. . . . He wished he had sent his son. There was absolutely nothing I could say to that except, "Well maybe you should do that. But not with my children." I was so upset at the time. But he actually helped me.

"He helped you to realize how much your children needed you and how much you needed your children."

I thought that I couldn't live. I never lived alone. I always had my father before I got married. I was never on my own. I was a dictator. That was the problem. All my wishes were granted. That is why I felt that this time I would do differently.

"Well, you may already know this, but I feel it must be said. It's not at all a betrayal of those who are still in danger or those who have perished, for you to enjoy playing with your children—to get down on your hands and knees and have fun."

I am not interested in everybody in Bosnia. I am really concerned about my own children right now.

"Understandably so. Is there something else you want us to talk about?"

There's nothing special because everything seems to be so special, and in the end very little can be said.

"You have said a lot. You spoke from the heart. It's important to remember that you have not lost that."

I think that in the end I may not have the strength.

"This is the worst of times. All times won't be this bad. What would you like for us to do now? Talk again?"

I don't feel that I have really anything to say. I am alone in my sadness and sorrow, and I feel that YOU ARE MY ENEMY. I am sorry to say that. I am sorry. So sorry. If only I were a believer, that would help. If I had faith.

Up to this point our conversation seems to have been going well. But when she says that and sobs, it feels like we have hit rock-bottom. If the result of our conversation is that I am the enemy and she is embattled, then something is very wrong. Maybe it is not the right time, or I am not the right person. What have I done wrong? I feel sorry for getting us into this. So awful that I want only to apologize and leave. But there is something about the way she is condemning me for being me that invites a response. I want to tell her, without rejecting or conceding, that I cannot be anything other than who I am. At that moment, it just feels like something I have to say.

"I know that you are working on rebuilding your life, and that it will take time. You know that I am in a very different kind of life situation, essentially an outsider to your experience as a survivor and a refugee. I am not going to apologize for my life any more than you would have apologized for what you had in your life. Still I can be your friend and listen."

I feel that you are a friend and a good person and you want to help me as a friend in spite of the fact that you may have other reasons for doing this. On the other hand, it's just so awful to see people who have their lives; who can and do get on with their lives without having to see this kind of thing.

"But the feelings were really there. You don't have to apologize. But you are going to have to deal with those feelings with just about anybody you meet. I think it would be good for us to talk more about it. Unless you felt that it was going to be too painful."

Let's be in touch.

She is right. Nothing I can say can help those in Bihac. Neither I nor anyone else—short of military intervention—has an answer to the darkness surrounding her.

Helpless

It's still happening and there's nothing I can do.

This was the unhappy refrain spoken so often by the refugees as ethnic cleansing ground on in Bosnia. The recognition that "it" was still happening was ubiquitous and unavoidable. Nearly all the refugees I saw actively kept up to date on the daily unfolding of events in Bosnia through the mass media, the World Wide Web, and through letters and phone calls to family and loved ones.[3] There was a great willingness, even a great pressure, to know at all times what was happening in Bosnia. At the same time, there was also a recognition of the substantial emotional price to be paid for staying aware. Nightmares, images, crying spells, despair, and worst of all, sleeplessness, all were openly displayed in their weary, terrified faces. But for most survivors, there was never any question that one had to stay involved. Whatever emotional cost was being paid became part of the burden one had to bear as a survivor from Bosnia. Their symptoms were not an affliction so much as an obligation.

It's my nation, people, land. I feel very connected to that. I am very attached to them. Whatever tragedy they go through, I feel it is my tragedy as well.

I can't be happy as long as other people suffer over there.

Very often they experienced no clear demarcation between past and present atrocities. Even though the refugee had reached a safe haven, there was no escaping the awareness that the genocide was continuing in Bosnia. The memories of one's prior traumas during ethnic cleansing and the images of another's present traumas became intertwined. Memories of ethnic atrocities from World War II and earlier also got yoked in, both for older refugees who were actually survivors two or three times over and for younger ones who carried handed-down memories of their parents' or grandparents' traumas. All these memories clung together, and it was as if all of them were happening to you, here and now.[4]

Survivors in the United States struggled daily over whether to talk about their memories.[5] I remember sitting with one survivor in his living room, with the television blasting CNN. I am inviting him to tell me his story, and he is resisting.

Now you can see it on TV anyway. We saw the people on TV just yesterday. We saw the people on TV, so skinny. I went through all of that. I cannot help them. There's nothing I can do. If I see it or not, it's still going to be the same.

The proliferation of the genocide on television and the absence of consequential action served to exacerbate a breakdown in basic communication for the survivor.[6] If the media's telling of the story was unable to accomplish anything, then what could one survivor say that would make any real difference? After all, whether I say it or not, it's still going to be the same. Because it was meaningless for them to speak of traumas, survivors began to feel it was meaningless even to recall them. For most refugees living in America while the ethnic cleansing was happening, it seemed there was nothing they could do about the collapse of their world other than to watch it on TV like the rest of us.

Sometimes I feel guilty being here, in America. I think I would rather share it with them—no matter if it is hunger, death, or hardship.

In the refugees' minds, it even seemed as if their efforts at rebuilding their own life, and that of their families, were opposed to their efforts at staying connected with Bosnia. They found apartments, got jobs, learned English, made friends, bought cars. Each of these steps became another degree of connectedness with America; each came to seem like another degree of separation from Bosnia. When feeling obliged to know what was happening in Bosnia, to feel and to suffer the deaths, atrocities, and losses, refugees were less available to commit to the process of rebuilding their lives in America. Some were tortured by a sense that they had betrayed their Bosnia by leaving. They saw themselves as complicit with all the other betrayers of Bosnia in the West—those who refused to look past their noses to see the suffering of others or those who refused to put their own lives on the line. Other refugees attempted to sever their ties with Bosnia, its sorrows and hardships, so as to begin anew.

Among Bosnians there was a great deal of sniping at one another, a great deal of bickering about who was the greater betrayer of Bosnia. Those who stayed in Sarajevo mocked those who had left. Dizdarevic wrote, "I consider it a duty to remain in my city until the end."[7] Those who left and then wrote or talked about Bosnia were derided, unfairly so, as if they were false survivors and should have surrendered their voices once they crossed the border into exile.

The fact that it was still happening pressed the refugees to find ways of demonstrating their commitment to Bosnia and to their loved ones who remained there.

The news from Bosnia is really stressful for me. I feel a duty to be there with my fellow citizens. I think I should share their destiny.

But what could one do? What ways were available? What form could sharing their destiny take? Some refugees talked openly about going back. But their going back was contingent upon so many factors over which they had absolutely no control: if they could get a visa; if they had the money; if the arms embargo were lifted; if they knew their families would be safe. Still, some actually went back, to fight with guns or to fight for Bosnia's survival in other ways; to visit loved ones dearly missed, or to try to get them out of Bosnia. But for most refugees, it seemed, going back to Bosnia was not a real option. Others took up the fight in their new home, becoming activists for Bosnia in America, or advocates for the Bosnian people trying to establish a new life.

Losing Our World

A refugee in Chicago found a flag of Yugoslavia in a garage sale. A flag that came from a time *when it was my country, before they changed it.* He bought it on the spot. *Now I have no country.*

I am looking for a new life, but Bosnia is still in my heart and in my mind.

I left my country and I went somewhere, but now I am going through the world without my home country.

We lost our first country—Yugoslavia. Now we've lost our second country—Bosnia-Herzegovina. . . . Can you imagine how people feel without a country?

Our sense of opposition to extreme ethnic nationalism can keep us from imagining how much the entity of nation gives structure and meaning to life. Nation is political, ideological, cultural, historical, geographical, spiritual, aesthetic, and more.[8] Not only Bosnians, but all the world's refugees know the suffering entailed when one is forced to be without one's nation. Is it any wonder, then, that the mourning over the world they have lost is not only incomplete, but barely understandable?

It begins with the recognition that the Bosnians who came to the United States are something other than immigrants or economic refugees. They are survivors of genocide.[9] Their countries that died, Yugoslavia and Bosnia-Herzegovina, did not die of natural causes—they were murdered. And the murderers came in part from within. So this is not only a loss (as if that in itself were something straightforward), but a traumatic loss and a crime. What you lost was ripped from you violently, brutally, and wrongly by someone who was a part of what you once had. You are not only saying good-bye, but also protesting that this should not have happened, and that its happening can only be explained by human evil, folly, and indifference. What's more, you might also feel guilty, thinking that you were not sharp enough to catch on until it was too late.

Given the intensity of these feelings, it is inevitable that survivors would often reminisce over their world lost, and in doing so produce memories that bear traces of an understandable desire to recast the past in a more favorable light. We did not just coexist, we really lived together. Tito didn't oppress divergent voices, he actually kept the peace. Merhamet was not just for some, it was for all. I listened to the ways survivors talked about the world they lost.

Many draw attention to the Bosnian landscape that they so miss. Their Yugoslavia stretched from the Central European mountains and plains to the Mediterranean coast. Herzegovina is rocky and dry, hot and wild. Bosnia is a mountainous paradise of soaring peaks, dramatic green valleys, cool running rivers. Among its ridges nestle jewel-like villages and cities, enveloped in their sense that the dirtiness of Europe and the rest of the world had been kept out by its formidable mountain passes.[10]

City dwellers also spoke of the loss as something cultural. They were painfully aware that they were part of a unique multicultural enterprise, and took great pride in celebrating it on the world stage at the 1984 Sarajevo Winter Olympics. This made their loss all the more painful.

"If you don't realize what you've lost, then you've lost nothing. I know very well what I have lost: the experience of that singularly rich identity—the product of a unique, challenging, yet uncommonly charming cosmos—to Belgrade's military ambition."[11]

They recognized that without Yugoslavia and Bosnia-Herzegovina, merhamet was far less welcome. Bosnians could feel the difference in themselves and those around them.

For the generation born after World War II the loss of this cultural experience was especially hard. The youth culture within which they were raised was committedly multicultural. And their immersion in that multicultural experience was not mitigated by commitments to a particular ethnic experience, as it might have been had they directly experienced the traumas of World War II.

Young people recall Bosnia's strong youth counterculture, with Sarajevo the undisputed rock and roll capital of ex-Yugoslavia.

> I am convinced that rock music will never be the same for me, thanks to Yugoslavia's violent disintegration . . . the original songs from Bijelo Dugmo, the Idols from Belgrade, Leb I Sol from Macedonia, and a host of other bands whose half-forgotten names once signified a genuine sentimental education for the generation that long ago, oh, so long ago, turned out in the tens of thousands for Yugoslavia's first Woodstock in a village outside of Belgrade. That experience led us to believe—naively—that the good vibrations of our collective transcendence would mark a new life in harmony, like stars, like the four seasons. (Debeljak, *Twilight*, 55)

Had we met in high school, young Bosnian rockers and I might have traded albums and talked about our favorite groups. Now, sometimes I reminisce with survivors about those old rock songs we have in common, or they turn me on to Yugoslav rock and roll. At a dinner party for a group of Bosnians in Chicago, the hostess put on some tapes of her favorite bands from Sarajevo. It brought back to them incredibly strong feelings of their euphoric and idyllic youth in Bosnia—a life they loved, yet could not save. Listening to those songs was too much for these Bosnians to bear. Before too long, our hostess switched it off and put on some American jazz.

All the Bosnian refugees I met were painfully aware of how miserable it felt to be away from their countries.

People are not willing to accept me the way that I am.

My presence here is only physical. My thoughts are in Bosnia.

Now all I can do is talk about Bosnia.

Debeljak speaks of "the homesickness that has become the state of mind of so many displaced Yugoslavs" (*Twilight*, 38). To say that this feeling is actually homesickness is to presume that the sufferer still has a home to return to. The prospect of "going home" was and remains very unlikely for most Bosnian refugees.[12] The state of mind of Bosnian refugees seems closer to the mentality of homelessness. Still, it is understandable that the nostalgia of homesickness is preferred over the nothingness of homelessness, a grimness for which there are far fewer words. I am struck by the many Bosnian refugees I meet who say they are terrified of homelessness in America. It is a sign of their worst fear—to be once again without any place. Homelessness is how they think we turn people into animals in America.

Families Afloat

Bosnians often tell me that the family is the most important element of the Bosnian way of life:

We are our families.

We live for family and through family.

If you want to understand Bosnians, you must know the family.

It is plain to see that after surviving ethnic cleansing, Bosnians have seen these beliefs proven true in a new and unexpected way. For scores of refugees, their family has become the only social entity left standing, the only part of their shattered world they have left.

Worse yet, for many survivors, ethnic cleansing has also destroyed or seriously damaged their family as they knew it. There are husbands without wives, wives without husbands, parents without their children, children without parents, and all other possible configurations after an irreparable rupture or hole in the family that was.

In addition to families shattered by death, innumerable families are rocked by separations of tremendous distances.

"My parents and my sisters are in Slovenia. I wonder when, if ever, we will live together again as a family."[13]

"My family are now completely scattered across the globe" (Gordon, *Bosnia*, 50).

In mental health work with Bosnians, we often try to meet with the whole family, being that it is the most tangible remaining part of their former life in Bosnia. We try to understand and to work with families. But it isn't easy. We find ourselves facing problems unfamiliar to us as mental health professionals. After their world sank, these families trying to stay afloat were made up entirely of family members who were also, each in and of themselves, victims of history.

It is obvious that the members of such families can have serious difficulties contributing to each other's recovery. Family members' individual traumatic experiences are as different from one another as they are alike. This contributes to their sense that they may not know each other the way they once did. They can have problems communicating with one another.

One young refugee mother says of her toddler son, *I really don't have any control. I don't keep an eye on him and watch him growing up.*

Another woman says, *There I was a victim of war. Here I am a victim of my relationship with my teenage children.*

But these are by and large healthy and strong families who knew how to be together before. These survivor families can hold onto one another in the most powerful ways. One important aspect concerns how the family relates to its traumatic memories: whether or not they talk about them; how they approach the dilemmas of memory and what meanings they derive. Clinical scholars have noted how the family itself serves as an important structure for containing, transforming, and transmitting historical memory, especially across generations.[14]

Difficulties in communication often center around the experience of traumatization.

My family knows something but not absolutely everything because they suffered so much. I think they suffered more than I suffered. I think they don't need to know all the details. Regarding other people I don't want to explain what happened. Everyone has his story and his experiences and I don't want to put my problems above theirs. . . . I want to protect my children. My wife, she knows enough. And I want them to be children. Many children during that war matured more than they needed. They are a lot older. I want my children to have a normal life and be occupied by science and sports. Not stupid things like war. Not to put an idea in them to hate somebody.

Families often seem to be good at grasping what it takes to survive. They work very hard, pitch in together, and make sacrifices. In Bosnian families one often finds the attitude that in order to keep the family afloat, it is necessary to put those memories aside. One can hardly blame parents for not wanting to burden their children with memories. However, in choosing not to give memories a more central place in family life, could these families be drifting into the currents of a historical memory they do not grasp? Silence presents certain advantages, but it is not without risks. Memories that are kept locked within the family, and are dealt with in the public arena only latently and selectively, do not enter into and enhance the totality of the system of values that guides social and political life. And memories not openly named or discussed can still flutter about family life—they can haunt, and return later in another guise. That is what seems to have happened with the ethnic nationalists and their memories of World War II. And it can happen again.

Life's Seasons Shredded

Ethnic cleansing ripped millions of adults, young, middle-aged, and old, out of the fabric of their lives.[15]

You have everything, and somebody comes and takes it away as if nothing ever existed. I have no hope for anything.

I worked for thirty-eight years, and now everything is gone.

Ethnic cleansing tore people away from much of what they had considered to be the core elements of their lives: families, friends, jobs, homes, communities, culture, and values. It is the totality of its impact on many if not all realms of life that accounts for the enormity of survivors' suffering.

I had my life the way I wanted to have it. My home was very sturdy. I built it out of stone. Not like homes here, of wood and aluminum. Everything I worked for was lost.

In Bosnia-Herzegovina, it was common for people to own their own homes, to live in them for most of their lives, and to continually invest their money in them. The house and the land served as a fundamental anchor for the self. A home was something a person and a family would develop over a lifetime, not simply a material possession to be bought or sold like any other commodity. A home was irreplaceable.

Ethnic cleansing not only removed people from their jobs, but often completely derailed them from the career path on which they were advancing. Once you have been shoved off, you cannot simply hop back on. Some may get back on years later, but many more never will. I know many doctors who, after years of practice, were having to study for entrance exams that would allow them to repeat a residency—all before they could practice medicine again. In the meantime they would work in grungy factories, drive taxis, or deliver pizzas. One woman had enjoyed her work as an executive in a bank, but now stays home with the kids. The odds are very low that she will ever land a job that will allow her to establish a foothold outside of the context of her family, a job like the one she had enjoyed in Bosnia.

These components of life—home, work, and family—are fairly clear; others may be as hard for us to appreciate as the water is for the fish.[16] Life is also about a person's participation in a community. It is made up of many tiny experiences that remind people of how interconnected their life is with that of others. Sitting with friends in the coffee bar. Greeting a friend on the street. Asking a neighbor for a favor. Having a block party. Sitting on the grass for an outdoor concert. Being part of the fantastic celebration of the winter Olympics. Riding the tram. Strolling past a mosque, a church, and a synagogue on an evening walk in Sarajevo. Bosnians will tell you again and again that it was vitally important to them that those others with whom they connected included persons with small differences of ethnicity or religion. Because those communities were destroyed, survivors' lives cannot ever be what they once were.

I wanted to see lives that changed like the seasons, not frozenness and deadness. Sometimes when I saw the markings of a life cycle transition, the survivor saw not even a life. This was not something they were going to be talked out of, no matter how hard I tried. I stuck close to them and kept watch to see what evolved. Talking with some of these same refugees some years later, I was so often surprised to see how different things were turning out to be. Where there had been only deadness, I now saw signs of life. Where life had seemed to be flourishing, I now glimpsed indications of an encroaching gloom. Life went on, but always with the dark shadow of ethnic cleansing still undeniably present.

D. seems fairly settled in her role as a mental health worker for Bosnian refugees until something comes undone. A middle-aged Bosnian woman she sees in session at the refugee center confesses that she was raped by Serbian soldiers. D. is the only person she has ever told.[17] D. keeps it to herself for two weeks, but the woman's story eats away at her and brings her down and down and down. Without talking to me or anyone else, she keeps silently asking herself, *How could anybody do that to a woman? They treated her like an animal.*

I become aware of all this one day after politely asking D. to do some small job. No! she says, taking me by surprise. This isn't like her. D. lets me know that she is in a crisis and needs some "psychotherapy" from me. When we find a few minutes to talk later that day she confesses:

I thought everything was going all right with me. I didn't think I was necessarily happy. But I didn't think I was unhappy. I never asked myself if I like my life now. Now I can truly say that I do not like my life. I have no life. I used to have a good life. I wasn't rich, but I enjoyed my life. I think about our dog a lot. We used to have a dog. We took our dog for walks. Now we don't have a dog anymore. I don't even want to say what happened to the dogs in Sarajevo. Now I am like an animal. That is what my life is like now.

As a professional woman approaching middle age, D. should be taking satisfaction in advancing in her career and shepherding her children through their teen years. But on this day it all comes crashing down. Suddenly she feels that her life, which once had a human shape, has been stripped of so much of what she valued, rendered something less than human.

Many survivors have reported that they suffered the most crushing encounter with the nonhuman shape of their own existence only after being exceptionally open to another survivor's trauma story. It is in part via contamination mechanisms such as these that the damage done to peoples' lives by the traumas of ethnic cleansing—both from the beginning and from later on—has not dwindled or disappeared with time, but has persisted and multiplied.

The condition of many Bosnian refugees reveals what it means to be alive but to be without a life. Of course, their lives will never be what they would have been had ethnic cleansing not occurred. Will they ever regain some semblance of the evolving seasons that adult lives are supposed to have? As one survivor asked: *Will I have a life or an appendage to my life?*

Survivors look for acceptable ways to even begin to conceive of this sort of massive change. Is it like turning a new page, or starting a new chapter? Like letting one life die and another be born? The mind searches for a usable metaphor that does not do away with one's dignity. Zlatko Dizdarevic says, "That's what this war is, nothing but a long good-bye."[18]

It takes a kind of courage to say good-bye. Courage to acknowledge what one has lost and will never regain. Courage to see the long path that lies ahead. Courage to face the hard choices one must make to rebuild one's life. It can never be easy to deal with a loss so staggering as the loss of one's own life.

The Bosnian refugees who know better than any others what it means to be alive but to not have life are the older adults—those who had built their homes, made their careers, watched their families grow. Those for whom the rest of their adult life was to have coasted on the foundation of what they had already done, known, and seen. The losses they suffered are impossible to recoup. Adolescents and young adults can imagine starting over, but middle-aged or older adults cannot.

We would have had a very nice retirement. Now it's all gone.

I don't feel young enough to start again.

If God wants to punish you, he first lets you have things and then takes them away.

I wonder if I will ever. . . . My whole life is destroyed.

There is no way that I can change at my age.

I will never be happy again.

Bosnian refugees like to say that the aggressors have left the life that they once shared together and therefore no longer exist. They like to say that they, the Bosnians, still exist. Even as refugees in a strange country, we still have our pride. We still believe in our way of living. We try as we may to make something of this life. Do not say that it cannot be done. Because if it can be said that we have lost our lives, then we have lost that which matters to us the most. If that can be said, then we are defeated and they have won. And that is unspeakable.

Humiliation

I'll say it again. You can't forget the humiliation. For me that is the main thing. I spoke with my father in Sarajevo on the telephone today. He'll never say it. He tries to put up a good front. But I hear it so clear. This has been so humiliating for all of us.

Bosnian refugees often emphasize that Bosnians are a proud people. The ethnic cleansing struck them at the heart of who they were, individually and as a people. This is another kind of mass rape—to destroy a people's living pride in what it means to be Bosnian.

Survivors speak directly about humiliation when they are describing the process of their deportation. A middle-aged man told me: *We were insulted and humiliated because we were driven from our homes.* It is seldom articulated as sharply as by the writer/survivor Zlatko Dizdarevic:

> But to forgive the humiliation of deportation to a concentration camp—
> that is not possible in Sarajevo, nor will it ever be. When a bullet in the
> back ends your life, there's nothing left—no distress, nor any conscious-
> ness of distress. The rifle butt in the back, and the truck ride to the
> camp, cause a distress that cannot be forgotten. That rifle butt shatters
> everything civilization has ever accomplished, removes all finer human
> sentiments, and wipes out any sense of justice, compassion, and forgive-
> ness. (Dizdarevic, *Sarajevo*, 54)

The refugee often details the markers of humiliation they can plainly see when they compare their life now with what it was before.

It's a great humiliation for me. An old man, poorly paid.

I feel like I have no value compared to what I had before. Like I'm not worth anything. . . . Like now I am nothing.

Living the life of a refugee is total humiliation. You have been stripped of nearly all attributes that render you human. Then driven from your home and thrown out of your work. Transported in trucks, trains, or buses in lethal conditions. You watch people die like flies and are helpless to intervene. You wish only for your own survival, or perhaps for death. You have been reduced to the condition of an animal. Even if your death comes, it will be part of the same bestial slaughter.

But say you are fortunate enough to be liberated. Then you are again herded—into refugee camps. There you sit for months or years like cattle in what seems like a pampered concentration camp. Again you have nothing. You are one of millions of refugees. Maybe you are given permission to resettle. Traded like horses, it seems to you.

To the refugee resettlement agency, it seems you equal x dollars received from the government for resettlement. The agency tells you what you should and should not do. Do not end up on welfare. Get a job. Learn English. Do not drive without a license. You can't find your way around town. People treat you as if you're an idiot. As if you have never seen currency before. As if you are a native from a savage land.

When they talk to you about Bosnia, they seem to be making the assumption that in the Balkans slicing each other's throats has been a nationa pastime. So you are supposed to feel fortunate that you have now entered the civilized West. We do things differently here, they tell you. Yet in the factory where you work, the other immigrants spit on you. You are the lowest of the low.

I doubt anyone has been confronted by the refugees' humiliation as directly as the social service workers who have managed their resettlement from Bosnia to their new host countries. When I talked with the workers at the nongovernmental organizations in Croatia, I repeatedly heard statements like this:

I have worked with refugees all over the world, but I have never seen a group behave like this. In Africa, in the Far East, in Central America, the refugees know they must wait, that the process takes time, and they accept all this. These Bosnians do not want to accept any of that. It's like they experience each and every thing as an insult, to which they defiantly protest.

Refugee resettlement workers in the United States say, *Never before have I seen an angrier group of people. They come into my office, sit and yell at me and refuse to leave.*

Rage is a common pathway of response to humiliation, and it is often present in the refugees. One refugee said, *Don't ask me anything. I am so angry. I am so full of anger. At everybody. Everything. For all that happened. They put me up against a wall and shot bullets above my head. And my knees, my ribs, my back—It's all been broken.*

One refugee in Chicago was so furious at the health care workers who were trying to get him a new prosthesis that he says, *I'd rather kill them than get my new leg.*

In America, it is common for the refugees to call the other Bosnian refugees who work as resettlement workers *kapos*, and to openly despise them.[19]

When they are unable to live with and contain their own humiliation, the refugees often let go on whoever comes along with the next small insult with a major barrage. They aim their weapons and fire on an unsuspecting, often undeserving victim. Rage can be directed at oneself, at one's family, at authority figures, at persons who try to help, or at persons one has good reason to hate. Not enough time has passed to see all the ways that this kind of rage can eat away at the goodness in human lives. We certainly have every reason to be concerned about the possibility that this rage, born of surviving the Serbian nationalists' ethnic cleansing, might be transformed into a hatred of other ethnic groups.[20]

Memories Come Alive

I have been meeting with a group of Bosnian survivors on Saturdays in a Queens school. On this occasion I have brought along my wife and two daughters. The girls play together with the Bosnian children while I sit with the adults in our small group. Afterwards all the families have a pizza lunch in the school cafeteria. I walk into the cafeteria carrying my infant daughter in one arm and her blue diaper bag on my shoulder. When Z. sees us he starts screaming at the other Bosnians, *See, that's what they do! That's what Serbs do!* The next hour is spent trying to help him to contain the torrent that has so suddenly erupted. The story comes out in bursts and fragments, but with some support, he is able to tell me about the morning when he was on a forced march with his sister and her baby and they came to a Serb checkpoint at a bridge. You had to throw all your belongings over the bridge into a net. He tells the soldiers, *We need diapers for the baby.* The soldiers grab the baby and throw her into the river. When the child's mother tries to jump in after her, she is shot dead. As he paces, shouts, and kicks the air for a tense hour, the school cafeteria is that bridge. Eventually he calms down and says, *I saw your child, and the memories came alive.*

I would never have brought my children to the psychiatric hospital where I once worked, but it seemed O.K. to bring them to this community setting to play with the Bosnian children. But after you provide a cue that triggers another's fall back into hell, it makes you feel responsible and causes you to wonder. Did I do something wrong? Is it my fault? Maybe it would be better for me to go away. In that tense moment, I hold fast to the role of the therapeutic listener, and endeavor to stay with Z. so that he will be less alone while he is reliving that memory on the bridge, and then help escort him back into the school cafeteria where the others are eating their pizza. Still, it is hard to watch that kind of fall, without feeling that you might have been the one who pushed.

Memories can be triggered by a sight, a smell, a sound, or a feeling. To the survivor, it often seems to come out of nowhere. As with J., who is overcome by memories of Bihac when she is frustrated by a rude nurse at a hospital clinic after waiting for hours to have her son seen for a strange colored splotch on his scalp. Very often it is only afterwards, with the help of another to listen and reflect, that the survivor can understand precisely what triggered this release and reliving. Most refugees' days are filled with these explosions of memory, both tiny and huge, but usually they are all too alone in trying to piece the fragments together again.

I never cease to be impressed at how completely these memories can take over the survivor, hurling them out of their involvement in a current life situation and dropping them back into the abyss.

I see it like it's in front of me.

When I tell these things to you it is like I am there again. You brought me back into the camps.

A refugee in Chicago carries soap, towel, and a toothbrush in her purse on her bad days. If the shells start falling and she has to go into the shelter, she wants to be ready.

The veracity and intensity of the remembered images drown out all else, and the person is in the grips of the world of atrocity. I could fill a book completely with such recollections of the intense moments of being there with survivors. It would be unreadable.

Bearing memories of genocide can make one anxious, nervous, and tremulous—some of the symptoms of what psychiatrists call Posttraumatic Stress Disorder (PTSD).

I am shaking as if I am in a state of electric shock.

Trauma's mark upon the mind may come as memories that can be readily verbalized, but it may also appear as memories encoded on the body. Many survivors report that as a result of their traumas, their body no longer works the way it used to. They may feel "broken" throughout their body, or the symptoms may be localized to somewhere specific that begs for the psychiatrist's interpretation.

A survivor comes into the interview room for his first meeting to evaluate symptoms of "strangling" for which the internist has found no medical explanation. Within minutes he starts feeling the strangling and has to leave the room. We pace the hall with him until he feels calmer, then encourage him to come back into the room to tell us about what's going on. For the first time ever, he

speaks of when the soldiers took him to prison, beat him severely on his chest
and neck, and let him go home. The story he is telling us has been spoken first,
and most persuasively, through his body.

Memories of ethnic cleansing leave the survivors with gloomy feelings that
have no ready place in their lives.

*During the war I felt good. I was trying to fight to live. . . . I am feeling worse
than during the war. With memories of the dark side of life. Always thinking negative.*

When this happens, the refugee's tendency is not to attribute the gloomi-
ness to the memories, or to the traumatic experiences that brought them on,
but to lay blame upon oneself:

The worst thing is that I disturb myself.

Behind this common reaction there seems to be a hidden assumption, shared
by many survivors, that war is simply part of life and that one must bear it. If
one cannot, then it is a sign of personal weakness of some sort, a character flaw
for which the individual is responsible.

The person you once were stands by stunned and helpless, as I did in the
Queens school gym, while the traumatic memories slam into some other part of
you. And it crosses your mind that maybe you could have done something to
stop it from hurting you. And each time you don't, a strange thing happens:
the sense that you should have grows and grows. You start to feel like a person
who can't help yourself, who makes things worse for yourself, who is no good
for yourself. You may not even recognize who you are or who you used to be.

Relentless and terrifying, these traumatic memories gnaw away at those thousand tendrils of understanding and connectedness that would otherwise enable
the survivors to find a place for the memories in the saga of their lives. Unable
to find their niche, traumatic memories evolve into yet darker growths upon
the self, which may overwhelm and confuse.

*All kinds of things come together. Being expelled. Things we lost. Twenty years
of work—then suddenly being without anything. The exchange. How they mistreated
kids. It gets mixed up and overlapping. All the memories come at the same moment,
and it's too much. I will make a cocoon for them.*

Memories crowd each other out.

For many, permitting the memories to resurface has the effect not of working things through but of working oneself over. It is no wonder, then, that refugees try to push their memories away in any way they can. Being with other
people. Keeping busy. Drinking. Trying not to talk about it with others. Keeping the TV off and not reading the newspapers.

Not until after lots of sitting together with refugee families did I realize the
complex ways in which having traumatic memories occurs, not in isolation from
other survivors, but in complex relationship to others, most often in the con-

text of one's family, where traumatic memories ricochet from family member to family member.

One adolescent girl says: *Everything I remember like it happened yesterday.* Her father said, *I don't forget.* Next he said, *I never think of those things.* His wife says, *There is no point in talking about what happened yesterday. It's gone now but it's difficult to forget. It's always coming up. I don't see how it would help to talk about it though; when we would talk about it, we would live it again. The best thing is to think of other things and just start to live again.*

One family member's remembering prompts another to remember, and a third to want to forget. When the first to remember sees what it does to the next person, or the one after that, it may be enough to convince them that it is better not to share one's memories, and if possible, not to remember at all.

Survivors worry that memories are contagious. Mothers do not want to transmit them to their children.

A woman gives birth to a child in the middle of the siege in Sarajevo. *I tried to please the baby as much as possible—so the baby wouldn't feel what my fears were.*

But is this a problem that can be solved by simply choosing not to speak about memories? The infant might not notice, but the grown child will, and it becomes a part of who they are. How many young children will grow up longing to reconnect with a Bosnian history their parents did not want them to know?

Maybe you can keep them away during the day, but who knows how to chase the memories out of one's dreams? I met only one refugee who said she had a way of keeping nightmares away. She was able to sleep without traumatic dreams only by using a nightly ritual:

I lie down and go through every step of the house in Bosnia—the stable, everything they took, the rugs, the horses, the doors. I see it all again.

Try as they may, so many survivors continue to relive ethnic cleansing in their dreams.

Nightmares

It is not even necessary to ask survivors if they have nightmares or traumatic dreams about ethnic cleansing, because they usually speak of them spontaneously, often within the first few minutes. Dreams wake them in the middle of the night. Are there pills or anything else I can give that will help them to get some sleep?

Traumatic dreams tend to be dreamed again and again, hovering over the survivors' existence, turning out images of terror and death, night after night. The impression left in the dream can embody crucial information about the agonies and struggles of the survivors, information that hours of conversation would never reveal.

One predominant theme that appears in the refugees' dreams is that of fleeing:

I dream about fleeing.

I am in a field and we are running. The Serbs are behind us. I wake up before anything happens.

I am always running away. I have to jump out a window and then I wake up. That is the fear of being shelled. When you are always looking where the hill is. I am always dreaming that the hills are always within sight.

These dreams do not have the scary but thrilling feel of those fleeing dreams most of us remember from our youth. In ethnic cleansing, the monster doesn't go away, it stays to terrorize and destroy.

I dream that everything is happening. . . . That they are killing A. I run into a big factory hall and I see her dead. I keep running around.

I dream about home, my people, my family. The Serbs killed my sister. I see the home where the massacre took place.

When you ask refugees to say more about the killings in their dreams, they are often reluctant to give more details. *I saw it exactly how it happened. That's all.* When I sense that those traumatic memories are too much to bear, I back off.

Survivors dream not only of the killings, but also of the psychologically dev-astating betrayals:

I see my colleague—a Serb—who worked with me and who called us Muslims brothers and then turned on us and did so many horrible crimes. I see them all the time in my dreams. I feel that they destroyed me completely. That I have fallen to such a low level of being.

Some survivors report with great relief that once they got out of Bosnia and Croatia their traumatic dreams simply disappeared.

No nightmares. It would be better if they didn't come back.

I had nightmares only when we were in Serbia. Since then I have slept like a baby.

For some, no nontraumatic dreams have emerged in their place. They used to have dreams, and now they don't dream at all.

Some survivors report that their dreams have changed over time since leav-ing Bosnia. For the survivors living in exile, when dreams change, they may take on elements of experiences from life in their new locale.

The unusual thing was that the dream happened here.

Some report in detail the evolution in their dream imagery.

I dream about my husband. That something is going on with him. The two of us used to go up a hill—it was strenuous and stressful. In the dream I am staying with him to help him so that we can succeed and get up. From that strain I wake up. . . . Maybe it's related to the time the Serbs came and took the big hill—I feared they'd come. I look at the hill as being our future and the blockade being lifted so we can continue climbing and see.

At first my dreams were about animals being slaughtered, and there was blood everywhere. Now I am having better dreams. Not like the dreams with blood and violence. Now in my dreams I see my mother, and very often my wife, and I dream of places in Bosnia where I felt like I was in paradise. Before the war. It looks like paradise. Bosnia was a very beautiful country. . . . I like animals. My profession is with animals. Piglets, cattle, rabbits, dogs, cats. In my dreams I see the farm. Piglet farm. Rabbit farm. The farms where I had very good friends and good colleagues, and I would like to walk with them and with the animals. Everything is O.K.

I still have dreams of being chased but also pleasant dreams. Being surrounded by flowers, being with my husband, these come more often. Dreams about exams—a result of my efforts to learn English!

Dream reports such as these testify to the staying power of traumatic imagery as well as to the self's remarkable capacity to render even the most horrific of experiences into something other—if not affirmative, then at least not overwhelmingly negative. From rivers of blood into a land of milk and honey. From treating people like animals in concentration camps to a peaceful animal farm. Hills that drip terror becoming slopes to climb. Being with a loved one who is not there. Examinations, not interrogations. Flowers, not bombs.

As a child I stepped out from behind an ice cream truck and was hit by a speeding car. My clavicle was broken, I passed out, and spent a few days in the hospital. It happened near the end of our street, where there was a dead end with a metal barricade, and on the other side the end of another street. For more than twenty-five years, whenever I experienced some new and unwelcome stress, image fragments from the end of my block—permanently burned into my retina at the instant I was hit—would come back in dreams. Dreams of going down an up escalator, in an out door, two rivers flowing in opposite directions straight into each other, a sea that flows into a river, a city in the country or a farm in the city, cars passing on the road.

I am crossing boundaries here by talking about my own dreams. But I know of no other way to begin to fathom what happens to one's dream life when one has lived through ethnic cleansing and experienced countless traumas, losses, deprivations, and humiliations. For survivors of traumas immeasurably worse than mine, I expect multiple dream reiterations, revisions, and reappearances of the ethnic cleansing experience. Once it gets inside, it never leaves.

Lifton's work with Hiroshima survivors found evidence of a "death imprint," the consequence of a total and precipitous immersion in death. In the case of survivors of ethnic cleansing, such imprints appear to be organized less absolutely around death than was true for the survivors of the atomic blast. Death is surely present in these dreams, but not in the complete way reported in survivors of Hiroshima.[21] There is a different pattern to the dream imagery here.

The imagery of dreams of ethnic cleansing brings to mind animals being herded, hunted, captured, and slaughtered. A deer hears a gunshot, escapes into the woods, and runs for its life. Cattle or sheep stand in a muddy corral. Horses are transported to an unfamiliar place to be slaughtered. Rats are killed in experiments.[22]

The pattern of dream imagery suggests that it is not simply that one horrific flash of death or atrocity, or even a complete death immersion, but the total experience of dehumanization that is epitomized in the life of the Bosnian refugee. These dreams give free expression to the terrifying sense of being abandoned by the human world and turned into an animal. That tissue of humankind's culture, connectedness, and understanding has vanished.[23] There is the sense of being utterly alone and utterly vulnerable. Not even sink or swim, just sink:

In my dream it is as if all the ethnic boats sank.

Still, almost unbelievably, a desire for human connection may persist, as some dream of rescue by another:

I'm in a deep canyon and I am afraid. I am trying to make a connection to the other side of the canyon. After a while I am saved.

And others dream dreams that serve as an ironic defense of their own humanity. These are dreams of protest against the fact that the human survivor was made to feel like an animal by another human. They give us dream images of Chetnik beasts, bearded, drunken, bloodied. These dreams scream, "it's not we who are the beasts but they!" One dehumanization begets another.

Neither protest dreams, nor idyllic dreams, are enough to displace the haunting of the imagination that comes in dreams of returning to a Bosnia to which one no longer belongs.

I went to Banja Luka alone, and everything was covered with something in colors. It's a different color, with blankets and different letters. I went to the Hotel Bosnia, and it was covered with some papers, black and red, very strange. Same but different. I met people on the street. One, his name was Emir, like me, asked me why I left. He is an engineer but he is checking the road. No, looks like he is cleaning the road. Why didn't we help them to clean the road?

J., December 1994

We meet again.

I felt guilty about accusing you of being our enemy because I felt that I had no right to do that. Especially since I need you. I wanted to call you that evening. Not so much to say I am sorry but really to tell you how I felt. I really did think at the time that you were my enemy. But I have no right to accuse anyone else. If I hadn't been caught at a moment when Bihac was so terribly threatened I might never have uttered those things.

If I am surrounded by people who make me feel bad, then I can't cope. . . . I feel a bit relieved that I moved away from a building where there was one family from Serbia. . . . They were ordering me around and asking me to do the cleaning. It's that kind of behavior that really makes it difficult for me to cope with things.

When the time comes that you can't understand what people are doing . . . can't define it, then. . . . The next day instead of going to school I went to the Metropolitan Museum of Art. I went to look at the Impressionists because I never appreciated or liked them. What helped a lot was a painting by Monet.

I spent about an hour with the Impressionists and especially this particular painting. It reminded me of my childhood and the time I spent with my husband, and somehow it provoked nice memories for me in a way that only art can. This painting is particularly fascinating for me. For me painting brings out all the beautiful things I have experienced. Not everybody has this kind of gift or talent, but at least they could try and be good.

"I can't remember the painting."

I brought it with me! It's just like my childhood because we always loved the snow. Here . . .

She shows me a small photo of the painting from a museum brochure. It's Monet's *The Magpie*, on loan from the Musée d'Orsay.

This is just like a part of my childhood. I feel as if I actually walked through here. It reminds me very much of the place just outside of Zagreb where my mother comes from. This is like my grandmother's. There is a fence that looks just like this one. It reminds me very much of the time that I spent there as a child. You know it reminds me of the happy, carefree days of my life, and it also reminds me of the mountains just above Sarajevo, where the Serbs are now, and where we went skiing and how happy times were! What a wonderful life we had.

Not only do I see it in my mind, but I can smell and feel it, especially the shadows that come from the setting sun. I am really grateful to this painting because it really brought me to life and reminded me of those beautiful times.

"It's amazing to me how different are your feelings and images associated with this painting in comparison with the feelings that you shared during our last meeting."

When you reach a point where you can no longer be sickened by these horrors you feel as if your innards are about to explode, then you have to find a way out. I am so afraid that I will lose my dear ones again. That's what I am so scared of.

"If you didn't have that fear, then there would be something wrong with you. It's natural. But it's also good that you are able to find ways to give yourself a break from it, and to help soothe yourself."

I was very egotistical at the time because I left my children and I didn't think about what happened to them. I just went. I should have been in school but I wasn't, and I went to the museum. And I felt really sick about the children, and actually I may have neglected them that day because I wasn't thinking about how they feel.

"I disagree with you. I don't think you are egotistical. I think you knew you needed to take care of yourself and that in the end that would be the best for your children."

I understand what you're saying, but whenever people came to extend their condolences to me they would all say, well it's awful, but you know you have to do it for your children.

"And what do you think about that now?"

I think that I am studying the language and I am trying to be an example for the kids and I have needs as well.

"I don't see why it has to be all or nothing. All for your children or all for yourself. I don't see why you can't find something in the middle."

I think that I am doing what you said. In other words—both. But people actually thought and felt that I should live for my children. It's also a commentary on people back home, who shouldn't really be thinking this way—you have your children to live for—as if you didn't exist. There's so much meaning one can find in life.

Enduring Struggles

When J. and I meet for coffee one year later, things are better. Several Bosnians and Americans have offered friendship, and she is beginning to enjoy their company. I, who have unintentionally become a link to the dead and the suffering, am asked if it is O.K. for J. to be released from the chains binding her to her husband and loved ones in Bihac, and to the whole catastrophe of ethnic cleansing. "Yes, of course." We share a smile, but the look in her eyes, and the queasiness in my stomach, say it is still going to take more time. We still keep in touch. J. tries her best to provide a life for her children, to give a human shape to her own life, and to keep her family afloat.

The refugees' struggles will endure. The genocide that tore them from their embeddedness in the life course has entrapped them in traumatic memories and a shattered life that have rendered them something tragically nonhuman and seemingly untouchable by life's goodness and vitality. Yet at the same time, life serves to bring them into contact with new experiences, people, and ideas, which could form the basis for affirmative changes. Just being alive puts the survivor at risk of experiencing these changes. Their very existence is defined by a struggle between the dehumanizing genocide experience and the potentially humanizing experience of the life process. At no point does their involvement with the one make them totally immune to the other. In their lives, as in J.'s, we can find traces of continual struggle, which may take many different forms: between different parts of the self, or between individuals in a survivor family, or within survivor communities. Yet with each passing day there are opportunities for writing a new life saga less overwhelmed by negative signs. Survivors and refugees like J. are finding out that although there is no way for this to be the same life that was lost, neither must it be a lifeless appendage.

What is also happening is that a culture is fighting for its life. Stripped of the support and structure provided by individual lives, families, and communities, as well as by a political system, this tissue of humanity endeavors to persist, to assert itself over and around the horror and sorrow of war. One place where this struggle for survival is waged appears when Bosnian parents and adults ask, "what will we teach our children about Bosnia and its history, and especially ethnic cleansing?" Some try to put aside the memories of war and to conceive of living together in Bosnia as before, much as they did after World War II. Others make the memories a focus for reorganizing Bosnian identity along a new sense of ethnic nationality. A primary division between one coalition of ethnoreligious nationalists and another of secular multiculturalists seems likely to be the primary shape of the sociopolitical landscape in the short term; perhaps this will be followed by innumerable lesser fractures and fissions.

The ethnoreligious nationalists who now dominate Bosnian political culture appear to draw greater strength from the experiences of survivors and refugees than do the multiculturalists and their merhamet. That is in part because merhamet never was a political sensibility. It had the advantage of acknowledging and accepting ethnic and religious diversity, but the disadvantage of not recognizing the memories of aggression and the existence of enemies. The experience of surviving ethnic cleansing makes it far easier for the ethnoreligious nationalists to know and publicly express who they are, and who their enemies are, in comparison with the secular multiculturalists.

Given the absence of Tito, or of some other force to broker a nonethnic resolution, and given the continued presence of nationalistic leaders, the nationalist way will continue to derive far more strength than the multiculturalist. Although this certainly spells the end of Bosnian culture as it was known, Bosnia and its Diaspora is far from being a homogenous, singular entity. There is still room for hope that in the debates that will ensue among these different positions, that the place and significance of memories, of both living together and ethnic cleansing, and the struggle to reconcile them will this time be a central part of the struggle over a new Bosnia.

Part II

Producing Ethnic Cleansing

Introduction: Psychiatrists Colliding with History

When Dr. Vaso Cubrilovic, philosopher and Serb nationalist, spoke at the Serbian Cultural Club in Belgrade, on March 7, 1937, he revealed himself as one of the fathers of ethnic cleansing. He proposed to solve the problem of the Albanians' colonization of lands claimed by Serbia by expulsion and mass removal, "with the brute force of an organized state." In outlining his strategy, Cubrilovic stated: "The first prerequisite is the creation of a suitable psychosis. It can be created in many ways."[1] He suggested enacting intolerable laws, burning houses and villages, and arming locals to draw blood.

Fifty years later, Cubrilovic's writings resurface with the resurgence of Serbian nationalist ideology and the making of new plans for achieving a Greater Serbia. Ethnic cleansing is the contemporary embodiment of Cubrilovic's "creation of a mass psychosis." It is the deliberate effort to shatter the multi-ethnic self and its connections with its human and physical environment, and to push individual Bosnians into the abyss of madness. Just as Robert Lifton describes the Nazis' genocide against the Jews in biomedical terms as extermination by surgical excision,[2] so we may see the Serbian ethnic cleansing of Bosnia-Herzegovina in terms of psychiatric imagery: The primary goal is not to murder persons but to annihilate the intrapsychic and psychosocial structures that constituted the life and culture associated with merhamet—to make them fear so much that they would never want to go home again.

Genocides are known to have involved the participation of health care professionals. Lifton demonstrated the extensive involvement of the medical profession in the Nazi genocide in his *Nazi Doctors*. This not only involved "medicalized killing" (Lifton, 14–18), but also took the form of the "killing professionals"—those doctors and other educated professionals "who combine to create not only the technology of genocide but much of its ideological rationale, moral climate, and organizational process" (Lifton, 489–490). The involvement of medical professionals was so complete that the Nazi vision of genocidal destruction of the Jews became thoroughly merged with biomedical imagery. Psychiatrists were also active in perpetrating and supporting the Nazi genocide.[3] Since World War II, mental health professionals have been implicated in the systematic abuses of psychiatric diagnosis and treatments in the service of political repression and violence in totalitarian states such as the former Soviet Union, and in former governments in Central and Eastern Europe, Cuba, and China.[4]

What then are we to make of the fact that a psychiatrist, Radovan Karadzic, was the leader of the self-declared Bosnian Serb Republic that performed the ethnic cleansing? A psychiatrist creating a mass psychosis! Was Karadzic somehow deploying his psychiatric knowledge in the service of genocide? Had Karadzic ordered his soldiers to commit mass rape and other atrocities because he knew, as a psychiatrist, how effectively such acts could annihilate merhamet?

In 1993, the American Psychiatric Association passed a declaration condemning Radovan Karadzic for "brutal and inhumane actions," adding that "psychiatrists issue that condemnation with particular offense, urgency and horror because, by education and training, Dr. Karadzic claims membership in our profession."[5] A strong statement was needed. But the psychiatrists' condemnation could also be a sophisticated way of saying: Because of what he has done, we cannot consider him one of ours. As a psychiatrist, I wanted to give more consideration to the possible connections between Karadzic as a psychiatrist and Karadzic as a genocidal leader. There was also another psychiatrist, Jovan Raskovic, who had been a leader of the Serbian nationalist movement in Croatia just prior to ethnic cleansing. I never thought to suggest that psychiatrists were the only ones who contributed to ethnic cleansing. Genocide is a broad and ambitious project, requiring cultural elites from many different professions. Yet as a psychiatrist, I could not ignore the fact that two of the leaders inciting ethnic cleansing belonged to my profession.

I acquired their writings and studied them in detail. Raskovic wrote many professional books and articles. Karadzic wrote nothing of significance in the professional literature; however, he wrote and published several volumes of poetry. Both sets of writings were of interest because in them the writers were actively engaged with personal and historical memory.

Then it turned out that my work brought me into contact with several psychiatrists from Bosnia, Croatia, and Serbia. Because there were relatively few psychiatrists in the former Yugoslavia, most knew Raskovic and Karadzic from the same meetings and professional organizations. I got to know one Sarajevan psychiatrist who had supervised Radovan Karadzic for many years and others who had worked closely with him for most of his professional career. I listened to what they said about professionals and genocide.

In nearly all of these conversations, the speaker begins with a warning: *If you are thinking that being psychiatrists had anything to do with what Raskovic and Karadzic did in promoting genocide, then you are absolutely wrong!* They insist that whatever Karadzic was or did in the aggression has nothing to do with his psychiatric work or their work together. Commenting on these dismissals, one Sarajevan psychiatrist warns:

So what did the others tell you? You must take care that what they say is biased by current conditions. Now they see only black. But if he were a hero, they would be saying something very different.[6]

I had to keep reminding myself that these psychiatrists were not as comfortably removed from historical events as I was, with my laptop and books. They were psychiatrists who had encountered history because it had smashed into their lives. Just like most others in Bosnia-Herzegovina, they were unprepared for what happened when the nationalists came to power. Being psychiatrists did not give them any special insights into the evolving political catastrophe. And by and large they took no special interest in historical or political concerns. If anything, they tried to ignore all that. They focused on their work and their families, as they always had.

These conversations with former colleagues and friends yield useful biographical information. But more importantly, these dialogues also give a firsthand sense of what takes place when psychiatrists' professional and historical worlds collide. In my quest to know more about Raskovic, Karadzic, and the mentality of the ethnic cleansing and its leaders, it becomes apparent that there is more to learn by gazing upon the scenes of these collisions than by looking away from them.

In the meantime, I am involved in a collision with some psychiatrists from Serbia after publicly accusing them of being psychiatric apologists for genocide. They then publicly denounce my claims, and me, and they hire a lawyer who tells me to "cease and desist" addressing these matters. When I show the lawyer's letter to one of my Bosnian refugee friends, he shouts, "That is exactly what they do! 'Cease and desist.' Now you know!" This episode gives me a creepy feeling. When I open their letter I feel the long, dark hand of totalitarianism reaching across the ocean into my office. That afternoon I feel their fist in my face. No, these psychiatrists from Serbia did not actively lead the genocide, as did Karadzic, or promote genocidal ideology like Raskovic. But the story they tell in their books, as professionals, helps their government to avoid condemnation for the genocide.

In Part Two of this book I look at the three different contributions to the ethnic cleansing project made by the psychiatrists Raskovic, Karadzic, and the Belgrade group. I explore the common theme of how each was working with the memories of collective traumatization as a part of the effort that produced ethnic cleansing.

Chapter 4

Jovan Raskovic's Fall and the Ascendance of Serbian Nationalism

Confession after a Fall

On January 24, 1992, an interview with the psychiatrist Jovan Raskovic appears in the Zagreb periodical *Vjesnik*, where he says:

> I feel responsible because I made the preparations for this war, even if not the military preparations. If I hadn't created this emotional strain in the Serbian people, nothing would have happened. My party lit the fuse of Serbian nationalism not only in Croatia but everywhere else in Bosnia and Herzegovina. It's impossible to imagine an SDS in Bosnia and Herzegovina or a Mr. Karadzic in power without our influence. We have driven this people and we have given it an identity. I have repeated again and again to this people that it comes from heaven, not earth.[1]

There are many ways to read this statement. You can read it as a truthful confession. Or as a boast, perhaps somewhat exaggerated. Or even as a sincere apology. To be sure, there aren't yet too many examples of Serbian leaders apologizing for their part in promoting nationalism and aggression. Raskovic's confession also raises a central question for our discussion: how does a psychiatrist make preparations for ethnic cleansing? Raskovic, the psychiatrist, did so by receiving, documenting, and communicating survivors' stories of Serbian suffering, so as to build a collective memory that could work synergistically with nationalist ideology to propel a mass movement.

Raskovic's confession is made after a fall. In 1992, Jovan Raskovic was relieved of his duties as the leader of the Serbian Democratic Party (SDS) in Croatia and retired to Belgrade. A few months later, Serb aggression in Bosnia-Herzegovina begins, and the violent consequences of Serbian nationalism are realized there. Even in January 1992, Raskovic sounds as if he already knows of the genocide the Serbian aggressors are about to initiate.

Raskovic wants us to know that he had a part in it. Not a military part, but a big part nonetheless. But why? His confession seems as self-serving as it does self-effacing, as is often the case with victims of what Robert Lifton has mockingly called "retirement syndrome."[2] This sudden moral reading of his prior work is hard to take seriously when it comes only after his forced retirement. And there is also the smell of a loser in his having to remind us: don't you forget about me.

But before his political fall Raskovic had climbed to considerable professional heights as a psychiatrist in Croatia. He was born in 1929 in Knin, Croatia. His father, Dusan Raskovic, studied law in Padua and Graz, and practiced in Knin. Raskovic writes: "I lived in Knin until 1941 when the winds of war carried me out of the Independent State of Croatia in order to avoid massacres there."[3] After the war, the family moved to Zagreb, where his father worked for the Ministry of Justice. Jovan Raskovic completed high school and then studied medicine at the School of Medicine at the University of Zagreb, receiving his degree in 1956. He did his internship at Sibenik, and quickly rose to become the hospital director in 1958. He passed his psychiatry boards in 1962 and worked on the neuropsychiatry ward at Sibenik Hospital. He studied electroencephalography and electromyography, and lectured within Yugoslavia and internationally.[4]

Raskovic wrote many papers that were published in professional journals. These included: "Social Aspects of Aggression" (1979), "Ontology and Psychoanalytic Anthropology of Death" (1980), "Social Meaning of the Scapegoat and Psychiatry" (1980), "Paranoiac States" (1982), and "Ontology and Anthropology of Jealousies" (1987). Although these writings deal with social and cultural topics, they are not overtly political in the way that the later writings were. He also wrote a number of books dealing with more explicitly political topics, including *Narcissism* (1988), *Depersonalization* (1990), and most important for this discussion, *Luda Zemlja* (1990), which means "The Mad Country."

Raskovic eventually became widely known in the former Yugoslavia, not primarily as a psychiatrist, but through his political work, which did not begin until late in his life. In 1990, Raskovic met the Serbian nationalist intellectual Dobrica Cosic, upon the recommendation of Jovan Opacic, a Serbian dissident in Croatia who had been jailed in Sibenik, where Raskovic lived and worked. Together, Opacic and Raskovic formed the Serbian Democratic Party in Knin on February 17, 1990. Raskovic wanted it to be a broader "Democratic Party," but Opacic prevailed in making it a group specifically committed to promoting Serbian national interests. This tension persisted between Raskovic and the nationalist politicals and is what ultimately led to Raskovic's fall just two years later.[5]

But before the fall, Raskovic functioned exceedingly well as a celebrated spokesperson for Serbian nationalism. His writings were generously excerpted in many periodicals in the former Yugoslavia. Dobrica Cosic celebrated Raskovic's mass appeal in his introduction to *Luda Zemlja*:

> Jovan Raskovic is a new personality in the Yugoslavian political scene. Only the current circumstances in Yugoslavia—the destruction of the social order by internal differences and ideological utopia, the multifaith and multinational community about to be consumed by the fires of hatred, a society mentally and morally sick, a dangerous and painful period for all Yugoslavs, and especially the dangerous situation of the Serbs in Croatia—and these circumstances alone, have made this doctor from Sibenik, this psychiatrist with a national reputation, this pensive Freudian, this Dalmatian hedonist with prophetic traits, who at the age of 61 had never practiced politics nor even been a member of any political organizations, into a politician, President of the Serbian Democratic Party, a national defender, a charismatic figure, the most famous Serb this summer. (*Luda Zemlja*, 7)

In 1990 and 1991, Raskovic stood before large crowds in Croatia, Montenegro, and Bosnia-Herzegovina. His public appearances were splashed all over the newspapers and the television. With his full, graying beard, dark eyes, and dramatic style, he cut a prophetic figure that was a big hit in the Serbian movement. He always drove a BMW to political meetings, like Croatian President Franjo Tudjman. When he got out of the car the people started shouting, "Jovo, Jovo Jovo!" His bodyguards encircled him, he held his hands above his head and clapped. The people yelled loudly, "Caca! Caca!" then "Jovo Jovane," and "Jovo Srbine" (*Luda Zemlja*, 27). Cosic continues:

> when he begins to speak, the Serbs listen attentively, considering everything he says to be the truth. In the shadows of fear and disillusionment shines a ray of hope. This scrupulous doctor brings the remedy of truth to a people sick from lies; this generous intellectual uses reason to awaken the Serbian people, who had until this moment been misled by a univocal ideology. Jovan Raskovic has agitated the cheated, resigned, and desperate Serbs in Croatia and Bosnia-Herzegovina, leading them to an awareness of their true historical, national, and civil worth. (*Luda Zemlja*, 13)

Stories of Serbian Suffering

According to Raskovic, the mentalities spread by the communist system of the preceding forty years stand between the Serbs and truth. The era of Titoism was a "time when the total lie was ruling. When false states and false myths were created. False autonomies and false regions, not to speak of false peoples" (p. 126). The truth the Serbs are searching for is to be found in their long history of oppression and suffering, Raskovic writes: "Nothing is more successful at establishing a national collectivity and a national consciousness than genocide" (p. 56). Raskovic's speeches and writings for the nationalist movement derive their force from the stories he tells of Serbians surviving genocide. Some of these stories appear in *Luda Zemlja*.

When he tells the story of his own family, Raskovic speaks of their ethnic origin in Raska. Raskovic could claim special status among the Serbian people, having hailed from Serbia's most ancient southern territories and the fortress of traditional Serbian culture. This adds to his credibility as a teller of the Serbian people's sacred history.

He tells the story of how his family survived World War II and speaks of the frightening moment that changed their lives forever:

> In May 1941 the organized persecution of Serbs in Knin region began. My father Dusan Raskovic, a very well known attorney in Knin, was a high ranking Serb of the region. . . . Into our house comes a decently dressed and imposing peasant. He wants to talk to my father. He remains behind the door, but then enters cautiously, saying something in a low voice to my mother. She calls my father, who enters the room sleepy and half-dressed. He recognizes the guest. They go to another small room. My father leaves for a minute to get dressed. The guest is nervous, doesn't want to accept anything. He just wants to relay the news. My father is now awake, normally dressed, but obviously worried. In a low voice as if frightened, the guest informs him that last night the Orthodox priests were killed in three villages. "We are expecting persecution of all important Serbs and then after that of all Serbs. It is time to leave Mr. Dusan." Now my father realized that evil times were upon us. He was frightened by this news. Everybody in the house started running. My mother, though it was a rather warm morning in May, put on her fur coat. Our housekeeper, who had been with us for years, suddenly brought a hammer to remove the Raskovic name. (*Luda Zemlja*, 23–24)

The story Raskovic tells about his family is much less grim than those of many Serb familiess during World War II. The Raskovic family was most fortunate to have escaped from Ustasha-controlled territory and to have avoided the horrific atrocities and killings perpetrated there. The Ustasha slaughtered hundreds of thousands of civilians in Croatia, especially Serbs, with a brutality that disgusted even the Gestapo.[6] The young Raskovic was placed in a monastery in Kistanje, Croatia, where he remained for most of the war years. His stories about World War II are not about atrocities that happened directly to him, but rather about what he heard and saw during that time. When he tells the story of life in the monastery, Raskovic speaks of the horrors he witnessed from his safe haven in Kistanje, which he says received more than 7,000 refugees fleeing the Ustasha.

> Slowly the victims from across the river started coming and telling their horrible stories. One story is about the merchant from whom we used to buy shoes. They put nails in his head and then wondered, "Why is he still alive?" Finally they cut open his abdomen and chest and pissed and spit on his wounds. Another story is about a musician who used to play in a church orchestra. They cut his toes one by one, and then his fingers. Then they decided to leave him, let him go, so that he again can go and help the priests in church. But finally they killed him.
>
> One evening I heard sounds by the river. Something slowly and hesitantly slips into the river. I hear the sounds of swimming. It seems to be an animal. I hear breathing. I come closer and I see a very tall, corpulent man coming out of the river, first his left leg and then the right one. Then he lies on the ground. Helping himself with his left hand, with his right one he is supporting his head. I help him to get up and now he is supporting his head with both hands. I run to the monastery, calling out to everybody saying that there is a very seriously wounded man, come and help him. The wound was deep and very ugly. We put him on a bed and called for an Italian doctor. The doctor is a small man who comes with an enormous soldier to help him. He enters the room and after some time comes out saying that the man will live, but at the same time, he says, "What kind of people are you, you damned Slavs!"
>
> During the summer of 1941 our small town Kistanje received more than 7,000 immigrants. One morning a strong and tall man with enormous hands appeared. He didn't talk with anybody. He sat in the sun and didn't look for shade. And in this heat he wore a warm sweater and a dark hat on his head. The story went that one of his neighbors who became Ustasha killed all his children and threw them in a pit. (pp. 28–29)

These memories of genocide against the Serbs stayed with Raskovic for decades and shaped his identity and his professional interests. He writes: "The flight from our family home in May 1941, and that frontier between Knin and Kistanje, which divided two worlds, and also divided my own life, remained deeply impressed in my conscious and perhaps brought the prejudice for all my understanding, for all my ways of thinking. The first and most permanent thing was that I was and am preoccupied by the idea of death in its various aspects" (p. 54).

This is evident in many of the psychiatric topics on which Raskovic wrote well before his political involvement with the nationalists began. It also appears that, being a psychiatrist who himself had survived war, Raskovic gravitated toward other survivors, and took an interest in helping them and hearing their stories. In Tito's Yugoslavia, this could not be done in any way that elevated Serbian suffering or collective identity above that of any other group. Partisan stories about World War II portrayed victims of fascism without identifying them as Serbs. But with the passing of Tito's era it became possible to speak critically of its falsehoods, and specifically about the Serbs' surviving genocide. Raskovic's survivors' stories make suddenly available a whole experiential world of suffering and knowing that can connect powerfully with the Serbian nationalists' ideology.

Raskovic discovers that his clinical case histories have an appeal that goes beyond psychiatry, and that they actually carry strong memories and truths that can serve to awaken the Serbian people from their slumber in a way that ideology itself cannot. Raskovic tells the story of Stojan, who was brought to him in 1964:

> He lived alone in a shabby village house. He left the war as a sergeant and there were some indications that he had lost his whole family in the war.
>
> He never had any trouble with anybody. He lived in peace with his neighbors. When they found him he was lying on the floor with a wooden vessel of stale water beside him. There was no food. He had probably remained like that for days. He was immediately transferred to a hospital bed. He accepted everything they gave him. But he kept returning to an abnormal position, keeping his head upright in the bed. Never putting it on the pillow. Whenever we put his head on the pillow, he would accept that but then a few minutes later he returned his head to the previous position. He looked like a stone sculpture.
>
> He didn't eat. He didn't drink. He permanently kept his eyes closed, and had a typical clinical picture of catatonia. I tried to talk to him and said whenever you wish to speak, you call the nurse and they will call me. For days and days, we were feeding him with a tube, and discussing his case.
>
> I heard many stories of people who remained in these regions of north Dalmatia and Knin and after World War II living in a strange condition, almost like in a desert, with no social contact and no need to know the truth. Sometimes they lived in the shells of old lorries or even automobiles. One of them lived in an old tank and even today there are two men living in the leftover shells of cars from which everything useful was removed. So my man was of the same kind.
>
> You cannot say that he lost his identity. To the contrary. He is probably carrying with himself all his profound fears. He is frightened of any relationship with people, with things, and even with his own self. His identity is stronger than the identity of those who are integrated.
>
> One morning I was called by a nurse saying that Stojan has woken

up. He sat on the bed, and asked that the tube be removed. Then he went to the bathroom and washed himself. Then he went for his breakfast and ate it, though without much enthusiasm. Then he came in front of my room and was sitting there, waiting for me. Then he told me his story.

It was long ago in the summer of 1941, as you know, it was that great massacre. My neighbor, Ustasha, took all my 4 children and me and took us out of the village. For some time we were walking to a big open space where the people were being collected. There were children, women, young and old men. They encircled us and started humiliating us. For some time they made us walk and then they put us into the trucks. They took us to a pit where they killed us and threw us in. They used long sharp knives, hammers, and only very rarely firearms.

My neighbor was all the time looking at our little group. My children started crying, asking for help. I was only waiting for the end of it all, since there was no other solution. I bent my head and waited. With a lot of crying and resistance my beaten and killed children were thrown into a pit.

When I thought that my time had come, my neighbor came closer and said that he will make me stay alive. He said, "You Stojan, will remain as a testimony of our power and revenge. If I would kill you now, it would be a great advantage for yourself. Therefore stay and live." (*Luda Zemlja*, 64–69)

Raskovic continues:

This is not the end of the story. When our forces occupied these regions the two sons of his Ustasha neighbor, who had already been killed, were brought to him. With a small pause, and without any expression on his face Stojan said that he killed one of the children. But after he saw what he did, he started trembling, and for some time felt paralyzed. The other child he took to his aunt in a village. That was the end of his story which was told in a way as if he had rather told it to himself than to me. (p. 69)

It is these survivors' stories, such as Raskovic's account of Stojan, or his first-hand story of his own odyssey, that provide the ground upon which the nationalists' ideology can stand. These stories of Serbian suffering bear powerful historical truths that could not be spoken in the communist era. It is easy to see how for Raskovic, Stojan's case becomes an archetypal story. It powerfully connects with his own personal and familial story of survival in World War II. It supports his sense that there are many Serbs who survived Ustasha persecution who have been suffering in silence. Raskovic, the psychiatrist, wants to heal what ails them, but he also knows that this can only be done through a broader social and cultural process.

Raskovic recognizes the power in these stories. The stories contain certain historical facts that had never been acknowledged or taken seriously in Tito's Yugoslavia.

> I remember that the talks that proclaimed the forgetting of the evil are neglecting the evil of forgetfulness. I couldn't forget. Because what happened to us, the dead and alive, the people of the same language, that lived together, but with a different truth about themselves, different truth about the crime and punishments, which represents our destiny, and still not our past, because it's going to last until the doom of permanent lie is not anymore with us. (p. 54)

The stories also carry psychological and spiritual truths that must be faced.

> From the hell in which we were, and perhaps still are, we don't get out without a great purification of our consciousness. We don't get out without doubt in ourselves. Without doubt of us and of our un-knowledge and our non-fitness to know about the other and to hear the voices of the others. That kind of doubt is the sun of the mind. We should start talking about consciousness instead of permanently talking about the guilt. (p. 93)

Raskovic, this listener and holder of many stories, wants others to know the stories and grasp their truths, and then enter into the struggle to redefine themselves. He isn't the only person who held on to these memories. Presumably, Serbs all over the former Yugoslavia have nightmares and memories of World War II. But he is one of the first Serbs to put these memories into stories and to tell those stories publicly. Being a psychiatrist must help in a number of ways. His ability to listen and to receive the stories in the face of the survivors' terrible aloneness and despair is clearly important. As a psychiatrist, he has the conceptual and methodological capacity to articulate those stories as a part of a growing body of knowledge about human behavior and suffering. Putting a doctor in relation to the Serbs underlines the realness of the Serbs' suffering, and the seriousness of the ailment now facing the Serbian people.

The nationalist politicians had to like these sides of Raskovic. He told stories that communicated truths in a more prophetic and electrifying way than their ideology ever could. The sufferings his stories brought to life propelled people toward the nationalist ideology, around which they could organize their newly awakened ambitions and frustrations. But there was another part to Raskovic, the theorist, that got in their way.

Psychiatric Proto-Nationalism

Raskovic the psychiatric writer and educator was committed to exploring and discussing clinical psychiatric theory. He did not shy away from theorizing about the history that was then unfolding in Yugoslavia. His book is full of his psychiatric analyses of just about everything: fascism, communism, leadership, ethnicity, nationalism, genocide, and so on.

Alexandra Milenov, who was reading Raskovic with Professor Cherif Bassiouni for the United Nations Commission on Experts for War Crimes in the Former-Yugoslavia, asks me if the theoretical ruminations in his book are "accepted" theory in psychiatry. I ask her to read me what she is questioning. She reads me this:

> Due to my work as a psychiatrist for decades at the border of three
> republics, I had the opportunity to treat people from different ethnic
> groups and religions. For example, Catholics, Orthodox, and Muslims
> experience different kinds of neuroses. To put it simply, the Serbs
> exhibit a very strong Oedipal situation, with all of the problems that
> accompany it. On the other hand, neurotic problems that afflict the
> Croats are fixated on the Castration complex. The Muslim people, as
> Freud would say, are afflicted with anal frustrations. (p. 128)

"No! Absolutely not," I tell her. Raskovic's theoretical writings are undisciplined, sloppy, confusing, repetitive, and emotional. Venturing into territories where a subtle and steady intellectual approach would be required, he wields an ax and a flamethrower.

Raskovic's most outrageous theorizing concerns ethnic identity and interethnic conflict. He applies Freudian theories of unconscious intrapsychic conflict and psychosexual development willy-nilly to social issues concerning national character and intergroup conflict. He pronounces: "What surprised me most was the fact that the majority of Muslims cured by me had anal fixations" (p. 128). Accordingly, Muslims "possess an aggressive component, precision, and cleanliness" (p. 128). They are thus "disposed to gather property, to rule, to judge people by the measure of their fortune and achievements, by social success" (p. 128). These attributes are etiologically related to "the Muslim laws and demands concerning the particular hygienic treatment of anal channel" (p. 128).

How does Raskovic come to these conclusions?

"I didn't reach these conclusions from the Koran. They are rather founded on my personal experience from my observing certain social and psychological characteristics" (p. 128).

Though his characterization of the Muslims is clearly the most dehumanizing of all, and in and of itself can be seen as contributing to extreme ethnic nationalism, Raskovic does not spare the Croats or even the Serbs from his analysis. He interprets the historical conflicts between Croats and Serbs as a psychic "conflict between Oedipal Serbs and Castrated Croats" (p. 124), in a not entirely flattering way. "Sometimes the Castrated and Oedipals agree, provided the Castrated accepts the Oedipal as a fait accompli and submits. But when the

Castrated character begins to watch the Oedipal suspiciously and begins to defend himself against his suppressive character, their relations become very unpleasant and their confrontation becomes a shock between the peoples, the historical confrontation of their politics" (p. 125).

In emphasizing the inevitability of conflict between Serbs and Croats as a result of a psychologically driven need on the part of the Croats to challenge the Serbs' power, Raskovic is using psychiatric and psychoanalytic principles and language to provoke, explain, and justify the prospect of Serbian aggression. You don't have to be a psychiatrist to recognize how intellectually irresponsible Raskovic's thinking is here. But lay persons, especially the uneducated, may regard statements such as these as lending professional and intellectual legitimacy to the aggressive leanings of the Serbian nationalists.

There are many examples where Raskovic is trying to make some clinical theoretical point while at the same time making a statement that supports a nationalist position.

> Human reality enriches itself through the crisis and destruction of the inner worlds. The ethnical being of the Serb people is closest to himself and most intimate with himself when cataclysms occur. . . . The Serb people have always been a nation of tragic destiny, a kind of heaven-born people, a people from Heaven and a people of Death. The connection between heaven and national destiny has created specific psychological and social conditions. It has created conditions for the religious destiny of an ethnical being. (p. 125)

In some passages, the merger between the psychiatrist and the nationalists appears seamless. "The Serb has been locked up in a dark chest, beneath a veil of shame and modesty. Right now, we are opening up this gloomy box, removing the veils of the Serbian people, a people that was hidden from its self, and we are bringing them out into the light" (p. 126).

But overall, the more Raskovic brings clinical theory into the discussion, the greater his divergence from the nationalist position. At times the criticism gets a little sharper, as when he writes of the paranoid leader in a paper titled "Social Forms of Paranoia," which can be seen as anticipating Radovan Karadzic: "The leading figure of such an institution can even be admired for his infantile style and his permanent pseudology tendency to lie instead of doubt and irony bring him glory and popularity. Just because it abolishes reality" (p. 148).

Yet, unlike some of the other examples cited, where the theorizing lends support to the nationalists' agenda, in these passages Raskovic puts some distance between himself and a nationalistic agenda, and even criticizes that way of seeing reality.

Raskovic uses clinical theorizing as a way of building upon what is learned from the stories of Serbs surviving genocide. But he does it in a way that differs from the nationalist politicians.

Raskovic says of the relationship between Serbs in Croatia and Serbs in Serbia: "Those people should be spiritually and politically united. Here I am not thinking in terms of space" (p. 149). Theory entered at the point where Raskovic is unwilling to fully commit to a Greater Serbia.

Raskovic's writings came under attack from prominent psychiatric colleagues in their reviews of his book. The prominent Sarajevo psychiatrist Dusan Kecmanovic wrote: "Discipline is not a strong side of Raskovic's writing. He is prone to digression. His definitions are not sufficiently precise. Though he can be sometimes very inspiring. The main problem is, whether it's possible to enlarge individual psychological phenomenon to groups or even to social systems."[7]

From this critic's professional scientific orientation, Raskovic's writings are clearly flawed. But such professionalism is no longer an important aspect of Raskovic's writings as his involvement with Serbian nationalism deepens. He is not writing a professional text to guide clinical work so much as presenting a hot-blooded narrative to persuade a people. One prominent Serbian psychologist writing about Raskovic's *Narcissism* seems to grasp this:

> The language of *Narcissism* is meant for a general audience, to the community of the readers who are fans and supporters, who in its author see the wise teacher and leader. It's not meant for the skeptical reader or critically disposed individual who would try to verify hypothesis by himself, to challenge the proofs, to try the author's deductions and conclusions. Therefore the author of *Narcissism* most probably unwillingly trying to decipher the narcissistic language started himself to talk this very same narcotic language.[8]

Especially in the stories he tells, but evident also in his theoretical reflections, Raskovic's writings are not organized around testing a hypothesis or building a theory. They are a confessional and argumentative narrative that is actually far more provocation than explanation of the evolving genocidal mentality within the Serbian nationalist movement.

Pushed Aside by the Memorandum

The Memorandum of the Serbian Academy of Arts and Sciences is a seventy-four-page text written by a group of Serbian academics in the mid-1980s to express their nationalistic frustrations and aspirations. It is rumored to have been partially written at the home of Raskovic, but it is clearly the product of other writers with an entirely different approach to the dilemmas of the Serbs. It consists of a rather technical and dry first section, "Yugoslav Economic and Social

Crisis," and a second half entitled "Position of Serbia and Serbian People," which more fully carries the arguments and passion of the radical Serbian nationalism voiced by Dobrica Cosic,[9] identified as a "moral crisis" (Memorandum, 307).

When excerpts are first published on September 24, 1986, in the daily paper *Vecernje Novosti*, the Memorandum shocks Yugoslavia.[10] It brashly says what could not be said under Tito's reign. It becomes the defining text for the Serbian nationalist movement, claiming, "A worse historical defeat in peacetime cannot be imagined."[11]

The Memorandum declares that the Serbs have been oppressed: "The Serbs were imposed the historical feeling of guilt, but, unlike other nations, they were the only ones who did not solve their national problem or get their own country" (Judah, *The Serbs*, 335). The Comintern and the Communist Party are accused of a policy of "retaliation against the Serbs as the oppressors" (p. 334): "The attitude towards the economic lagging of Serbia shows that the revengeful policy towards Serbia has not weakened as time went by. On the contrary, fed by its own success it has strengthened, which has finally resulted in genocide" (p. 321). The Memorandum speaks of the crucial importance of the "genocide in Kosovo" (p. 315) for the Serbs: "The fate of Kosovo remains a matter of life and death for the Serbian people . . . the demand for an ethnically clean Kosovo (which is being put into practice) is not only a direct and serious threat for the minority nations but, if triggered off, this wave of expansionism will represent a genuine constant threat for all Yugoslav peoples" (p. 326).

Many have commented that it was Kosovo, where a Serbian minority had resented dominance by and oppressed the Albanian majority, that really ignited the Serbian nationalist movement. When Serbian President Slobodan Milosevic visited Kosovo on April 24, 1987, he realized a totally new connection with their cause that transformed his leadership, their movement, and history in Yugoslavia. Milosevic told the Kosovo Serbs:[12] "You should stay here. This is your land. These are your houses. Your meadows and gardens. Your memories. . . . But I don't suggest that you stay, endure, and tolerate a situation you're not satisfied with. On the contrary, you should change it with the rest of the progressive people here, in Serbia, and Yugoslavia."[13]

The way for Milosevic's transformative encounter with the Kosovo Serbs and his stirring speech was paved by the Memorandum, which envisions for all Serbs a contemporary "moral crisis" (p. 307) that demands immediate resolution: "But for the period of the existence of the NDH (the Independent State of Croatia), Serbs in Croatia have never been as threatened as they are nowadays. The solution of their national position has emerged as a top priority political issue. Unless solutions are found, the consequences might prove harmful and manifold, not only within Croatia but within Yugoslavia as a whole" (p. 329).

The Memorandum calls for an invigoration and redefinition of Serbian identity. Given the "depressive condition of the Serbian people. . . . The Serbian nation must gain the opportunity to find itself and to become a historical subject, to regain awareness of its historical and spiritual being . . . to find . . . their moral and historical self-awareness" (p. 335).

In comparison with Raskovic, the Memorandum more crisply defines what kind of psychological transformations are necessary: "the first and most important thing is to remove this historical guilt off the Serbian people and to confute officially the claims that they had an economically privileged position between the two wars, and that there would be no denying of their liberating role throughout their history and their contribution in the creation of Yugoslavia" (p. 335).

The Memorandum is also far more clear in defining the problem as political, and locating it in the 1974 Constitution of the Second Yugoslavia, which it claims "does not possess a minimum coherence necessary to secure further social development" (p. 312)

But the Memorandum's bottom-line grievance reads:

> Not all nations are equal: the Serbian nation, for example, did not gain the right to its own state. Parts of the Serbian nation, who in considerable numbers live in other republics, do not have the right, unlike the national minorities, to use their own language and alphabet, to get politically and culturally organized, to develop the unique culture of their nation. The undeniable expulsion of the Serbs from Kosovo drastically demonstrates that these principles, protecting the autonomy of a minority (Albanians) were not applied when it came to a minority within a minority. (p. 313)

The Memorandum's primary focus is upon the "great number of Serbs living outside Serbia": "Outside Serbia Proper there are 3,285,000 Serbs or 40.3% of the total number. In the general disintegrating processes sweeping across Yugoslavia, the worst disintegration hit Serbs. . . . The process is aimed at a complete break-up of the national unity of Serbian people" (p. 330).

In the government of Yugoslavia, the Memorandum finds "a historically worn-out ideology, general stagnation and increasing regression in the economic, political, moral and cultural spheres. Such a condition imperatively demands radical, deeply thought-out, scientifically based and energetic reforms of the entire state structure and social organization" (p. 337). It concludes: "The biggest trouble is that the Serbian people do not have a state, while all the other nations do" (p. 335).

This Memorandum may be seen as having its roots in the historical idea of a Greater Serbia, which has been manifest in a stream of texts published over the past 150 years.[14] For example, Ilija Garasanin's 1844 "outline" proposed that "a plan must be constructed which does not limit Serbia to her present borders, but endeavors to absorb all the Serbian peoples around her" (Cohen, *Secret War*, 3–4). As another example, in 1902 Nikola Stojanovic published a piece demanding that the Serbs fight to dominate Croatians: "This struggle must be fought until extermination, yours or ours" (p. 4). The contemporary Serbian nationalists could draw upon this historical ideology, but they would then face the challenge of how to build a mass movement around these ideas. That is where Raskovic comes in. His stories are the flesh on the ideological bone. The nationalists wanted him for his stories, which are powerful repositories of the knowledge of Serbian suffering, but ultimately not for his confusing, contradictory, and non-nationalistic theorizing.

As a set of organizing principles for the nationalists' project, the Memorandum succeeds where Raskovic's theorizing fails. It brings Serbian nationalistic frustrations and aspirations to the forefront in a far bolder way. Grievances are not couched in psychobabble, but can be spoken openly and clearly in political terms. It is not conflicted about its desires for the Serbian peoples of Yugoslavia to achieve a new and larger state. Milosevic ascended to power on the path the Memorandum opened for him. Raskovic, on the other hand, has been likened to the rabbit used to set the pace at a dog race. After circling the track for the first lap to get the race going, it is time for him to disappear.

But before disappearing, Raskovic had moved the masses. "A miracle is happening before our very eyes" (Raskovic, 265), he reports. "Serbs from Bosnia-Herzegovina have got back on their feet and are starting to stand tall. The days when they were on their knees are over" (Raskovic, 265). Raskovic got them on their feet, assembled them, and, if you will, put them on the bus. Yet Raskovic asked only for recognition of the Serbs' right for cultural autonomy as part of "an uprising without weapons" (Judah, 168)—not for political or territorial autonomy. For Raskovic, the SDS's purpose was to create an international community for Serbs, not a Greater Serbia. He used to say, "Wherever there are Serbs, there is the SDS" (Raskovic, 282), whereas the extreme nationalists repeated the claim, "Wherever there are Serbs, there is Serbia." Once the masses were on the bus, they got a new driver. Raskovic took a fall. He retired to Belgrade, where he died in July 1992.

The exact circumstances of Raskovic's fall involved his dealings with Tudjman, who had courted Raskovic after the 1990 elections. Recognizing the importance of the Serbian movement in Croatia, Tudjman invited Raskovic to become a member of his government. Raskovic refused. Tudjman wanted an independent Croatian nation-state for the Croatian people, whereas Raskovic wanted the Serbs to have equal status with Croatians in Croatia (not minority status). Although Raskovic was not asking for land or autonomy, Tudjman was unwilling to give the Serbians in Croatia even the right not to be a minority.

Ignoring Raskovic's warnings, Tudjman pushed ahead and drafted a constitution for Croatian independence that essentially ignored the Serbs. In an effort to ruin Raskovic in the eyes of his supporters, Tudjman leaked a transcript of a private conversation in which Raskovic said that the Serbs were a "crazy people."[15] So much for the psychiatrist serving the masses.

Where Raskovic fell short, there were others, including Milan Babic in Croatia, second in command of the SDS, who would step up with a far more militant brand of Serbian nationalism (Judah, *The Serbs*, 169–190). They would do the job the way it had to be done. They wanted Serbs to take up arms, get out of Croatia, and fight for a Greater Serbia. Even then, it would still require more than cold-blooded ideology. They would require the use of state-controlled television and print media as extraordinarily effective vehicles for spreading the nationalistic message amongst the Serbs in Yugoslavia. The nationalists found the leader they needed in Bosnia-Herzegovina, in the person of another psychiatrist, Radovan Karadzic.

But sitting in Belgrade, the ailing psychiatrist Raskovic wants to say: Be aware that what you are finishing began with me and what I told the people. There is no doubt that Raskovic believed in his stories of Serbian suffering, and sensed the power they carried. It is even possible that Raskovic believed in the reawakening of a Serbian community, but not in a genocidal nationalistic project. But he also believed too much in his own theories, and mistakenly thought they could contain what the memories he shared had released in the Serbian people. If he really hadn't wanted it to lead to violence, he should have handled those stories with far more care.

Chapter 5

Radovan Karadzic and the Metaphors of Terror

RADOVAN KARADZIC was a village boy from Montenegro. At age fifteen he moved to Sarajevo, and came of age in the city. He dabbled in poetry, got a professional education as a nurse and then a doctor, and eventually became a psychiatrist. In his forties, he became active in politics, founding the Green Party in Bosnia before being appointed leader of the Serbian Democratic Party. Then in 1992 he became the first leader of the self-proclaimed Bosnian Serb government and left Sarajevo to oversee the Serbian nationalists' ethnic cleansing of Bosnia-Herzegovina, eventually to become an accused war criminal.

Because many Sarajevans considered him one of their own, and never imagined that he had the cunning or evil to do what he did, they wanted to know: How did he change and turn against us? Karadzic's exit from Sarajevo and journey into the historical nightmare of ethnic cleansing cannot be understood without knowing of his struggles with the historical nightmare of World War II. His father had fought as a Chetnik and was sentenced to die by the victorious Partisans. They spared his life, but the Partisans, who were savage and vengeful toward the Montenegrins, killed many others from the extended Karadzic family.[1] We may ask: What nightmares of history were haunting Karadzic even before ethnic cleansing? How did Karadzic respond to the history bearing down upon him as a Montenegrin, a villager, and an Orthodox when the communist era in Yugoslavia drew to a close? How did Karadzic contribute, as psychiatrist, poet, or otherwise, to the collective transformation that culminated in ethnic cleansing?

Causal explanations of genocide and terrorism are thought to be futile, especially those that evoke clinical psychopathological constructs.[2] Complete biographical and historical information is presently lacking, and the story of Karadzic's life is not yet finished. At the time I was researching and writing this text, though indicted by the United Nations' War Crimes Tribunal, Karadzic nonetheless remained in power, in open noncompliance with the Dayton agreement. Apparently, even after having resigned, he still wields considerable political influence.

The people I interviewed in Sarajevo about Karadzic were themselves just awakening from the historical nightmare of ethnic cleansing that he had brought upon them. Moreso than anyone who had not endured the nationalists' violence, they appreciated the "obscenity of understanding," to borrow a phrase from Claude Lanzman.[3] In looking for Karadzic, they knew they were crossing into uncertainties and gaps that understanding could not possibly bridge. Thus, this is not a straightforward study of objective truths concerning Karadzic's role as a genocidal leader.[4] Rather, it is a quest for truths concerning his mentality, and that of the Serbian nationalist project as a whole, via pieces of narrative that Karadzic left along the way. It is an exploration of the language, images, and stories by which Karadzic escaped from one nightmare only to produce another.

Montenegrin

No person on this planet knows more about Karadzic than I.

Thus begins Marko Vesovic, Radovan Karadzic's former close friend, who has lived and worked in Sarajevo for more than thirty years, and who also comes from Montenegro.[5] Marko's proposition has a touch of the extreme: he claims to know more about Karadzic than Karadzic himself! But this is not an empty claim; among other things, Marko was the best man at Karadzic's wedding. We speak over coffee and cigarettes in his book-cluttered apartment in Sarajevo, while Karadzic is upland at his presidential headquarters in Pale.

Straight off, Marko challenges one of the most commonly held misconceptions about Karadzic:

The tendency of journalists is to present a story about how Karadzic had been prepared for years by the Yugoslav army to take the leadership of this slaughter. It is a fabrication—because I know for sure that he was the fifth man who was offered leadership of the Serbian Democratic Party.[6]

This invalidates a set of explanatory hypotheses that have attributed the "success" of the Bosnian Serbs' ethnic cleansing to the special preparation for leadership that Karadzic underwent—for instance, the belief that the success was due to Karadzic's psychiatric knowledge or even special training from military psychiatrists. Perhaps the attractiveness of such an argument is that it is easier for us to make some sense of ethnic cleansing if we can say that it was organized by one very well prepared, strong leader who brainwashed the people.[7]

Marko says of Karadzic being chosen:

It was sheer chance. But it was an extremely good match that came by chance.

It wasn't special professional or political training so much as a confluence of personality, family, and cultural history. To Marko it is both totally unpredictable and completely understandable that Karadzic would have taken this path toward being a politician and genocidal leader. Yet each time Marko attributes some quality to Karadzic, he also takes something away. It is as if Marko is divided between his desire to confirm Karadzic's significance as a man who has done something really remarkable and his need to deny Karadzic that distinction, to just wipe him out.

To Marko, Karadzic is no psychiatrist.

I think I can be a psychiatrist for Karadzic.

To Marko, Karadzic is not a man of truth.

Everything about him and everything about his family and children is so special and so great. He is the best psychiatrist, the best poet, and his children are the best in the world, although we all know that is not true.

To Marko, Karadzic is not ambitious.

He is essentially an extremely lazy person. A classical Montenegrin lazy boy.

To Marko, it is Karadzic's wife.

His marriage is the greatest catastrophe in his life. At least half of what he did, half of the awesomeness and cruelty, was her personal contribution.

As a youth, he was tall, good-looking, with long hair. He had this air of being a student of medicine. And he was also a poet. He was extremely humorous and charming, and he could have picked up any girl in this city. Even a rich, good-looking, smart girl.

Who he married was a complete surprise to all of us. He sort of died when he married. Her father actually forced him with a gun to marry her because she let herself become pregnant. She was quiet for long enough for them to do something, and then she announced the good news. He wanted to run away but her father forced Karadzic to marry her.

When he got married he had two alternatives. One was to face reality and the other was to escape to fantasy. And he decided to escape. He is one of the biggest falsificators of reality that I have ever met.

To Marko, Karadzic is no poet.

Karadzic was not without talent, but first of all he was uneducated. He didn't go to gymnasium like the rest of us, where we got a really broad and solid education. He went to nursing and medical schools. Of course he was too lazy to get educated and then too lazy to read poetry. I remember him bringing me a series of his poems. They were good but I never saw Radovan in them.

The reason that I think he would have never made it in poetry, and his characteristic that again makes him a perfect leader of the Serbs in Bosnia is that he is a man of clay. A clay that has not been baked. It is soft. It can be formed in whichever way you want it. He was a perfect material to create a leader for Serbs that was good enough to reign in the two sides, the Serbian nationalism of Milosevic and the Bosnian Serbs.

To Marko, Karadzic was no Serb.

I think it's extremely important to stress that both Karadzic and Milosevic are Montenegrins, because Montenegrins in general are very crazy people. And because the Memorandum and all that talk would be nothing if there were not two crazy Montenegrins connected with all that. I actually think that this war is an experiment of the Montenegrins upon the Serbs because I cannot picture a person from Serbia implementing it in this way.

Serbs are not a mythological people or nation. In this war we have to understand that the Montenegrins are the mythological people. You can say that in this war the Serbs were infected with Montenegrin's mythology.

Marko explains this Montenegrin craziness, cautioning, *I mean this metaphorically:*

You have to picture, a tiny Montenegro, in the middle of a too-wealthy Turkish empire. A tiny country of only 100,000 people with nothing in that country except limestone and men. If you live in a place defined by stone and nothing, stone nothing, stone nothing, then you have to develop a mythology to feel something. They all know that they are living in a place where nobody normal would live. Not only do they know that but they pride themselves on that.

The main expressive tool of Montenegrins is hyperbole. In one moment they go to extremity. That tendency toward exaggeration goes in two directions, of course, both towards good and towards evil. They often say, when a Montenegrin is good, he is really angelic, and when he is bad, he is really evil.

It was a source of my poetic inspiration and an experience par excellence to sit in the winter nights in Montenegro and listen to the stories that were so rich with fantasies. I have never heard stories that were so detached from reality, stories miles away from reality, like in some South American novels.

When the Montenegrin throws away restricting morals, then he is without any boundaries. The vastness bursts and explodes in front of him, and he is lost. He has no way, and there is nothing that he cannot do.

The greatest words of the poet Njegos[8] come to mind. He says "Let the impossible be. Let that happen which is not possible." We find the same message in Dobrica Cosic's communiqué to Karadzic when the war began. He told him, "Do so and do that long, until the impossible becomes possible."

In Bosnia, it was done, so that the Muslims would start believing that it was never again going to be possible to live together.

Without being aware of this we cannot understand the cruelty of the war in Bosnia.

Marko condemns Montenegrins, even if only metaphorically. He sees something dangerous there that he wants to name. National character arguments are frowned upon for obvious reasons. Nonetheless, there is something inspired and true in Marko's testimony about the mentality of Karadzic as a genocidal leader. It seems that his anxiety is not only about Montenegrins, but also about villagers and their hostility toward the urban way of life. Marko also points a finger at himself. Why so? Perhaps there is guilt for what Montenegrins, his people, did in Bosnia. And for what he himself did not do to somehow stop Karadzic before he went back to the hills.[9]

Condemning Montenegrins serves other functions too. It is one of the ways, perhaps the most powerful way, to take something away from Karadzic, this leader of the Bosnian Serb nationalists. Yes, Marko is incredibly ungenerous toward his old friend in every possible way. He gives him no credit whatsoever—not as friend, poet, husband, father, psychiatrist, Sarajevan, nor chosen leader. Only for being the right man for this dirty job. Marko's extremity may stem from his own cultural heritage, but his ungenerosity would seem to point more toward Karadzic. It is a measure of the scale of the human disaster he oversaw.

Perhaps one of the most important facts to be learned from Marko is that he—the man who knew more about Karadzic than Karadzic—himself never suspected that Karadzic could become a nationalist or genocidal leader in the years before the war. This of course must be put in context; it was completely unimaginable to Marko that genocide would come to Bosnia.

Nonetheless, Marko says that neither Karadzic's political views nor his personal style seemed hateful or intolerant. He was egotistical and ambitious, with a craving for money and greatness. But he was also lazy and uncommitted. He had a tendency toward exaggeration, fantasy, and lying. But these fiery sides of his personality always seemed to be modulated by his charm, reasonableness, and incompetence. Many of us have known a Karadzic. We never take them too seriously.

Neither Marko nor anyone else took Karadzic seriously. Rather, he bordered on the comic. If not into psychiatry or poetry, where would Karadzic channel his ambition? Perhaps the worst they could imagine had already come true. His entrepreneurial forays into business ended miserably; he pled guilty to corruption charges and served an eleven-month prison sentence.

Curiously, Marko said nothing about Karadzic's father or family history, which I believe to be critical to an understanding of Karadzic and ethnic cleansing, until the very end of our conversation, when I asked if he thought it was important that Karadzic's father was a Chetnik.

It was very important that his father was a Chetnik. Because the Partisans did very bad things in Montenegro at that time. I have heard rumors that Mosa Pijade[10] himself killed twenty-seven Karadzics. I thought it was a rumor at the time, but later when I read Milan Djilas's book I found it confirmed. It is a very significant family burden that was critical to Karadzic's orientation.

I knew all the time that Karadzic hated communists, but he never showed a bit of hatred towards Muslims. Now it is very clear to me that his intention was to erase Partisan history, to go from one place in Bosnia to another that was famous for its

Partisan history, and to inscribe a new history in those places. But I could never understand the origin of his hatred towards Muslims.

However, the multi-ethnic way of life in Bosnia is a product of the communists. In 1946 there was no coexistence here. It was all butchering. It was the communists who succeeded in persuading these people to live together. And that to me explains the pleasure and thoroughness with which Karadzic wanted to eradicate it. I know that there was coexistence because I lived in it for thirty years, and Karadzic knew that that was a product of the communists. And he decided to destroy every trace of it with great personal pleasure. The only motive that I can think of for the atrocities and horror that he produced was that he wanted to make the communists pay for what they did to him and his family.

Although he hated communists, that did not prevent him from personally sending a copy of his first collection of poetry to Tito. Some people saw it in the presidential headquarters in Belgrade, and they reported back to him what he wrote—"Beloved president, Comrade Tito, it would fill me with happiness knowing that this book was in your hands," R.K. So, no matter how much he hated the communists he liked to flatter people of power, and when he wrote that inscription he was really down on his knees in front of Broz. He signed it Radovan Karadzic, Sutjeska Street, which is the street he lived on, but also the name of the famed Fifth Offensive victory of the Partisans in World War II.

We roar with laughter. This Radovan Karadzic, who gives people a lot to laugh at. These Sarajevans, who choose laughter and forgetting even after this disaster.

Psychiatrist

The story most often recounted by Karadzic's former colleagues at the Kosevo Day Hospital was of a famous episode in the annals of group psychotherapy, recalled by Karadzic's cotherapist at the time.

There was a psychopath in the group who liked me, but he had a big resistance to Karadzic. Karadzic liked to repeat the saying, "With a fist between the horns," which is how we kill our bulls. When he said it to this patient as some kind of interpretation, the patient jumped up and pulled out a knife! I was able to calm him and get the knife. Karadzic wasn't hurt. He ran one flight down the stairs and locked himself in an office![11]

Invariably, after sharing this story, the teller laughs, then shakes his head and sighs—this story, which contains so much of what Karadzic was to them.

Radovan Karadzic's primary job as a psychiatrist was at the Day Hospital of the Kosevo Hospital Department of Psychiatry in Sarajevo from 1979 to 1992. He also had a small private practice in Sarajevo and did some consulting, including a stint as the psychiatrist for the Sarajevo soccer team. He had earned degrees in nursing and then medicine from the University of Sarajevo.

Because he was not a strong student, it took some arm twisting for him to get the position at Kosevo. During his employment there, he left and returned twice. One time he resigned and went to Belgrade, but never found a job. The other time was when he was imprisoned for eleven months in Sarajevo. Each time persuasion was required to get him back to Kosevo. But when he returned, Karadzic insisted on having his old office back. The third time he left the Day Hospital was in the spring of 1992, when he left Sarajevo for Pale along with several nurses who had worked with him.

I learned about Karadzic, the psychiatrist, from conversations with more than a half dozen of his former colleagues at the Kosevo Hospital in Sarajevo. They spoke with some reluctance, and in some cases only because they were asked to by one of the senior psychiatrists at the clinic. Their reluctance was understandable, given that these psychiatric professionals had been condemned in the international media for contributing to what Karadzic brought to the genocide; then condemned by other Bosnians for not recognizing and stopping Karadzic's genocidal potential; then victimized like all the other Sarajevans by Karadzic's siege. And who could I be, but another internationalist on safari, come for a sensational story about how psychiatrists lead genocides?

Karadzic's colleagues did not regard him favorably and told me why. He hardly showed up for work. He was pompous, he dressed funny, and he had that posh haircut. He diagnosed everyone with masked depression, provoked psychotic patients, and never finished his case reports.

But the psychiatrists and other mental health workers who knew Karadzic had no idea that he would end up as a nationalistic and genocidal leader. Still, this not-knowing must be put in its proper cultural context. One colleague said:

I spent my whole life with people and sometimes I didn't even know if they were Orthodox, Muslim, Catholic or Jewish. Only at the funeral did I see.

It is hard to tease apart their particular not-knowing about Karadzic and his family history from their overall not-knowing about ethnic and religious differences. Another thing they did not know about Karadzic was his poetry, despite the fact that he had given out innumerable autographed copies of his books and spoke of it incessantly.

The stories the psychiatric professionals told were less about how a psychiatrist became a nationalistic genocidal leader, and more along the lines of questioning how this man, who happened to be a psychiatrist, could end up as he did. The last thing they were trying to do was to explain how a psychiatrist becomes a genocidal leader. I came with my biases, but I tried to keep an open mind. I invited them to tell me, in their own words, whatever seemed important. Here I will share two doctors' stories of Karadzic. Dr. B. is a Bosnian Serb and Dr. C. a Bosnian Muslim. Both remained in Sarajevo during the siege and worked at the clinic.

Dr. B. is very businesslike in his account. His dislike for K. is plain, as is his need to create some distance. Dr. B. wants to dispel certain misinformation about Karadzic, but he also sees evidence of personality traits that explain Karadzic to him.

For us who have worked with him, it is ridiculous to often hear many things about what he supposedly was. We are told that he was a great expert, a great psychotherapist and that he graduated from the best schools of higher learning in the West and occupied special positions. It is all ridiculous.

Part of this is of his own making. Ten years ago he was walking around the city and telling everybody that he is the best in everything. The lie was very close to the truth, in some ways. He was a doctor. If he said that "I have just returned from London, where I was for two months in a specialization," then his neighbor believed it.

He always had this tendency to make you think that things were bigger than they are. To exaggerate. For this he had an enormous talent.

Often he could be very polite and very decent. He always did favors for people. He'd act like he was very reliable and he was always smiling.

For him it was very important every day to meet as many people as possible. If I was walking down the street with one of my friends, and we met Karadzic, he would stop, ask the time, and insist that I introduce my friend to him. And the next morning he'd ask me, "Who is he?" "What is his profession?" and "Could that man be of some use to us someday maybe?" If that man was somebody he really needed, like the director of a bank, then he would approach him. If somebody could be potentially helpful to him, then he had no qualms telling the person, "I am a famous doctor. If I can be of any use to you, you can come to me."

Karadzic talked about how he wanted to have his own people at every place in town. But I am claiming, because I know the man, that there is no connection between that and the humanity of a doctor. He was paid for that service very well, not in money but with some kind of favors.

According to Dr. B., Karadzic's characterological problems were always plain to see. They were recognized, often disliked, but essentially tolerated. In contrast, his political leanings were not so apparent.

He was proud of his knowledge of history and about his political knowledge. Nobody here was interested in politics, not even in reading the papers. He couldn't talk to us about politics. We had no interest in politics.

I claim he was a nationalist even fifteen years ago but his nationalism was hidden behind his traditionalism. All the time he was preoccupied with Serbian tradition, and for the last two or three years it was very unpleasant to listen to him talk about all that. He could sit around and talk for hours about it.

I see him as a sociological and cultural phenomenon. In the period from World War II until today, there were many like him, who came from villages, from underdeveloped areas and poor families which raised them within the Serbian culture, the myth of Kosovo, and taught them about the age-old jeopardy of Serbs from others. Then this young man of fifteen years found himself in the big city. And he wanted to succeed. But he always carried with him his mythical idea about his people who are endangered and need to be liberated.

However, he hid his nationalism through the very intensive quality and quantity of meetings with Muslims. His best friends were Muslims. All the time at his house there were Muslims. With them he made dinners, socialized, and everything that goes with that. In 1993, people had every right to ask those of us who worked with him: "Did you know that he was like that?"

Dr. B's explanation—that Karadzic hid his nationalism all along—is hard for me to accept. It sounds as if Karadzic's personality would not allow for him to keep anything hidden. Was this the only way for Dr. B. to make sense of how he had not seen how completely Karadzic had changed?

Karadzic is a man of lies. And also, a man of evil. To him the lie and evil are the same thing. So the lie is the product of the evil, and the lie produces evil. I think that Karadzic is one enormous lie. I like better the word "falsify," because he made a forgery of reality, even his own reality and the reality of others.

"What was your relationship like?"

He was my colleague. I had a completely correct relationship with him. But we were never friends. Outside of work, we didn't socialize. He had a style and manners that personally didn't suit me.

There's a credo that he used which suits him well: "Your own enemy you should take to lunch and pour him wine." I am absolutely at the other end of the spectrum. I am one of those people who gets very angry at their enemy and doesn't have any intention to take them to lunch.

At the end of December 1991, I saw him in the hallway and said only hello to him. It was obvious that my orientation was not like his. I didn't give him any signs that it might be.

"Did you ever think that you or others could have done something to stop Karadzic from giving himself over to nationalism?"

I think that no one could have done anything. Including me. The process had been prepared for decades. The people who entered that process carried ideas which had lasted for centuries. They are archetypal ideas about their people. There is nothing one can do about that.

The momentum toward nationalism was powerful, but was it as unswerving and inevitable as Dr. B. claimed? Karadzic, like others, got drawn into its flow. Yet Karadzic and other leaders certainly pushed it along and spread it to others. What did Dr. B. think of that?

"Were you aware of any specific ways that Karadzic contributed to this process as a doctor before the Serbs took up arms?"

In our culture and in the primitive population with which he was working on the idea of Greater Serbia it is crucial that he was a doctor. A doctor is some kind of a spiritual advisor equal to God. These people idolize and trust doctors. And here, it happens that the doctor plays "gusle," that he is a poet, that he says he wants to set them free. They do not have their own country where they can live in freedom, and not be poor.

I heard his first talks in the villages on television and radio. It was a classic incitement of the masses. He was very familiar with their language. He was making jokes, and he was insisting on religion. The others were also religious but nobody kissed the arm of the priest. He couldn't shout too much about Bosnia, because he is Montenegrin, but he could have his wife kissing the hand of the priest, and he could insist on religion.

"Did you think that Karadzic used a psychiatric approach in his political role?"

There was a psychiatric construction of the message. It employed basic psychiatric concepts.

"Can you give an example?"

He used some sentences that are common to use in group psychotherapy. In a group of very uneducated peasants it was a big success. However, he used much more his knowledge of the culture, of the spiritual archetypal needs of the Serbian people, than psychiatry, to seduce them. Because of that it is ridiculous, when we heard that he was educated in mass brainwashing. He was using stories, legends, gusle, and religion.

He went to the valley at Pale where the peasants were cutting grass, drank something, asked them if the grass is good this year, and gave them a blessing. That is custom, not psychiatry. With that he controlled the masses. Not with brainwashing. Besides that, these people were already brainwashed.

I remember one time he received a call from Slobodan Milosevic at the clinic and told one of the nurses. The nurse said, "Doctor please, when he calls next time, give me the handset just to hear his voice and to pronounce myself to him." A few days later, Milosevic called back and the nurse got to say hello. He was shaking, he was very flushed. That conversation between the nurse and Milosevic lasted only for ten seconds. But his wish came true to him in the summer of '91. The young man was thirty-five or thirty-six years old, born near Pale, and Bosnian Serb. He carried the fear, believing Karadzic that when the war began in Sarajevo, he would be slaughtered by the Muslims. He trusted Karadzic and he escaped with him to the other side. Karadzic put him in a trench and he was killed.

Only a handful of the 120 clinic employees went with Karadzic to the hills. Most, like Dr. B., didn't go for it at all. Before that time came, the person they saw in Karadzic was abrasive, cowardly, foolhardy, egotistical, manipulative. But concerning nationalism and genocide, they were completely unable to imagine the fire, nor recognize the lighter in their colleague's hand.

Dr. C. is even more tentative in talking about Radovan Karadzic. When Bosnian and international journalists approached him to ask about Karadzic, whom he had personally supervised for years, he said nothing, because there was nothing to say. He had had no thoughts of Karadzic—none at all. Dr. C. had wiped Karadzic out of his mind.

Then, in the fall of 1993, after the psychiatric clinic was bombed and badly damaged, Dr. C. started to think again of Karadzic. Thoughts and images broke through, and he even dreamt of Karadzic.

Something similar happens in our conversations. Dr. C. begins with the feeling that there is really precious little to say. He submits to my questions out of kindness. But as we go on, he starts to remember that which he had forgotten, and gets curious about the stories he is surprised to find himself telling.

I try to explain to myself, and to my mother, my wife and my sons. Because everybody knows that we were very close, as colleagues and friends. His family came to our house. I try to explain but I absolutely don't understand what is going on concerning him. I had the obsessive habit that I didn't like to watch TV when Radovan was on talking about the political situation.

But I'd hear about his television and radio appearances from people who watched them. Every time I was surprised. Not so much because I did not know the real Karadzic, because I did know him very well. I came to separate what I felt was really his own statements from what came from his supporters, Milosevic and others. Day after day, for months, I made those excuses for him.

Now I see Radovan and smile. It is all absolutely empty of any ideas. It's only sentences. None of the thoughts are real. It's full of tradition, of a connection with history from the seventh century. One thousand years of culture. It's absolutely stupid.

I believe that his psychological profile was always the same, but that power absolutely changed him.

Dr. C is searching for a way to explain what seems inexplicable. He recalls what Karadzic told him, after his notorious pronouncement in Parliament.

"Well, chief, let's drink a cup of coffee. You remember I said something in the parliament. Those were not my own words. It was some others." This is some kind of excuse. Very naive, like a child. At that time, I began to have some resistance to Radovan and I tried to formalize our relationship. I spent time with others and tried to stay away from him.

At that time I lost Radovan in my eyes. For one and a half years I absolutely didn't think about Radovan. I repressed Radovan's picture, Radovan's personality, Radovan as a colleague, as a friend. Some journalists asked me what I thought about Radovan. I said, "I am surprised that this man exists. I think nothing about Radovan."

Dr. C's losing Radovan in his eyes is perhaps a more profound truth than what the others have said. Whereas Marko is saying, "Now I can see he was being Montenegrin," and Dr. B. is saying, "Now I can see he kept his nationalism all hidden," for a time, Dr. C. is confessing: "There is no possibility for me to see him because he completely changed in a way that I do not understand."

After one and a half years I start to think about Radovan, after our clinic was hit with thirty grenades, destroying the building we finished just before the war.

Dr. C. shakes his head.

It's absolutely unbelievable. It's very interesting that he had Muslim friends.

Dr. C. speaks of his two dreams of Karadzic during the war.

One was just after the shelling of my house when my mother was wounded by a grenade, the pictures on the wall were damaged and the furniture was damaged, I dreamt about Radovan, but during peace, as if he was in the department, talking with me. As if it was normal like before.

The other dream came after somebody told me that Radovan was looking through binoculars and telling his soldiers that sometime soon they would capture Sarajevo and destroy it all. I dreamt that Radovan and his wife came to our house. I said to them, we haven't any coffee, tea, wine, or anything. When I woke up I smiled. You see, it was normal that he would come at any moment that he wanted—as he did in my dream. But this time we had nothing for him. I felt bad.

Dr. C is haunted by his generosity toward Karadzic, both in his dreams and in his life. If it had not been for Dr. C., Karadzic might never have gotten a job in Kosevo Hospital's psychiatric clinic or made it in Sarajevo. That is a thought he finds hard to let go of. Only after our conversation does he realize how much he really needs to talk about that guilty feeling.

And just what is he being accused of? Helping a young person along at the beginning of his career. That is no crime. It is actually admirable. Still, Dr. C. asks, shouldn't I have known? All too often we do not know until it is too late. Like so many other Bosnian Muslims, Dr. C. did not want to see the signs of collapse, even when faced with fairly compelling evidence. The pull of the normal was too great. Operating within the merhamet way of life, Dr. C. would rather see and say nothing at all, than be ungenerous to a colleague and friend. But now that whole worldview itself, and the blindness it conferred, is on the line.

Karadzic had actually tried to warn both Dr. B. and Dr. C. of what was to come. Dr. B. recalls the shock of suddenly getting the message.

In the last days of December 1991, three months before the war started, we had an annual party for the New Year. We were all sitting together at a big table, more than thirty people. He came and sat across from me. It was the first time in six months that we met face to face. It was a very short interlude, but I will never forget it. He picked some meat and put it on the plate. He looked at me and said, "How old is your child?" I answered, but immediately I realized he was alluding to war. Until then I didn't believe it would be war. I told my wife what he asked me. I told her that in a few months there would be explosions. Children would get killed.

He is one of the few people I speak to who actually anticipated the siege.

Much more common is a response like that of Dr. C., a Bosnian Muslim, who refused to believe that it was possible.

We last talked March 23, 1992. He spent one hour in our department. I met him in the hall, I asked him what was going on. He said that the situation was very dangerous. I said, "Don't worry Radovan, the war is not on our street." He said, "Maybe the war is closer than you believe." I said, "Don't worry about that, it's not a problem at all."

Both Dr. B., who could see, and Dr. C., who could not, remained in Sarajevo for the siege that saw Karadzic direct the shelling of Kosevo Hospital, where they all once worked together.

Poet

Decades before he became a political leader, Radovan Karadzic was a poet. He wrote and published several volumes of poetry before, during, and after the period in which he practiced psychiatry.[12] His psychiatric colleagues remember him boasting that he was the best poet in Bosnia, and even more outrageously, the fourth best contemporary Serb poet in Sarajevo. Karadzic claimed a connection to Serbian epic tradition. His colleagues took these claims no more seriously than they did his boasts that he was the best psychiatrist in Bosnia and that his wife was the most beautiful woman. Even within the Sarajevo literary scene Karadzic was a gadfly, and his poems were not well regarded. Ferida Durakovic, a leading Sarajevan poet, said: *We all knew it was bad poetry, so no one bothered even to read it.*[13] If neither literary figures nor psychiatrists took Karadzic the poet seriously, why should we?

My experience of these poems as a reader, not a literary scholar, is that they are awful. They are replete with empty abstractions, and lack the precise detail and imagery that makes a poem stick with you. When Tvrtko Kulenovic, the writer and intellectual from Sarajevo (and former acquaintance of Karadzic), and I started going through the poems one by one, it became abundantly clear just how monotonous and unappealing they were. Nonetheless, when you compare the early poems to the later poems, you see that Karadzic had somewhat advanced his technical skills as a poet over the years. However, even this is only partially satisfying.

More disturbing than these structural problems was the visionary nature of Karadzic's poetics. One day, after a few hours spent together reading the poems out loud, Tvrtko remarked, *I thought this would be simple poetry, like mountains and the sun, but this is a program.*[14]

The first Karadzic poem I read was an untitled verse, published in 1968, that offers a chilling representation of the poetic vision that came into genocidal reality in the streets and buildings of Karadzic's city under siege.

There is no doubt anymore
all things I have elucidated at last
in each thing there is a part of my body
in my eyes the forest is near its end
in my blood I hear the last cries of cuddly little animals
this moment my right hand
is turning calm seas into hell
while ships keep rolling on the waves
to the endless joys of my vultures
this moment my lips jeer everything and anything
laughing aloud in every place in the world
this moment I have knocked down all existing theories
first of all that ugly theory of relativity
all relative things I have turned into absolute nothingness.
And everything will come again
Everything will under my hand grow strong and powerful
And everything will be as you have never seen or dreamt
Relativity, what stupidity
(1968, untitled)

One does not require the context of the violence the writer eventually visited on the world to recognize this poem as a fundamentalist narrative. Fundamentalism is described by Robert Lifton as "any movement that embraces a fierce defense of its sacred, literalized text in a purification process aimed at alleged contamination—all in the name of a past of perfect harmony that never was, and of an equally visionary future created by a violent 'end' to impure, profane history."[15]

The protagonist has found absolute truth, although it is not clear what particular ideology he serves, if any. His hatred of "relativity" is typical of fundamentalists' disdain for intellectual complexity. Violence is everywhere. The imagistic fluidity between the body and the external world, reminiscent of schizophrenic delusions, perhaps reflects the psychiatrist's familiarity with those bizarre mental states. Most impressive is that the protagonist is under the sway of an "end time" vision.[16] He declares that the end is near, and actively wishes to hasten its arrival by initiating extreme violent actions. He is also possessed by the fundamentalist's vision of the world's rebirth, which is to come from his own magical hands. Pushed aside is the whole historical reality of living together in Bosnia-Herzegovina, which Karadzic himself experienced and benefited from.

When this poem is read alongside the history its author helped to produce, the response is shock and outrage. He not only wrote it, but he brought it into being as an actual historical event! The fundamentalist in the narrative is not only a figure in the world of the poem. He is a core figure in Karadzic's living self and in his notorious life's work as a political leader. The ideology is extreme ethnic nationalism, the project is genocide, and the method is terror.

"Petnica" is a longer, more ambitious poem, published in 1990. This poem shows an entirely different side of Karadzic. Unlike the first poem, this one is not fundamentalist, but can be regarded as a survivor's narrative. It tells the story of his father and the memories his father has left him. The poem, dedicated to his father, Vuk, begins:

> An enormous yard we made
> My mountain breaking father
> Desert in garden, and in the age.

Linking Karadzic with his father, the poem draws attention to a darkness they share:

> As if the necklace broke
> As if there were no childhood
> No healing herbs
> Petnica lies like a broken nest
> Like empire destroyed as a devastated empire
> as if the bad spirit has passed this way.

This darkness belongs to the memory of the vain sacrifice of those Montenegrins killed by the Partisans in World War II, including those who fought for the Chetniks. The nightmarish memories live in the mountain village, in its very trees and houses.

> Oak trunk where we were shot
> Oak, the history of this house
> Waves its vein shadow to call us.

The memories cannot be spoken in public, but they live on in trees and things. They are passed from father to son, even if all in silence. Feelings of loss are everywhere. The poet welcomes those feelings.

> The cemetery is deserted. The mocking word bites the hearts of
>   ancestors
> Breaks the crosses and shakes the bones
> Whose names now irresponsibly uses. Lost people
> No hat and barefoot . . .

> Calm down your axes
> Slow down your heart
> There is nothing here for destroying[17]

In the poem Karadzic returns to the old village, its graves, old bones, and tree stumps; to the memories of his father and the other Karadzics cut down by the Partisans. It is not clear what he desires to reclaim from this return to the past. The part of the father's experience with which he identifies ominously suggests the pull to follow a path of violence. Yet the poem's openness to the feelings of loss, its acknowledgment of the suffering that comes of war, and even its quasi-moralistic call for an end to violence qualify this as a survivor's narrative.

Retrospectively, we know that for Karadzic the political leader, the survivor's openness and sorrow gave way to the fundamentalist's closedness and destructiveness. As represented in the discrepancies between these two poems, this change involved a drastic shift in the narratives of the self in history that shape identity and morality. In the fundamentalist narrative, Karadzic erased any knowledge of the multi-ethnic life, and rewrote history.

Karadzic's poems bear traces of his psychological journey from a Montenegrin village boyhood to a Bosnian urban adulthood, alluded to earlier. We find the poet struggling to live with the historical nightmare fated to him and his family. A major psychological happening in the poetry is the birth of the poetic figure of the nationalistic and genocidal fundamentalist—a figure that resonates all too well with Karadzic's role in the genocidal project and with the mentality of the Serbian nationalists. The journey begins with the tracing of a personal and a historical nightmare, and the appearance of a dreaded and feared other. Then there is a self-awakening, a movement out of darkness. This then leads to the actual birth of the antihero. What follows is the antihero's call or order to his flock and the elaboration of the apocalyptic and messianic nature of the antihero's vision.

Many poems create an atmosphere of fear and dread that is the nightmare. "Mother" reads, "The peace is over / she can see the trembling of things / and she can hear the pale of his eyes."[18] One of the untitled "Midnight Verses" reads, "the streets are trembling in front of me and my look" (*Mad Spear*, 21). "Nightmare" reads: "the abyss is just next to your eye" (p. 18).

This nightmare is more than personal. Some poems historicize the nightmare in a Montenegrin context. "Peace" describes the situation after a battle between Montenegrin tribes. "There is no song because they are killed in the mountains / the long hair swirls over their cut off heads / Whilst the river of time gives them the glory, there is no song" (p. 11). It repeats, "There is no song," again and again. Other poems associate the nightmare with the father, as in "Petnica." For the most part, the reader is left with the overall sense of a nightmare, but without the complete expression of any specific dream story—only a vague, intolerable, silent presence. This nightmare that remains silent can be thought of in relation to the social experience of living with memories of World War II in Tito's Yugoslavia. Memories of the Serbs' suffering during World War II, especially their mass murder by other Yugoslavs, could not be publicly discussed in the former Yugoslavia, except in the most rigid ideological way. Yet citizens still had their nightmares.

Curiously, in Karadzic's poetry the nightmare does not translate into direct animosity toward Muslims or Croats. Rather, the dread and fear in the poems is drawn toward cities and concentrated upon life there. In Karadzic's poetry, it is urban existence, not any specific ethnic group, that becomes the target of dread and fear. The poet is out of place and uncomfortable in the city:

Why the street?
Why the stones in pavement?
Why the lights?
Why metal is screeching?
Why this huge building and your poor room
except for you in this dark midnight? (p. 12)

And in "Sarajevo" he declares, "The pestilence resounds" and "The misfortune, I can really feel it coming / Transformed in an insect."[19] One of Karadzic's important poetic discoveries (important from the perspective of lending a metaphor for ethnic cleansing) is that the city comes to embody the nightmare.

To the villager within Karadzic, the city was objectionable on a great many grounds. The city was the embodiment of pluralism, especially in the case of Sarajevo. It was home to sophisticates who preached intellectual, aesthetic, philosophical, and spiritual subtleties and complexities.[20] The Bosnian city was the heir to Ottoman, Austro-Hungarian, and communist rules, whose policies were responsible for its growth. The city was the opposite of the rural-mountain-village life of his youth; it was the repository of the society that had destroyed his father and attempted to impose its will on the villagers. Ironic, though, that Karadzic clearly benefited from the city in becoming a poet/psychiatrist/intellectual. That he then gave voice to the anti-urban message is an illustration of Robert Jay Lifton's claim that "fundamentalism is attracted to what it opposes."[21]

The poet looks for a way out of the nightmare. In "Gentleman I feel like crying", he notes his misery, but also hints at a possible escape:

You can hide in its shadow and become bigger than yourself
That's where this crying could bring me[22]

But the poet will not stay locked in the nightmare's shadow. The motif of awakening from a darkness appears in many poems. The poet often uses images from nature, which he sets in contrast to the unnatural physicality of cities. "Nightmare" reads, "The grass is trying to rise to the sky" (*Mad Spear*, 18). In "Slavery" he writes, "In this desert there is a flower that arises from defiance / From defiance it doesn't want to wilt / It demands the freedom from the ceiling and from them" (p. 14). Other poems develop this awakening theme with imagery that moves from darkness to light. In "Midnight Verses" he writes, "The big word / You are awakening my senses / From you I become blind / I've seen you with my eyes closed" (p. 15). And in "Slavery" he writes, "And from my thoughts the sword has become / which is longer than the ray of the sun" (p. 14).

The poet is drawing upon classic romantic imagery—darkness to light; blindness to seeing; nature growing and changing—to illuminate the possibility of getting out from under the nightmare and shaping a new identity. This is yet another important poetic discovery for the future genocidal leader and movement: appealing metaphors that can be used as propaganda to inflame the followers and make the plan for ethnic cleansing more compelling.

After the reawakening comes the actual birth of the antihero. In "The Mad Spear" Karadzic writes that the spear is "in love with its own blade / it becomes mad / thinking of the possibility to become a hero" (pp. 7–8). In "Interpretation of Dreams," he writes:

> The sky is full of your presence
> but the earth is expecting you
> Your arrival it would declare an event
> As the sky declares the work of the clouds an event
> (p. 75)

In untitled:

> Don't believe that midnight is black
> That it can't be changed
> That the God wanted it that way
> Don't believe that you are doomed
> That there is no salvation for you . . .
> Believe that summer is winter, and winter's autumn and make it so since
>   you have a word.
> Don't believe that the midnight is black
> That this is unchangeable and think God wanted it that way
> There is something in it made according to your will
> (pp. 52–53)

The figure that takes shape has the characteristics of an antihero. It is a man who assumes the supernatural powers of a god. The antihero is driven by a megalomaniac's thirst for power; he wants to change the natural order of things. The figure looks at the world as his toy, and does not see his natural place there. Needless to say, this is a figure bereft of genuine empathy, compassion, decency, kindness, or generosity toward others.

The antihero needs followers. The identity of the antihero takes further shape out of the call he utters to his flock. In "The Tribunal" he writes:

> You have to become a member of my new faith
> I offer you something that nobody ever offered
> I offer you mercilessness and wine . . .

O jump to my call brother, people, crowd
How should I call you?
How should I bring you?
The deaf amorphous doe?
Subscribe to my new faith before its too late
(1968, pp. 31–32)

The antihero elaborates a messianic and apocalyptic vision for his flock. In an untitled piece he writes, "I created the world to chew my head" and "I feel contempt for the souls that don't radiate anything." And this:

But I can't look at you, the line of scums resembling a line of tortoises
So be faster in you scummity
Be faster because if I make a thunder of my word
I'll make a paralyzed swamp
When I am in a kind of mad fire
I could do anything
(pp. 33–34)

Another untitled piece contains the following lines:

. . . My creation is a war making falcon
The mountains are created only according to my will
Behind the love there is only my idea
I consist of everything that in this world exists
My will makes things die
When my eye blinks to the color it becomes color
My eye moves the light
Without me you would be in eternal darkness
(p. 37)

Karadzic's antihero envisions a world in total ruin which he alone can rectify through extreme action. If you do not share his belief, then you too are doomed and hated. His vision requires sudden, dramatic, and violent action. His antihero has the supernatural power to carry out his vision and bring on the end time.

Karadzic may never have discovered a unique poetic voice in a literary sense, but in a political sense he found something here of use to the genocidal project. As an obscure poet, Karadzic made an unwitting contribution to the future genocidal project, by articulating some of the metaphors around which the collective movement of Serbian nationalism and the ethnic cleansing would unfold in Bosnia-Herzegovina. These are the birth of the figure of an antihero and the elaboration of his apocalyptic vision. The antihero is mad, bloodthirsty, power-hungry, ruthless, and anti-urban. His vision promises deliverance from personal and historical nightmares, and guarantees immortality.

The Serbian nationalists led by Dobrica Cosic already had an ideology and

an argument, in the form of the Memorandum of the Serbian Academy of Arts
and Sciences.[23] But the text itself is bland and uninspiring. Marko Vesovic says,
*The memorandum and all that talk would be nothing if not for the two crazy
Montenegrins connected with it.* He is referring to Slobodan Milosevic, the Serbian
leader, and of course Karadzic. Milosevic, the former communist, had made a
sharp turn towards nationalist ideology in order to maintain his hold on the
reigns of power.[24] Karadzic was no ideologue, but he accepted the ideology, and
brought to it hyperbole, imagery, character, and metaphor. He enlivened the ideology and made it more attractive and compelling. He fastened to it the power
of the nightmarish memories embodied in his poetry.

In his role as a genocidal leader, Karadzic, animated by his own poetic antihero, was spreading the terror and fear that was required for annihilating the
multi-ethnic way of life in Bosnia. (Did Karadzic's poems not anticipate the mad
terror of General Mladic and the parade of killing and terror he led?) When
paired with Milosevic's political might, and Dobrica Cosic's Serbian nationalist
ideology, Karadzic's apocalyptic, messianic, anti-urban vision would have deadly
consequences. This is not to say that Karadzic left the impression with his former
associates and friends that he was the sort of person who would do this. One
wonders: what did Milosevic and Cosic see in Karadzic that others did not? Was
it something in the poems the Sarajevans never read?

Genocidal Leader

Dr. C. wonders: what kind of genocidal leader could Karadzic possibly be?

*He was the commander of the Serb army and he was never in the Yugoslav army!
He decided on whether this brigade goes here or there, but he didn't know anything.
For me, all of this is a comedy. He went to Geneva and New York. He was absolutely ignorant in every one of these fields. Every project that had Radovan in it completely collapsed. And this project is collapsing too.*

There is no way to imagine that Karadzic could have done it alone. It is
not only that he had the full support of the most powerful sponsors of Serbian
nationalism. It's that he took on their project. Dobrica Cosic, its primary intellectual patron, was the one who first encouraged Karadzic to enter politics.
Slobodan Milosevic, with clear aggressive designs on Bosnia as well as Croatia,
had the political and military authority to produce this project. Without them,
Karadzic was nothing.

With Cosic providing the ideology, and Milosevic the backing of the Serbian
government and the Yugoslav National Army, Karadzic could then bring his
metaphor to life. They had the plan and the means to operationalize it. He
brought to it all the exaggerating, lying, and outrageousness he had been known
for in Sarajevo, and the imagery and metaphors he had developed in his poetry.

As political tensions grew in 1991 and 1992, Karadzic, the willing convert to the Serbian nationalist plan, proved skilled at adding fuel to the fire, both in his communications and in his actions.

He seized on the tensions surrounding the 1991 war between Serbia and Croatia to prepare for military aggression in Bosnia. He interpreted the Croatian move to independence as a bellwether of what could happen in Bosnia. When Serbs in Croatia were threatened in the winter of 1991, Karadzic responded by calling for the Serbian people in Yugoslavia to set up an armed force to defend themselves. He threatened, "if Bosnia were recognized as an independent state, it would be stillborn and not survive a single day."[25]

Karadzic made alarming public comments that created an explosive picture of a dangerous Islamic nationalism brewing in Bosnia. After Izetbegovic visited Turkey in July 1991, where he sought to join the Organization of Islamic Countries, Karadzic said, "Izetbegovic wants Bosnia-Herzegovina to become an Islamic republic" (Silber and Little, *Yugoslavia*, 213).

On October 14, 1991, Karadzic issued an ultimatum in an address to the Bosnian Assembly that was clearly designed to provoke anxieties and propel the situation toward militarization: "You want to take Bosnia-Herzegovina down the same highway of hell and suffering that Slovenia and Croatia are traveling. Do not think that you will not head Bosnia-Herzegovina into hell, and do not think that you will not perhaps make the Muslim people disappear, because the Muslims cannot defend themselves if there is war—How will you prevent everyone from being killed in Bosnia-Herzegovina?" (p. 215).

It is interesting to note that in response Alija Izetbegovic said, "At that moment I had the feeling that the gates to hell had opened and we were all burned by the flames of the inferno" (p. 215). Yet despite this terrifying illumination of the nationalistic threat, Izetbegovic's response to the Assembly still downplayed confrontation and attempted to reassure: "I want to tell the citizens of Bosnia-Herzegovina not to be afraid, because there will be no war. . . . Therefore, sleep peacefully" (p. 215).

Meanwhile, back at the Kosevo Day Hospital, patients and staff were feeling the heat. Karadzic's colleague reports:

When he said that the Muslims would disappear as a nation, it caused panic and fear in patients. They no longer wanted him to be their doctor. Colleagues from other clinics started to avoid him. They even said to me, "Why don't you kill him?"

He kept a certain number of patients. He was often not at work. I can remember many situations, when five or six patients were standing in front of his office, and he couldn't remember any of them. They told me they were sad because their doctor didn't recognize them.

Their conversations with him were very short, very confusing. He told patients that he didn't have the time. That he was very busy doing a serious job.

Karadzic brought bodyguards to the clinic for nearly a year, beginning after he was elected leader of the party, in the summer of 1991.

From day to day his security increased. Personally, I think he enjoyed the sense of importance of having bodyguards. Unfortunately, the bodyguards examined the patients. They did body searches. They asked questions. At the beginning there was one, then two, then three. At the end there were five, and they came in two cars. One in the front of the building, one in front of his door. One at the rear. One in the office when the patient was with him. They kept their machine guns in the cars.

Dr. C. reports:

Before March he was very politically active. But he kept up with the clinic very determinedly. Every day he came to the clinic. Other colleagues didn't like that, and pressured me to cut off Radovan's relation to the clinic. In 1991, at Christmas, I said to Radovan, well look, you are very engaged in political work, and people don't like that. You can go on leave without pay for one year, then come back to the clinic without any problems. Radovan answered that he had a plan to be politically engaged only two months. January and February 1992. After that he would try to leave SDS and to continue to work as a doctor.

At the same time that he was working as a psychiatrist, all indications show that Karadzic was actively preparing for the aggression in Bosnia. He sought to have the Bosnian Serbs in the JNA transferred to his command: "The entire Serb population was behind the Army and they were counting on the Army to defend Yugoslavia" (p. 217).

On the one hand, Karadzic disengenuously reassured the public: "We [Serbs] are truly a good and powerful people, who have never done any harm whatsoever to anyone. The Serbs in Bosnia have never threatened anyone, and they will not do so now. All they are doing is organizing themselves."[26] On the other hand, he confessed that at the time the Serbian Republic of Bosnia-Herzegovina was named, on January 9, 1992, "I was constantly aware that there was going to be war because we knew very well that the Serb nation would not leave Yugoslavia. No one could force them to leave. Territories had to be defined. As nobody respected this, a conflict had to follow."[27]

He also owned up to his aggressive designs as the leader of the Serbian Republic of Bosnia-Herzegovina: "Muslims are the most threatened. They are the most threatened not only in the physical sense, and I did not think that they might disappear only physically; rather, this is also the beginning of the end of their existence as a nation."[28]

An interview published in January 1992 further articulated Karadzic's strategy: "'There is no longer any retreat. We will fight.' When asked 'How far?' he replied, '[We will fight] until we achieve Karadjordje's objective of uniting all the Serbs and until we complete his struggle" (Cigar, *Genocide*, 39).

At the January 25, 1992, session of Parliament, Karadzic had also depicted the Serbs in Bosnia-Herzegovina as enslaved, and had claimed that "in Sarajevo all the skyscrapers are built on Serbian land" (p. 45); other Serbian representatives added that even the Bosnian Parliament was constructed on a Serbian cemetery.

As he also admitted in an unguarded moment in January 1992: "There is no return to a united Bosnia-Herzegovina. The time has come for the Serbian people to organize itself as a totality, without regard to the administrative [existing] borders" (p. 40). Two months later, when his forces were putting up barricades in Sarajevo, Karadzic said: "The Serbs were almost a hundred percent sure that they wanted to stay in Yugoslavia. The Croats and the Muslims were almost a hundred percent sure that they wanted to leave. It was clear then that Bosnia could not survive."[29]

On April 6, the day the European Community recognized Bosnia, Karadzic proclaimed the independent "Serbian Republic of Bosnia-Herzegovina," with himself as president, and Sarajevo as its capital. Karadzic wanted to partition Sarajevo and erect a wall through the city.[30]

Before the aggression began, a major part of Karadzic's role was to be the spokesperson for the genocidal project to both domestic and international audiences. He did so with characteristic flair. His messages often centered on the fact that there was an Islamic nationalist threat in Bosnia the Serbs needed to defend themselves against. He even expressed uncharacteristic openness to alliance with the Croatians with his anxiety to "not allow Islamic domination over the Serbian and Croatian—that is, Christian—majority in Bosnia-Herzegovina."[31]

In a domestic radio broadcast, Karadzic openly urged abandonment of Islam as the best solution for Bosnian Muslims. He claimed cynically that "Many Muslims who are well-educated and sensible are being baptized and are becoming Christians in Europe as a way of reacting against fundamentalism and the introduction of militant Islam into Bosnia" (Cigar, *Genocide*, 59).

To the Serbian nationalists, all South Slavs are actually Serbs. In 1994, Karadzic again argued that by rejecting their alleged true Serbian identity, the Muslims had made themselves "vulnerable to marginalization and even to the danger of annihilation. The Muslims could have mattered only if they were part of the Serbian nation. As it is, I do not see a future for the Muslim nation" (p. 186).

But the overwhelming domestic intention of the anti-Islam messages was certainly to fan the flames of Bosnian Serbs' fear and dread so that they would learn to hate and fight the Bosnian Muslims. Karadzic openly stated that the battle was against Asiatic darkness and reiterated that the "Serb state has no need to incorporate its enemies into its own state. The Serb state should be the home of the Serb nation" (p. 65). He reassured his domestic audience that "we defended Europe from Islam six hundred years ago. . . . We are defending Europe again from Germany [sic] and from Islamic fundamentalism" (p. 65).

After the ethnic cleansing began, with rapid catastrophic successes in Eastern Bosnia, Karadzic became the biggest *falsificator of reality* for the genocide, as an apologist extraordinaire to the international community.

According to Karadzic, there simply was no Serbian ethnic cleansing of Bosnia. "The Serbian authorities have never forced any Muslim or Croat to leave his home. I believe it is obvious that the Muslims feel uncomfortable in Serbian territory and are leaving, but no one is forcing them to do so" (p. 88). All this was "not deliberate," and it was "ethnic transfer" (p. 88). Karadzic set the tone of denial that local officials would follow, such as the Serbian mayor of Visegrad, who told foreign journalists: "I don't know what you mean by ethnic cleansing! The Muslims left voluntarily. We even supplied the buses. We didn't force them to leave, I swear" (p. 88). Nor were there Serbian-run concentration camps where prisoners were killed: "We, unlike the Muslims, do not kill prisoners; that is why we had camps, not extermination camps as has been claimed, but prison camps" (p. 88).

Later, contradicting his earlier denials of their very existence, Karadzic reassured the international community that "today we have dismantled them completely, and have freed everyone. The Muslims, however, still maintain theirs. Europe is being deceived by the media and by their governments" (p. 90).

There was no mass rape. Karadzic claimed that "there is no evidence," and labeled the accusations of rape "a horrible lie" (p. 90).

There were no sieges against civilians: "We do not conduct sieges. . . . We defend our territory" (p. 91). According to Karadzic, even the apparent siege of Sarajevo was not really a siege: "It seems we are besieging the city, but in fact that is not true. There is no siege on our part, we have no aggressive intentions; we are only protecting our people who live in the outlying districts around the city" (p. 97). In an interview he claimed that "The National Library was destroyed by Muslims. They took away all the Muslim Islam books out of this building and then they burned it down."[32]

After the February 5, 1994, mortar attack on the Sarajevo marketplace, which left more than sixty dead and almost two hundred wounded, Karadzic accused the Bosnian government of masterminding the entire incident in order to convince NATO to launch air strikes against Serb artillery positions surrounding the city. He argued that the Muslims had used mannequins, actors, and cadavers supplied by the Croatians (Cigar, *Genocide*, 97).

Above all he claimed: "We can affirm with certainty that our [Bosnian Serb] army defended our people and their borders in a model manner and that it did not commit a single crime, rape, or attack against civilians" (p. 91). "Our generals are extremely sensitive about moral behavior" (p. 88).

It served Karadzic's apologist aims to play to the West's fears of Islamic fundamentalism. "We are doing that for Europe—to make sure Islamic funda-mentalism doesn't infect Europe from the south" (p. 91). Karadzic's apologia had its desired effect in the West. He was sometimes despised, sometimes pitied, al-ways found entertaining. He was considered a pathological liar. He himself be-came a kind of a sinkhole that drained off opposition to the war. He was outrageous and maddening to the point of being disarming. He played on West-erners' preoccupation with neutrality. He got inside their heads enough that they started to accept his mythological view of the Balkans' ancient ethnic hatreds, and that those hatreds could not be understood or contained in any other way. With his shock of hair and his outrageousness, Karadzic drew attention away from Milosevic and the other calculators who stood behind the ethnic cleans-ing of Bosnia-Herzegovina.

All in all, there is little evidence to suggest that Karadzic was acting as a psychiatrist. When prompted by Western journalists to say something about being a psychiatrist, Karadzic, the *man of clay*, would at times say something that had a psychiatric cast.

When asked what was his "diagnosis" of Bosnia, he replied: "A big erup-tion of the subconscious. You can't control it" (p. 100).[33] His recommendation: "In psychiatry we just try to understand the patient, try to preserve him from harming himself, to communicate with other people. That's what we should do for Bosnia."[34] The world should allow "antagonized nations to separate and to live their own life."[35] Why is it that the "international community should want people who hate each other to the point of extermination to live together again?"[36]

Karadzic also used the psychological concept of intergenerational transmis-sion of memories to justify the Serbs' atrocities: "It was a continuation of World War II. People recalled about this war which family had done to them, they were afraid it would be repeated and said, 'let us kill them before they kill us.' People did not forget who killed their fathers, grandfathers and mothers. Everybody feared vengeance and began first."[37]

This has an entirely different quality to it than does the Nazi doctor in Auchwitz explaining how his work in a death camp that killed Jews fit with his allegiance to the Hippocratic Oath: "Of course I am a doctor and I want to pre-serve life. And out of respect for human life, I would remove a gangrenous ap-pendix from a diseased body."[38] There is no fundamental conflict to be reckoned with, between Karadzic's work as a psychiatrist and his work as a genocidal leader, as there was with the Nazi doctors, because he did not really deploy himself as a physician in anywhere near the complete way that the Nazi doctor did. On the other hand, most Nazi doctors were middle managers of the death machine, but not genocidal leaders as Karadzic was. So there were not the same opportuni-ties for the two elements to connect.[39]

Indicted War Criminal

Many people look to The Hague to provide some kind of closure on Radovan Karadzic's role as a genocidal leader. The accused war criminal should be made to face justice, as did many of those accused of perpetrating Nazi war crimes. Yet the Republika Srpska is not militarily defeated, as was Nazi Germany, and the United Nations War Crimes Tribunal will not try suspects in absentia. It was not until the spring of 1995 that Karadzic was actually indicted by the U.N. War Crimes Tribunal. IFOR was still reluctant to arrest Karadzic.[40] In July 1996, bowing to international pressure, Karadzic resigned from the presidency, though he continued to be a political force in the Republika Srpska. Will he ever go to The Hague?

Back in January 1996, those who knew him were conflicted about what would happen next to Karadzic.

Marko Vesovic says:

Now that Milosevic has skimmed all the cream, and assumed his call to glory as a peacemaker, Karadzic will have to flee to South America to save his life. The only angle now is to get all those millions of German marks . . . because he has been dreaming about being a rich man all his life.

Whereas Dr. B. says:

I'm afraid he will somehow miss The Hague. Some think that he will commit suicide. Some think he will escape to Cyprus because Milosevic arranged everything for him. He now has a lot of Serbs who are expelled from their homes and won't be able to come back. I think some of them could try to kill Karadzic.

And Dr. C.:

I know Radovan. He is a coward. He will do everything to save his own skin. And because of that I believe that there is very little chance he will go to The Hague. Only to save his neck.

I have accepted the prospect of Karadzic going to The Hague as the best possible option. If Karadzic is found guilty, some measure of justice can be served. Testimony could even lead to the indictment and prosecution of those in Serbia who directed Karadzic, perhaps even Slobodan Milosevic. Western institutions, particularly the United Nations, would then have a chance of partially redeeming themselves for all their failings in Bosnia. A Karadzic trial could help establish a precedent for the establishment of a permanent war crimes tribunal.

For Marko, Dr. B, Dr. C, and scores of other Sarajevans and Bosnians who see Karadizic in their nightmares, a successful prosecution is barely imaginable. Of course they would like to think that justice could be served. But given all their experience with the international community's handling of Serbian aggression, including of course the United Nations, why should they expect anything more?

The prospect of a high-profile Karadzic trial, even with a successful prosecution, conjures up another disturbing image. His defense and imprisonment could add to Karadzic's status as a cult figure of ethnic nationalism, with the absurd parade of press conferences, books, websites, films, and further poetic ruminations to come. Still, this is nothing compared to the very real possibility that he will never appear in a court of justice, and become the next Professor of Psychiatry at the Republika Srpska University Medical School in Banja Luka.

"Petnica" concludes:

Future, you traitorous word!
O, my mountain breaking father
(Karadzic, Black Fairy Tale, 12)

There is a refusal to recognize the real future or the real past—only the sacred past of epic myth and its projection ad infinitum. The fundamentalist mentality of Serbian nationalist ideology cannot imagine a future that adequately takes into account the historical reality of living together in Bosnian multiethnic society. Its desired Greater Serbia depends on its end-time vision of violent ethnic purification, not on any realistic social achievement rooted in the historical past. Witness the ruins of Serbia, Republika Srpska, Croatia, and the singular achievement of the destruction of Bosnia-Herzegovina.

Regarding the future, Karadzic's poetics is additionally noteworthy in that it contains not only the possibility for rebirth through purification ("The eyes are shining from the happiness of being a member of something / There is no other" (p. 7), but also the visualization of its own demise of "an enormous desert yard" (p. 12). And in that sense, the future did indeed have a face: a face taken from the past. And the poet's father's tree stump, that plum tree that was once a place for children and birds, is now the whole of Bosnia-Herzegovina, laid waste by the axes that Karadzic helped to put in the hands of the Bosnian Serbs. The nightmare begot not a dream, but another nightmare. In the poems, and in life.

If poetry mattered at all when it came to these things, then the end for Karadzic would come not in The Hague, on a brilliantly lit world stage, but dumbly in some cellar, consumed by the flames of his mad fire.

Figure 1. Kemal Hadzic, "Untitled" from double grave series. *Reproduced with the kind permission of the photographer.*

Figure 2. Kemal Hadzic, "Untitled" (The National Library). *Reproduced with the kind permission of the photographer.*

Figure 3. Kemal Hadzic, "Untitled" from Sarajevo street series. *Reproduced with the kind permission of the photographer.*

Figure 4. Photograph of Zoran Bogdanovic's "Memory of People." *Reproduced with the kind permission of Obala Gallery.*

Figure 5. Photograph of Mustafa Skopljak's "Sarajevo '91, '92, '93 . . . '94." *Reproduced with the kind permission of Obala Gallery.*

Figure 6. Photograph of Mustafa Skopljak's "Sarajevo '91, '92, '93 . . . '94." *Reproduced with the kind permission of Obala Gallery.*

Figure 7. "Vraca 1996," Stevan Weine. *Reproduced with permission.*

Figure 8. "Vraca 1996," Stevan Weine. *Reproduced with permission.*

Figure 9. "Vraca 1996," Stevan Weine. *Reproduced with permission.*

Figure 10. "Grbavica florist," Stevan Weine. *Reproduced with permission.*

Psychiatric Apologists and the Denial of Genocide

Chapter 6

Letters from a Colleague

Shortly after I presented a panel on Bosnian survivors of ethnic cleansing at the November 1993 meeting of the International Society for Traumatic Stress Studies, a young colleague wrote to me looking for some advice. He had received several letters from some senior psychiatrists in Serbia. They wrote that the people of Serbia were experiencing hard times which were causing psychiatric consequences. They sent a copy of their 1993 book, *The Stresses of War*,[1] in which they claimed to have tried to record and understand this suffering. It was written in English.

The Serbian psychiatrists knew of this colleague because he had published in the traumatic stress literature. In their letters to him, the Serbian psychiatrists talked about their interest in Post-Traumatic Stress Disorder and asked for assistance with their research. My colleague was confused. He knew enough about what was happening in the former Yugoslavia to think twice before answering. But he was not inclined to simply dismiss them.

After all, they sounded pleasant and reasonable in their letters. The suffering they described appeared plain, as did their professionalism. Understandably, he was somewhat flattered by the interest of professionals half a world away. Part of him was thinking, "just like me, they are committed to clinical care and research. Besides, they do not sound too political. More like humanistic professionals who believe that their psychiatric work serves a larger purpose. Perhaps we can connect on that level. It may be a chance to do some work in a very timely and topical context." That is what he told me when we first talked about it.

Like many Americans, this colleague was slow to conclude that what was happening in Bosnia was genocide, and slow to hold the Bosnian Serbs and

Serbians responsible as aggressors. Even when it was relatively clear to him that the Serbian and Bosnian Serbian governments were responsible, he still wondered; perhaps these doctors were different. They said that they weren't being political; that they were primarily concerned with refugees and their suffering because of war. Perhaps these psychiatrists were dissidents, opposed to nationalism and genocide. If so, then they would need international support. Part of him was prepared to give them the benefit of the doubt.

I was glad that he had written to me; that he hadn't simply agreed to their requests. And I was also happy that he hadn't just ignored their letters. We both came to believe that there was something important to be learned here concerning the ethics of professionals and genocide. We spent hours talking about the psychiatrists from Serbia, and eventually concluded that their writings were essentially apologia for genocide. We wanted to know more about the topic of professionals who were apologists, but found little examination of the topic in the professional literature.[2] I wanted to know: in what ways do these apologists explain their professional involvement with the government that sponsored the genocide? Could they see the great disparity between their descriptions of Serbia as a victim of genocide and the realities of the genocide in Bosnia, or were they blind?

It was not possible for either of us to go to Belgrade to do face-to-face interviews.[3] So we tried to establish a dialogue with the Serbian psychiatrists by mail. My colleague wrote them back with some help from me (by then I had a public reputation regarding Bosnia and could not hope for a revealing response from them). His letters were friendly and curious, but he also threw in a few serious points for them to consider. I asked him to write,

> What is it like for you, as a mental health professional, to deal with such things as ethnic cleansing? How do you make your professional choices in this difficult and trying time? . . .
>
> You are not the only mental health professional who is reevaluating your professional posture in the context of the stresses of war. Radovan Karadzic is a psychiatrist. . . . How has Karadzic evolved from a psychiatrist to a governmental leader and how has he extended his commitments to professional skills, values and ethics into his important political role? Could you shed some light on these matters?[4]

Not surprisingly, the psychiatrists never answered these questions. But they wanted my colleague on their editorial board, and aked to start a collaborative project, cross-cultural in design.

This colleague of mine was not the only one to whom they wrote.[5] Other American mental health professionals received even more explicit appeals and requests. To a senior psychiatric leader, they wrote that the truth about the

Serbian people had not been properly told, and asked for help in representing the truth to international organizations.

There is no telling how many other such letters the psychiatrists from Serbia wrote. As for this last one, no response was written. It's the kind of letter you might just put aside like a piece of junk mail. But to ignore these apologist professionals, to not take seriously the possible impact of their writings, is to remain willfully ignorant about several critical dimensions of the contemporary genocidal project. One is the intended consequence of their work: to shape international opinion so as to avoid condemnation for genocide. Another pertains to the further consequences the apologists' denial of genocide might have in Bosnia-Herzegovina and Serbia in the post-Dayton era.

The World According to the Apologist Professionals

One need only glance at the title page of *The Stresses of War* to see that the book was produced with the help of the following Serbian Ministries: Science and Technology; Labor, Veteran, and Social Affairs; Information; and International, Scientific, Educational, and Cultural Cooperation. In other words, this book is explicitly a project of the Serbian government—the same government that sponsored genocide in Bosnia-Herzegovina.

No, this is not the Bosnian Serb government, and these doctors did not commit atrocities. Nor did they function as leaders of the genocide, as Radovan Karadzic did. They are bystanders to ethnic cleansing in Bosnia-Herzegovina, in the sense described by Ervin Staub—persons who have a great impact in shaping the memory and meaning of genocide.[6] The manner in which these mental health professionals served the ends of the Bosnian Serb and the Serbian governments' genocidal project was less direct, but nonetheless real and effective. They used their professionalism to produce apologia that would appeal to bystanders in the West and promote passivity or acceptance.

The authors state that they do not intend to make "political implications in the sense of judging who is guilty and responsible."[7] Yet when they report that "this war is the drama of tragically conflicting ethnic groups," they are presenting the Serbian government's view of the war. Not once do they speak of the Serbian nationalists' genocide (either directly or by its euphemism, "ethnic cleansing"). Instead, we find descriptions of "a civil, religious and ethnic war."

Although there certainly are religious, ethnic, and historical dimensions to Bosnia, placing emphasis upon historically conflicting ethnic groups obscures two central historical facts: the Serbian government's aggression against Bosnia, and the Serbian government's role in creating a situation where divisions predominated and drove people into the "individual and collective paranoia"[8] of nationalism, atrocities, and genocide. Rather than challenging their government's ideology or practice, these psychiatrists, by and large, stick with and defend it.

Yet it is curious that in making this defense of their government, these psychiatrists present themselves not as extreme nationalists, but as humanists and pacifists: "We condemn war crimes and genocide regardless of who is the perpetrator and who is the victim. We are against all spreading of hatred and aggression, and we are against war. We desire a just and lasting peace with equal respect of the rights of all nations and citizens" (1994, p. 14.)

Statements such as these espousing pacifism are likely calculated to appeal to the Westerner's reluctance to condemn the Serbs or to take sides in this far-off Balkan affair. But do they believe it themselves?

Platitudes can be tossed off rather easily when the discussion is kept at the level of vague generalities. But when addressing the topic of the alleged 50,000 rapes of non-Serb women by Serbian forces, the psychiatrists' humanistic claims are put to the test, and fail. They make their position crystal clear: "On the basis of our experiences it seems that there was not any systematical rape on either side" (Kalicanin et al., *Stresses*, 176). Their explanation is at best confused, at worst blind and misogynistic: "the number of persons who have been raped is almost the same on all three sides and that there are about 2000 persons who have been raped, but we also think that we shall never know the exact figure, the reason for it simply being the fact that women in our culture do not and will not talk about rape . . . even a psychotic woman, avoids giving a statement that she has been raped after receiving specialist psychiatrist's treatment. All that implies that the suggested number of the Muslim women who have been raped is absurd" (p. 177).

The psychiatrists demonstrate a complete inability to enter into the complexities of perpetrators, not to mention an utter lack of decency, when they state: "Kenneth Blackwell, the American ambassador, declared that the higher-rank officers of the Serbian forces in Bosnia and Herzegovina were issuing orders to their soldiers to rape at their command! According to this ambassador, erection can simply occur at somebody's command. This is really absurd, not only from the medical, but also from a layman's point of view" (p. 177).

The topic of mass rape, which has stimulated heated debate, is in need of further inquiry. Judging from their texts, it appears that the psychiatrists from Serbia have a slim chance of bringing clarity and understanding to the topic. Of course, that is hardly the aim of their books.

When the term "ethnical cleansing" appears in the text, it is taken entirely out of context and misrepresented as a threat to the Serbs: "Satanization along with ethnical cleansing are 'clean' weapons. Thanks to the powerful media, it can be applied easily, efficiently and in no time in the whole world, even on ethnically mixed territories. The victims just have to be marked. Therefore, Serbs all over the world have good reasons to protest against the media" (p. 13).

It is curious that the authors do not avoid the potentially problematic term "genocide," but use it again and again. However, they appropriate it to argue for a historical interpretation very different from the prevailing conception of genocide against multi-ethnic civilization in Bosnia. Their second book, *The Stresses of War and Sanctions*, published in 1994, centers on the threat of genocide against the Serbs.

"Is the genocide of the Serbian people and all the citizens of former Yugoslavia already under way?" (Kalicanin et al., *Sanctions*, 24).

Regarding refugees who have come to Serbia, "the proportions of exiles are large, resulting from renewed genocide politics against the Serbian people" (*Stresses*, 39). They make repeated analogies with the Holocaust: "today's satanization of the Serbian people is comparable only to the satanization of the Jews before and during the Second World War, leading to the Holocaust. In some components, it is even more harmful" (*Sanctions*, 22). "The satanization of the Serbian people and the U.N. Security Council sanctions have put the entire country and the general population in living conditions which, in many of their characteristics, are not very different from those in the Nazi concentration camps" (p. 25). Serbia itself is called a "concentration camp" (p. 26). "The genocide is being implemented on a much broader scope and in a manner which even the darkest Nazi minds were not able to grasp" (p. 25).

The authors also make analogies with Hiroshima and Nagasaki. In their hands, the image of nuclear warfare becomes associated with the dangers of a technologically sophisticated means of destruction via the contemporary media machine: "In terms of danger to people and mankind as a whole, satanization by means of and controlled by modern mass media can only be compared with the use of nuclear weapons" (*Sanctions*, 21).

The psychiatrists identify the psychological mechanism that propels this genocide. They call it "satanization," defined as "dehumanizing and disparaging other nations or groups of people" (*Sanctions*, 20). The danger lies in how satanization of the Serbs has "pave(d) the way for genocide to be perpetrated against them" (p. 11).

The psychiatrists also identify the practical mechanisms for committing genocide against the Serbs. First and foremost are sanctions. In May 1992, the United Nations imposed harsh sanctions on the Federal Republic of Yugoslavia (Serbia and Montenegro), forbidding nearly all scientific, economic, technical, cultural, and diplomatic contact with the outside world. The sanctions had their intended severe impact upon the economy and the well-being of the Serbian people. Ultimately, it was in large part these sanctions which drove Milosevic closer to the West, put a wedge between him and Bosnian Serb leader Radovan Karadzic, and opened the way for the Dayton peace accords.

In their books, written well before Dayton, the authors evoke the memory of another famous international summit: the landmark Convention on Geno-

cide of 1948, where the concept of genocide was defined and the commitment
to opposing it was crystallized as a principle of international relations.[9] The
Serbian psychiatrists issue the call for another Convention "on the prevention
and combating of satanization" (*Sanctions*, 21).

Once again, they appropriate a key event in the modern history of mass
violence and turn it to their own purposes. Along the way, they even find cause
to evoke the memory of Physicians for the Prevention of Nuclear War, the activist professional group that surged in the 1980s to protest the nuclearism of
the Cold War.[10]

"I suggest that we start an initiative in order to establish an Association for
the Prevention of Satanization (and depriving people and ethnic groups of human qualities on any basis). I have spoken my conscience. In my opinion, and
with respect to the current situation, this kind of Association is much more relevant than the Association for the Prevention of Nuclear War" (*Stresses*, 14).

With analogies and proposals sounding so preposterous, it is hard to accept
that the psychiatrists believed their own arguments. Yet regardless of this, and
of whether or not you accept their points, all this talk of satanization works to
put Western bystanders on the defensive and keep them silent. If to condemn
the Serbs for their actions is to satanize them, then who is certain enough and
emotionally prepared enough to risk being identified with the perpetrators of
genocide?

Trivializing Genocide

The story the psychiatrists from Serbia tell in their books helps their government to avoid condemnation for genocide. They offer as good an argument as
they can muster for a historical view other than the implication of the Serbs in
genocidal aggression. Some receivers of their message may even accept their arguments, as the study of bystanders has shown.[11] And yet the psychiatrists from
Serbia do not necessarily have to be believed in order to succeed. Merely in putting forth their text, they have to some extent succeeded, in that they have
trivialized the concept of genocide as it applies to Bosnia. *Satanization is genocide. Sanctions are genocide. Misuse of psychiatry is genocide. . . .*

Granted, there is some truth in these claims. Each of these actions, which
are real enough, is certainly hurtful to some Serbian people. The psychiatrists
from Serbia cannot be faulted for drawing attention to their suffering. Certain
of these actions may even carry with them some genocidal potential. This too
demands attention. But here we must make a sharp distinction between genocidal potential and genocidal aggression.[12] Genocidal potential can be found
among Serbs, Croats, and Muslims in Bosnia-Herzegovina and the other former
republic of Yugoslavia. Wherever there is ethnic nationalism, there is genocidal

potential. But it is the Bosnian Serbs and Serbs who are primarily responsible for actually carrying out genocidal aggression in Bosnia-Herzegovina.

The Serbian psychiatrists steer wide of these facts and all that they imply, because to address them would obviously implicate the Serbs. They do not try to make the argument that what is happening in Bosnia is not genocide. Rather, they claim that Serbia is a concentration camp—a reaction to the Sarajevans' wartime claim that besieged Sarajevo is the world's biggest concentration camp. Well, then Serbia is an even bigger one! Although they do not ever mention Sarajevo and the siege there, simply using the term "concentration camp" diminishes the claim Sarajevans have been making.

With these voices from the Serbian side talking genocide, the concept loses its sharpness and clarity. To the outsider, it becomes a war chant, a hysterical cry, yet another example of finger pointing. It becomes easier for the outsider to say "this is a dirty war," as the Serbian psychiatrists write, and talking genocide is just another way of calling foul. You are to conclude that in war, talk is cheap and all sides play foul.

Claiming the Mantle of the Victim

It is important that we notice and understand not only what the apologist professionals were saying, but how they were saying it. The psychiatrists from Serbia, who are not actually victims of genocide, claim the mantle of the victim and attempt to appropriate the rhetorical dialogue of the testimony.

The books give us Serbs who are "wrongly accused" (*Sanctions*, 38) and has them "discovering that we have all of a sudden been rejected by the world, and we do not know why. We have been accused and pronounced guilty" (p. 36). When each instance of rejection is recalled, it is with the intent to accuse others of their transgressions, but also to permit the Serbian psychiatrists to speak as survivors giving their testimony.

They claim that their abusers and aggressors come from many sources. First, there is the international community and its sanctions. The material and cultural deprivation and isolation imposed upon the Serbs is regarded as proof positive of the world's genocidal intent vis-à-vis the Serbs. Then there is "the media war that is being waged against it" (p. 22). The Serbian psychiatrists claim that the media takes the side of the Muslim and Croat peoples and has succeeded in propagandizing the world against them.

Then there are the international scholars from literature, history, political science, and philosophy who have offered explanations for why the Serbs did what they did. The psychiatrists from Serbia rally against arguments they regard as flawed, but at the same time make good use of these assaults to give themselves the possibility of speaking from the position of a victim. For example, they decry the writings of Richard Lauer, who wrote on the myth of the wolf and Serbian nationalism.[13] To them, he is "the author of this new racist theory" (p. 40):

> People are appearing who wish to bring some order into everything ugly that is being said about us, and to provide a theoretical background and explanation. As the anthropological measurements according to which the Jews were proclaimed a lesser race are no longer in fashion, a domain considerably more difficult to measure was embarked upon— the analysis of the Serbian myth that is branded guilty for everything. (p. 39)

They ask: "Why is it attributed to the Serbian nation alone?" (p. 43). They speak against the racist assumptions that underlie "warnings to the world that Serbs are even dangerous when they dream, when they write poetry, when they live their spiritual life" (p. 50).

From this position it becomes possible for the psychiatric apologists to offer a broader cultural criticism of the West: "Atrocities are a terrible fact of the contemporary age too. It has nothing more to do with the cultural heritage of the Serbs than it does with the cultural heritage of the Germans, the French, the English, the Spanish, or the cultural heritage of any other nation of Europe" (p. 43). The psychiatric apologists recontextualize Serbian atrocities in the hope of making them disappear.

The psychiatrists from Serbia respond with a special vigor to what they call the "misuse of psychiatry" (*Stresses*, 225): "In this destruction of the people through satanization and sanctions, particular use is being made of the achievements of the behavioral sciences" (*Sanctions*, 26). "The entire Serbian people has been put on a psychiatric couch and proclaimed to be Satan's people" (*Stresses*, 20). "In the religious, ethnic, and civil war waged in former Yugoslavia, medicine and psychiatry in particular are being misused in order to spread hatred against the Serbian people" (p. 227).

They draw the reader's attention to Dr. Eduard Klain's article for the *Croatian Medical Journal*, "Yugoslavia as a Group,"[14] which describes the Serbs as "primitive peoples" and psychoanalyzes their national character. Klain wrote:

> The Serbs are burdened with an inferiority complex compared to the peoples of the Western part of Yugoslavia, for they are conscious that they are on a lower level of civilization. They try to get rid of that feeling by means of various defense mechanisms, such as negation, projections, denial and destruction. . . . The Serbs are inclined to regress to a schizoparanoid position and exhibit an archaic type of aggression which can explain the torturing of the wounded and massacring dead bodies. (pp. 228–229)

In response, the psychiatrists from Serbia asked: "Are the Serbs a 'psycho-analytical' and other type of testing ground, since their behavior and manifested characteristics have been hitherto unseen in history, except in some primitive tribes and people of lower races, somewhere at the end of the world" (p. 229).Another psychiatrist is dismissed as "pseudopsychoanalytical, pseudoscientific, unscholarly kitsch" (p. 232).

One can more or less agree with their pointed criticism of certain Croatian psychiatrists, as I do, but still take exception to the way they use these arguments to raise themselves, their people, and their government to a higher ground. When the psychiatrists from Serbia propose that two articles be added to the Hawaii Declarations of the World Health Organization relating to the misuse of psychiatry, in the glaring absence of any mention whatsoever of Jovan Raskovic or Radovan Karadzic, they reveal how totally yoked they and their text are to the interests of the Serbian government. It is what Ervin Staub refers to as a motivated misinterpretation.[15]

More blunt and offensive is when the psychiatrists from Serbia deliberately draw the reader's attention to their peoples' victimization, which they dramatize in grotesque imagery: "Someone always has to die by fire, even in this contemporary age. . . . Like all others in the past, the stake being made will have to feed on human flesh. We, the Serbs, are the next in line" (*Sanctions*, 51).

This is not the romantic language of extreme nationalism,[16] but the language of survivors who, by virtue of their victimization, are entitled to speak with a special knowledge of humankind's problems. Thus the psychiatrists from Serbia permit themselves to say: "This speaks equally well of a deep moral crisis in modern mankind and the international community" (p. 22).

From this position as the survivor of so many abuses, the psychiatrists find it becomes possible to say almost anything. They can use their position as victim to claim to be speaking with the moral authority associated with that type of testimony. As a matter of fact, the words "testimony" and "witness" appear many times throughout their text: "The monograph originated from our desire to leave a written trace, testimony about the sufferings of the people" (*Stresses*, introduction). "The Institute for Mental Health is a witness and interpreter of its time" (p. 18).

From the position of the witness, the psychiatrists from Serbia are able to take on a duty toward history: "Our human and professional duty is to inform the world about what is happening. And this is furthermore our duty towards history, just as it is also the duty of physicians from other parts of our former common country" (*Sanctions*, 13).

The moral authority of the witness becomes merged with their notion of themselves as professionals who are already speaking from a position of medical authority. "We condemn any form of violence over health, above all as adherents

of Hypocrites [sic], and we are strongly determined to follow his path. We condemn any form of violence as a part of a nation that, in its long history, has
entered wars only to defend itself from violence" (Stresses, 7).

We also find these psychiatrists contending that they are acting on behalf
of a higher good: "We are firmly convinced that the Conscience of Mankind
will sooner or later say that we were right and that, at the same time, it will
condemn all those observers who kept silent in the face of the tragic consequences as well as those trying to justify the sanctions through politicization or
various other ways" (p. 7).

It is also worth noting that their use of the testimony is tinged with Serbian
nationalism. The psychiatrists do not speak of the suffering of people who happen to be Serbs, so much as the suffering of a people, the Serbs, once again
spurned by the world community.[17]

For those who want to believe in the purity of survivors' testimonies, the
Serbian psychiatrists' appropriation of the survivor's position as a witness is evidence that testimony itself can be corrupted. If you do not know any better, a
testimony such as theirs can come across with a moral certainty and clarity that
smells real enough to be received as the truth. Even if you do know better, it
may still disrupt your acceptance of the other side's truth.

For International Consumption

Because they wrote their texts in English, and assertively shared them with professionals in the West, it appears that the psychiatrists produced the book primarily for international consumption by Western bystanders. One psychiatrist
from Serbia, in discussing the books with me, dismissed the authors: Oh, they
did that just to get money.[18] Perhaps the human face their books showed helped
their Institute to get some money from providers of international aid. It did not
appear to play any role in lifting the sanctions, which were only rolled back after the Serbs began to comply with the Dayton agreement.

Why have the Serbian psychiatrists whom I call apologist professionals not
become the object of public scrutiny? In 1993, the American Psychiatric Association passed a resolution citing the denial of genocide and human rights abuses
as an ethical violation.[19] Why have the APA and other international psychiatric organizations not made the psychiatrists from Serbia and their work a focus
of ethical inquiry?[20]

Perhaps this silence is because the Serbian psychiatrists do not conform to
any known pattern of psychiatric abuse. Unlike Nazi psychiatrists, they did not
practice involuntary detention, eugenics, or extermination.[21] Unlike Soviet psychiatrists, they did not put psychiatric diagnostic and treatment tools in the service of oppression.[22] The psychiatrists from Serbia did not even directly

dehumanize the victims of ethnic cleansing, even though they certainly had at their disposal the medical and intellectual means to do so. If they had, it would have been much easier to criticize them, and they probably would have been condemned in the international community.

But the Serbian psychiatrists illustrate a different pattern of ethical abuse. It was left to others to create and spread the overtly nationalistic mentality that fed the genocide. They did not appear to fulfill any major role in that process. Rather, their role was limited to promoting the denial of genocide. Because they did so under the guise of being humanistic clinicians and researchers, they rendered themselves less vulnerable to criticism from other humanists. And because they appropriated the voice of the survivor, they spoke with a "moral truth" that was even harder to criticize.

The authors rarely slip. Only on occasion do they give a glimpse that there is, literally, another side: "We do, of course, have equal understanding for the victims and sufferings of the other side. But that has been the subject of discussion in the entire world for years. It is only on rare occasions that the sufferings of refugees and the population of this country can be heard" (*Sanctions*, 13).

This is no doubt true. These authors certainly have the right, if not the obligation, to open up the matter of Serbian suffering for us, so that we may know. But seeing as the government and the people on whose behalf they are speaking bear responsibility for the aggression that caused the recent suffering, there are complications involved in hearing only about one side. The reader is hardly reassured by the authors' claim: "As health care workers and humanists, we should have this very same viewpoint even if it did not concern our own people" (p. 33).

Would you want them to be your advocates? I would not, because to me despite their moral claim, even their concern about their "own people" is but an inch deep. Unlike the Nazi doctors, who fully entered into the madness and totally merged professionalism with genocidal ideology, the Serbian psychiatrists appear to be striking a pose calculated to save their jobs and their Institute, not humanity.

It seems to me that these apologist professionals are playing a sophisticated shell game with us. They lift up one shell to show you that only goodness is there. In the meantime, darkness and evil lie under the other shells. The apologist professional is a master, keeping the shells moving, piquing your curiosity, distracting you, and making you feel something good. The Serbian psychiatrists lift the shell to show you 800,000 refugees in Serbia—not the 3 million displaced by Serbian aggression in Bosnia. You cannot object to the things the psychiatrists from Serbia show you, for they are real enough. But you must never let yourself forget that they are showing you some things and not others, and that it is all part of their game.

The objective here, as in the sidewalk shell game, is first and foremost to take your money. The psychiatric apologists write quite openly about this motivation in their second book: "There was no single unfavorable reaction, nor was there even any contestation of what was put forward in the book" (p. 12).

> We have already received assistance from several foreign experts in the form of publications and research instruments. Cooperation in joint research has also been offered to us. With the assistance of these experts, the above-mentioned book was presented at meetings in the USA and in Europe. Some of these experts even expressed their gratitude, stating that the contents of the book had enabled them to acquire a view of the tragic events in our country from another angle. (p. 12)

"The book *The Stresses of War* enabled us to establish better contacts with a large number of humanitarian organizations and people of good will" (p. 12).

But they want more than money. They want to advance a view that shapes the historical record on the events in the former Yugoslavia. "The works contained in the book were entered into the computer data banks in the USA (Biosis, Pilot), thus making them more accessible to those who are interested. The book can be found in some university libraries, and it is increasingly in demand" (p. 12).

After Dayton, these psychiatrists' activities served not the push to get the sanctions repealed and to bring in money, but instead the enduring struggle to shape historical memory. The psychiatric apologists are very concerned about history. But as they themselves point out, the struggle did not begin with recent events in Bosnia or the breakup of Yugoslavia; it certainly dated back as far as the last World War: "History was falsified. In particular, events were falsified from the Second World War and the ensuing period" (p. 21).

Despite their claims, the psychiatrists go no further into the historical memories of World War II in their books. They do not attempt to retell history, or to tell any survivors' stories. That is unfortunate, because there is clearly a need for a greater depth of understanding of the historical nightmare of World War II through the telling of survivors' stories from all ethnic groups, including, of course, Serbians and Bosnian Serbs, who were the victims of Ustasha genocide. These senior members of the psychiatric profession could have been leading the way in teaching the younger generations about the history that could be derived from a knowing of these memories. Unfortunately, they appear to be prisoners of their own methodological and ideological approaches. Their quantitative methodology, and their rigid adherence to nationalist ideology, by and large keeps survivors' stories out of their books.[23]

That does not mean that their work was without impact, and should be ignored. Somehow, we must grasp the fact that in the current era, psychiatrists and other helping professionals may be called upon to become producers of apologia targeted at internal or external bystanders.[24] Their professional status enables them to make authoritative claims about suffering, both physical and emotional; to redescribe the memories of it; and to reframe the meaning of it, in powerful ways. When professionals have taken sides, and when they have something to say about survivors' suffering and stories and social injustice, I want to be absolutely clear about which side they are on, and to expose and prevent such ethical abuses.

A Blind Spot the Size of Bosnia-Herzegovina

The Serbian psychiatrists' two books have thus far made little impact in Bosnia, even in psychiatric circles. The fact is that they are but one tiny point of not seeing in an immense wave of blindness toward the ethnic nationalist aggression in Bosnia by Serbs and Bosnian Serbs. What I have shared from the Belgrade psychiatrists' writings on the war, is in actuality a terribly common affliction in Serbia and the Republika Srpska.

Blindness to the genocide in Bosnia has not been limited to psychiatrists, nor to that moment in time. The writer Lawrence Wechsler interviewed dissident Serbs protesting during the time of the Belgrade riots in 1997 and found that all possessed a remarkable "blind spot the size of Bosnia-Herzegovina."[25] We can find the same sort of blindness in many writings coming from Serbian intellectuals, academics, and politicians.

A book called *Serbian Side of the War*,[26] published in 1996 in Belgrade, and edited by Nebojsa Popov, raised (if ever so slightly) some expectations in Sarajevo for a more progressive view of recent history. However, it thoroughly shatters any such hopes, and more or less carries on with many of the same themes as the psychiatrists. A chapter entitled "Unelucidated Genocide" (pp. 159–170) says that "the Yugoslav authorities failed to make a tally of the country's fatalities," which "invited the incitement of revenge" (p. 778). Yet there is absolutely no critique of that revenge itself, or any curiosity at all as to its dreadful consequences in Bosnia-Herzegovina. There is a chapter on "Denazification in Germany" (pp. 726–730) and another on "The Problems of German-German Unification" (pp. 753–758), with acknowledgment of the "possibility of rectifying the injustices arising from wide-scale violation of human rights" (p. 786). Yet there is no genuine recognition of Serbian-sponsored human rights violations in Bosnia-Herzegovina or meaningful discussion of the dismantling of ethnic nationalist regimes.

These Belgrade scholars and intellectuals disappoint, as do the protesters who took to the streets in the winter and spring of 1997 for the Belgrade riots. I wonder, how long will their blindness continue? Will wartime apologists give birth to a veritable cottage industry of revisionists spewing out nationalistic interpretations? If Serbians cannot face up to the nightmare they produced, then the fate of their society, and that of the region, can only be darker.[27]

Skies did indeed grow much darker over Kosovo in March 1999, when Serbia finally implemented a planned, catastrophic escalation of their murder and expulsion of ethnic Albanians. This came as no surprise to Bosnians, who had seen it all before. But unlike Bosnia in 1992, the Western alliance did not stand by until the "cleansing" was mostly completed. NATO launched a massive air war against the Serbian forces, but Milosevic did not relent. Predictably, he seized the immediate opportunity to conduct purges and tighten his grip over Yugoslavia, and he pushed onwards with the widespread horrendous persecution of the Kosovars.

Once again, as with the ethnic cleansing of Bosnia, truth was a victim in the Serbian propaganda war. The Western media presented horrific images of refugees fleeing Serbs in Kosovo, but Serbs spoke only of their own suffering under Allied bombing and blockade. In the mass media, no Serbs came anywhere close to speaking the truth about what their government was then doing in Kosovo, much less their cleansing of Bosnia several years before. The Serbs partied at a rock concert in central Belgrade with the singer Ceca and her husband Arkan, the notorious indicted war criminal, whose Tigers paramilitary thugs had once done in Bosnia the same crimes that were annihilating life in Kosovo at that very moment. But the Western Allies can also be faulted their own persistent difficulties in seeing: the tendency to envision crises in Croatia, Bosnia, and Kosovo as disconnected episodes despite abundant evidence that all along Milosevic and the Serbian nationalists really did have genocidal program.

In the case of Nazism and the Jews, the work of the apologists and revisionists became an instigation for those who sought to tell the historical truth of the Holocaust. I am sick of lies, and know that others are too. What I want is for that sickness to yield to dissident voices from Serbia and the Republika Srpska to pierce the veil of denial and to soundly denounce the genocide. And in Bosnia-Herzegovina, I hope that the response to the affliction of blindness will be a great historical wave of seeing and knowing memories of genocide, in such a way that those who remain may build a better future.

Part III
Remembering Ethnic Cleansing

Introduction: Too Much History

The writer Tina Rosenberg, in thinking about challenges in postcommunist states, remarked: "Nations, like individuals, need to face up to and understand traumatic past events before they can put them aside and move on to normal life."[1] If that is so, then the Bosnian communality now faces a truly awesome challenge: learn to live and work with memories of ethnic cleansing in a way that will assist in the ongoing struggle to rebuild an acceptable way of life in a drastically new landscape.

And yet in speaking with Bosnians after Dayton you are far more likely to hear that there are many reasons to forget than to remember ethnic cleansing in Bosnia-Herzegovina. Current economic realities in Bosnia and in exile leave many preoccupied with meeting basic survival needs. In Bosnia-Herzegovina, the alarming number of deaths from suicide (often one a day in Sarajevo) and natural causes remind all of how easy dying is, even in peacetime.[2] One woman in Sarajevo spoke for many when she said, *Living is easier if you do not remember . . . so I forgot all those things.*[3]

The international community has unintentionally made a mockery of the memories of crimes of ethnic cleansing, by indicting so few for war crimes, and then by arresting even fewer. Nationalistic ways of thinking, so repugnant to many Bosnians, appear to be exacerbated by traumatic remembrances. *Besides,* one Sarajevan tells me, *for images of war. . . . All you must do is turn on the TV. This testimony, like Steven Spielberg and "Schindler's List," is on the news every night.*[4] The Bosnian communality is not about to face up, understand, and move on. They have suffered from much too much history, and if anything they are closer to being crushed by the burdens of memories.

As if that were not already hard enough, communist Yugoslavia did not provide the Bosnians with structures for processing personal and historical memories of traumatization, except in the most ideologically rigidified ways. Consequently, those persons most needed to lead Bosnia-Herzegovina—scholars, scientists, clinicians, intellectuals, educators, journalists, artists—find themselves lacking some of the necessary techniques, attitudes, or approaches for addressing the traumatic remembrances of war and genocide in a way that supports a peaceful, democratic, and open Bosnia-Herzegovina.

The international community has brought some of its own approaches to remembrances to Bosnia-Herzegovina. The United Nations War Crimes Tribunal was intended to be a means of shaping historical memory: if certain guilty individuals can be properly identified, then whole peoples will not have to be deemed guilty. The psychotherapeutic worldview, brought to Bosnia by international humanitarian nongovernmental organizations, provided therapeutic experiences through which survivors could abreact their traumatic memories so as to feel better. Related to this is the contemporary international human rights worldview, which advocates that survivors remember in order to affirm their commitment to human rights principles and actions. Such attempts to shape the collective memory of the Bosnian experience, especially externally derived approaches, are highly likely to have problems thriving in a land that has been known for its "decay over the abyss of memory," in the words of the Austro-Hungarian novelist Joseph Roth.[5]

Memory researchers and clinicians tell us that remembering is an important aspect of healing from traumas. The act of narrativization of traumatic memories can be especially important.[6] However, the historian Timothy Garton Ash emphasizes that there has been no single approach to remembrances after political violence and oppression, and that the role of forgetting has been underacknowledged.[7]

In Bosnia-Herzegovina and its Diaspora, remembrances may sometimes come out in conversations in the café or at home, but there is not yet any perceptible grassroots movement to narrativize the traumatic experiences. There have been some individuals and groups who have worked at communicating the experience of enduring ethnic cleansing and siege. During the ethnic cleansing and war, such activities seemed driven by the need to promote Bosnia's cause internationally so as to facilitate the military involvement of the United States and the West. Artists and writers, journalists, feminists, and health care workers were at the forefront of these efforts. After Dayton, Bosnians' desires and ability to relate more assertively to their traumatic memories seem to have been gradually worn down by the sheer enormity of all the difficulties survivors face.

This has not been helped by the totality and persistence of Bosnian Serb denial of the realities of ethnic cleansing. Some Bosnians have no hope at all for the "other side." Others wonder, just how can you make the Bosnian Serbs and Serbs face the truth of what they and their governments and their people did in Bosnia? How are you to undo their denial and lies about the crimes?[8] And yet it is in some says even more difficult for Bosnians to face the questions concerning the dilemmas of memory on their own side, such as: How do you live with the memories of the nightmare of genocide without becoming a prisoner to those memories? How do you reproach the historical memories of World War II that were silenced during the Tito years? How do you handle the many and profound contradictions in memories and redefine what it means to be Bosnian without nurturing a new extremism?

A special kind of memory work will be needed to manage these dilemmas and to promote peace, democracy, and pluralism. Nobody knows what will be the form or the results of this work. Timothy Garton Ash, in thinking about what has been learned from other historical experiences, endorses "what is sometimes called 'truth telling' (as) both the most desirable and the most feasible way to grapple with a difficult past."[9] It would have to center on survivors and the special knowledge they now possess by virtue of their traumatic experiences. At issue are not only their memories of atrocity but also the memories of living together and the mentality of merhamet.

Part Three of this book looks at several approaches that have been attempting to confront ethnic cleansing by working with the memories of that event: mental health professionals doing testimony work with survivors (chapter 7); creative artists bearing witness to genocide (chapter 8); and leaders, activists, and ordinary citizens of Bosnia attempting to give shape to a new communality in their nation as it awakens from ethnic cleansing (chapter 9).

Not separately nor together should any of these activities be viewed as a panacea for all the destruction wrought by the nationalists and their ethnic cleansing. Rather, each should be seen as the location of a certain struggle to rescue a human essence and put it to the service of the recovery from genocide and war. Each marks out a distinct but overlapping realm: self, culture, community.

Nor will any of these processes unfold rapidly. Citizens of Bosnia-Herzegovina, speaking about the prospects for recovery or reconciliation, almost universally say that it will take a long, long time. They correctly remind us that we are only at the very earliest point in the evolutionary process of living and working with memories of ethnic cleansing, with far more questions than answers.

Chapter 7

Doing Testimony
Psychotherapy with Survivors
of Ethnic Cleansing

Ending H.'s Testimony

I bump into H. at the Bosnian Refugee Center in Chicago about a week after our third testimony session with him. For the first time since leaving Omarska he has not seen the man in his dreams. A few days later we meet for our fourth session.

The last three nights I didn't have any dreams. . . . When I come here, however, I am reminded and I feel very bad that day. But after that I feel better. Better and better every day. Since I have been telling you my story I am much more social. Before I avoided people, but now I like to be with people and to talk with them. I had a terrible fear of people because I did not trust them. But now I like to speak with people and I don't withdraw anymore.[1]

"Can you say more about what happened to the man in your dream?"

When I saw his face and I recognized him, I stopped dreaming of him. He doesn't come anymore. I am not avoiding talking about him. But I have nothing more to say. Before I was able to recognize his face I heard terrible voices and had hallucinations. After I saw him I lost that voice—his voice.

I still have a lot of voices from different people. I know many of them who appear in my dreams. Many are prisoners. But when I awake, I forget them all. I know who they are, but when I wake up I forget them. I can give you lots of names of victims if you want. Just tell me and I will give you many, many names.

"Yes, we must take down the names for the record [and later we did], but what seems most compelling at this moment is to talk about those whose voices you still hear, so that we may come to know them like we did that man whose face you could not see."

One voice which I hear every day and I can't forget is the voice of the young boy whom they castrated. He is with me every night, and I think all my life I will remember that voice.

He speaks in detail about that poor boy and then turns to the other voices.

During the day I hear other voices, especially when I am alone. Sometimes I have the feeling that somebody is calling me. Very often, I open the door expecting to see somebody. I avoid being alone. I go out. I like to speak with people. Because when I am alone I always hear those voices.

"What do the voices say?"

They call me. They pronounce my name. I think that's because we were always afraid of the list. When they came with the list and read off your name, you knew that was the end. They would take you and kill you. Nowadays, very often I respond to that voice, answering like I would answer that voice in the camp. I hear them speak my last name. Sometimes if my family is with me in the same room they ask me, "Are you crazy? Whom are you answering?"

We tell H. how he can talk with his family about the voices in a way that describes it not as being crazy but as having strong memories.

Today I feel 70 percent better than the first day I came to speak with you. I was so afraid. I never visited my neighbors. Now I feel relaxed. I can communicate. I can talk with people. I can visit people.

But one thing bothers me. I am afraid of big working rooms, of warehouses, because they remind me of the torture rooms. I think right now that is the only problem—and I hope I will be liberated from that fear.

His voice trails off. We ask him if he wants to talk more. He shrugs his shoulders as if to say, I don't know. It can be immensely difficult to know how or even when to end a testimony. There is the recognition that the telling of the trauma story can be an endless venture. With H., there is so much more that can be shared. We can keep going and going. What happened in the warehouse? Tell us about the other voices. In those four sessions, there is no doubt that H. has only spoken a small part of all that he has endured in the camp. But still, we choose to stop there.

Testimony cannot be about telling it all. It would be unbearable. In testimony, you must enter into the world of the traumas, but you must also leave. Both the teller and the listener must survive. The story that has been told and received creates other obligations that then must be worked on.

A difficulty arises for the listener when the survivor is simultaneously leading you in and leading you out. Which path do you then take? We have the feeling that after four intensive sessions, H. has spoken a great deal and given reasonably convincing evidence that it has helped him. The nightmare is gone. So we surmise that he is primarily leading us out, and we follow. We talk about the possibility that someday he may wish to reenter that world, and we can go together. We meet the next week to read his testimony back to him. As we do,

H. listens intently. On occasion, he speaks up to add or correct something. At the end of the reading, we make the changes and he takes home a copy, thirty pages long. We arrange to meet again in one month to see how he is doing. We also give him some ideas as to what he can do with his testimony, and tell him we will keep him in mind and look for ways that his testimony might be publicly shared. That is all fine with him. He thanks us, shakes hands, and leaves.

This approach, the testimony method of psychotherapy, is one way mental health professionals have of working with survivors of state-sponsored violence. It is in part a straightforward proposition. Survivors tell the story of what happened when traumas shattered their life and the psychiatrist or psychotherapist is the listener who records it. Together they make a document of the trauma story, and then find ways to make that story knowable to others.

Yet testimony is not straightforward. Survivors do not speak only of their trauma story but also of their participation in the way of life that was, and what kind of future they foresee. The testimony yields a story that is shaped by both the survivors' and the witness's imperative to construct a narrative that is true to the events it seeks to represent, and true to itself. Remembering is itself a highly dynamic process, subject to interpersonal experience, social context, language, mental schemas, and brain functioning. Testimony has been used to reduce individual suffering, bear witness to human rights violations, collect legal evidence, and create art, and as a means of writing historical narratives. Assuming many different forms, testimony would appear to occupy a central position in late-twentieth-century Western culture.[2]

The benefits of testimony for the survivor are sometimes as plain to see as the departure of H.'s nightmares of a screaming man with no face. However, there is still much to be discovered about testimony as a means of working with survivors' remembrances of genocide or other social traumas.

Holocaust, Torture, and Ethnic Cleansing

I first learned about testimony from Dori Laub, the psychiatrist, psychoanalyst, and child survivor of the Holocaust who had cofounded the Fortunoff Holocaust Video Testimony Archives at Yale University. What Dori taught about Holocaust testimony helped to prepare my colleagues and me to respond to the call from refugee resettlement agencies when Bosnian refugees first came to Connecticut in January 1993. Our group at the trauma clinic first adopted a Holocaust testimony approach, although we knew very well that these historical events were not equivalent, and that consequently neither would be the survivors' psychological struggles. As we learned from working with the Bosnian survivors of ethnic cleansing, we kept reevaluating how Holocaust testimony could address, but was also changed by, this more recent human calamity.

The testimony approach to working with survivors of the Holocaust emphasizes remembering and knowing traumatic experiences from the distant past as a means of transforming identity, for self and community. "No one can become what he cannot find in his memories," wrote the Holocaust survivor Jean Amery.[3] And yet it is essential to note that most of the testimony work with Holocaust survivors was done forty to fifty years after the actual genocide. Consequently, what one finds in testimony is influenced by the many particulars of who one is at that time, individually and collectively.

Indeed, the scholarly work on Holocaust remembrances illustrates that the manner in which the genocide is remembered can be shaped by current sociohistorical context. There is James E. Young's study of Holocaust memorials, demonstrating a sharp contrast between how the Holocaust is remembered in Israel and in Poland. In Israel, where a Jewish nation was successfully established, the destruction and victimization of the Holocaust is collectively remembered in a way that feeds into an image of the heroic nation builder of the state of Israel.[4] In Poland, where the Jewish population of 3.5 million was annihilated, memorialization has taken the form of "broken tablets" made out of granite, railroad ties, or the shattered tombstones from destroyed Jewish cemeteries, in which "the fragments are not recuperated so much as reorganized around the theme of their own destruction" (Young, *Texture*, 185). I started wondering: which of these diametrically opposed archetypes—courageous "fighters" (pp. 209–281) or "broken tablets" (p. 185)—better captures the truth of survival in Bosnia and its Diaspora? Or is it something else still yet to be realized?

The testimony work with survivors of the Holocaust appears to be organized more around the psychology of "broken tablets." Dori Laub has characterized the experience of the Holocaust, as well as other forms of massive psychic trauma, as "an event without a witness" (p. 75). Echoing Martin Buber, he writes, "There was no longer an other to which one could say 'Thou' in the hope of being heard, of being recognized as a subject, of being answered . . . (and) when one cannot turn to a 'you' one cannot say 'thou' even to oneself" (p. 82). This yields "the loss of the capacity to be a witness to oneself" (p. 82). These traumatic experiences may not even be knowable to survivors, though their lives often bear unmistakable traces left by extremity.

Decades into their survivor experience, some kind of restoration becomes possible through testimony, when "this narrative that could not be articulated" can finally be "told," "transmitted," and "heard," and when the survivor "reclaims his position as a witness: reconstitutes the internal 'thou' and thus the possibility of a witness or a listener inside himself" (p. 85). However, Holocaust testimony is more accurately viewed as "dialogical process," "discursive practice," and "speech act," more so than the complete construction of a definitive statement, or the complete reconstruction of the "broken tablets," of one's own identity.[5] This theme is also stressed in the writings of Lawrence Langer, a scholar of

Holocaust testimonies and literature, who has argued sharply against any attempts to over-evoke the heroism of Holocaust survivors. Langer uses the concept "un-heroic memory," evoking far more anguish than hope.

An entirely different sense of the testimony emerges from the experiences of mental health professionals who were living and working in Chile during the time of political oppression under Augusto Pinochet. In comparison with Ho-locaust testimony, Chilean testimony was more explicitly a part of a political project—the active resistance of a military dictatorship. The Chilean profession-als sought to deploy themselves to help recent torture victims suffering from psy-chological difficulties as well as to oppose the human rights abuses and political repression. The victims themselves were mostly political activists and dissidents. The Chilean professionals had the survivors tell their stories into tape record-ers; these accounts were then transcribed, edited, and reworked into narratives of their torture experiences.[6]

The Chileans' understanding of their testimony work focused on its ability to mend the rupture in the self's relationship with the collective: "The thera-peutic process of testimony helps patients to integrate the traumatic experience into their lives by identifying its significance in the context of political and so-cial events as well as the context of their personal history."[7] This healing pro-cess was facilitated by the torture victim having been politicized even before the oppression, which again was not the case for Holocaust survivors. The au-thors report that the testimony works via a process of "catharsis," which leads to "symptomatic relief." However, testimony "does not simply express the emo-tional trauma, but facilitates its personal and social elaboration." This testimony "can have a wide distribution," through human rights and mental health net-works, both in Chile and internationally.

These authors seem to be making three very different (though not neces-sarily contradictory) claims about how testimony works: through integration, a reconnection; through catharsis, a letting go; and through acknowledgment, a making known. Overall, the Chileans convey a greater sense that individual heal-ing and social change is possible through testimony than is evident in the Ho-locaust testimonies of broken tablets. They make the claim that their testimony works effectively on several different levels. Survivors experience improvement in their traumatic stress symptoms; human rights abuses are documented; and the professional community becomes informed about this innovative method of treatment.

The Danish psychologist Inger Agger and psychiatrist Soren Jensen have also used the testimony method of psychotherapy in their work with refugee women survivors of sexual torture (from the Middle East and Central and South America) living in Denmark.[8] They too address the psychological complexities of how testimony works. Like the Chileans, Agger and Jensen focus on the survivor's isolation from the collective that was destroyed, her powerlessness in relation to the totalitarian regime, and her guilt over her own predicament in exile. For them, "testimony can be an offensive instrument for overcoming this guilt" and, as with the Chileans' emphasis on the political, in "strengthening the ideological commitment of the refugee."[9] Agger and Jensen also note testimony's dualism. Their testimony has a "double connotation"—that is, both "objective, judicial, public, or political" and "subjective, spiritual, cathartic, or private." Agger's *The Blue Room* provides an engaging exploration of what happens on the boundary between public and private life for these refugees.[10] Political violence is represented as an evil and brutish way of shattering a woman's capacity to achieve a more egalitarian place in society, forcing a retreat into a broken and humiliated private life. The testimony work took place in a blue room in Agger's apartment, and the figure of this room came to serve as a metaphor for the special healing space testimony offers the survivor, if not societies. How could testimony function in the very different spaces of Bosnia and its Diaspora?

Bosnians are also survivors of political violence, but under circumstances very different from these other three groups. Unlike many survivors of torture described in the literature, most Bosnians were not targeted because they were political activists. Rather, like Holocaust survivors they became subject to ethnic cleansing by the simple reason of their membership in the collective project that had been targeted for destruction. But unlike the Holocaust survivors, who gave their testimonies many decades later, the Bosnians were talking about ethnic cleansing proximate to (if not contemporaneous with) the genocide itself, and to their own desperate struggles to rebuild their lives and Bosnia, in the Diaspora and in Bosnia-Herzegovina.

Another important dimension is that for Bosnians, the genocide they survived came after over forty years of living together in a community of Muslims, Serbs, and Croats. And it bears restating that theirs was a communist society that had imposed substantial restrictions upon social, cultural, and political life, thus demarcating a rigid boundary between the realms of public and private existence. The giving of testimonies, and how they were received, communicated, and interpreted, must be located within the larger process of the "construction of social memory"[11] that has been preoccupying a Bosnian communality striving to redefine itself. All of these differences, which make surviving ethnic cleansing in Bosnia unique, also made the survivors' dilemmas of memory unique, and consequently the testimony work itself.

A Testimony Project

Our group started receiving testimonies in January 1993, when the first refugees from Bosnia came to Connecticut. This work continued in Connecticut through 1994, then moved to Chicago, when we established a small oral history archive for Bosnian testimonies as a part of our Project on Genocide, Psychiatry, and Witnessing at the University of Illinois at Chicago. Some seventy testimonies have been collected as of this writing.

It would not be accurate to convey that the testimony work proceeded with ease and that I and the other people involved were not often beset by struggle, confusion, and doubt. At first, we started videotaping testimonies, as in the Holocaust video archives. But survivors found that videotaping was too reminiscent of television interviews, which they experienced as intrusive and exploitative. It did not set the right interpersonal milieu for the giving of a more confessional and thoughtful testimony. So we stopped the videotaping. Compiling detailed, lengthy written narratives was more acceptable to these survivors, and indeed this form seemed better able to contain the narrative, sociohistorical, and cultural complexities of the testimony that were of greatest interest to us.

We also found that often enough the concept of testimony itself was not readily grasped by Bosnians. When Bosnians use the word "svjedocenje" for testimony, it is primarily associated with a legalistic meaning that denotes making a sworn statement before a judge.[12] One survivor said, *It is something official with legal consequences.*[13] We did not want the idea of the testimony to be constrained by this legal connotation, which could encourage the refugees to speak only in the kind of public voice that they would have been expected to use in Tito's Yugoslavia. Nor did we want the testimonies to be too closely associated with the United Nations War Crimes Tribunal, then so disparaged by Bosnians who associated it with the much-despised United Nations Protectorate Forces.

A number of survivors suggested that we use a phrase like "pricanje," or *telling your story,* as an alternative to the more legalistic "testimony."[14] Others dissented, feeling that this phrase put too much emphasis on the personal and did not draw enough attention to the social and political realities of this genocide. The effort to find a voice that could speak to both public and private dimensions of the Bosnian experience of ethnic cleansing involved continual struggle.

In one of our group discussions, a survivor defiantly counters those who are backing away from the testimony concept: *I will be glad to be a witness—to tell the truth.* Indeed, many survivors feel that they are in possession of a valuable and terrible historical truth to which they must publicly bear witness. Then there are others who back away from the nightmare of history, setting their sights elsewhere. One survivor speaking in a group meeting sums up the feelings of many who have given up on history, and who want primarily to rebuild a private life for their families, when she says, *It doesn't matter what we say. The winner makes history.*

This comment really depresses me. It is a negation of the survivors' bearing witness, of the power inherent in their remembering and telling, of the very proposition of listening to and documenting their stories. As we sit around the big table in the Bosnian Refugee Center drinking warm soda in the awkward silence that follows, Robert Lifton's teachings on the special knowledge of survivors come to mind. He wrote that what the survivor knows of genocide from personal experience can be a knowledge base for the work of making peace and preventing genocide. So I tell the group, "Survivors can write history too," and speak of the significance of remembrances of survivors of Hiroshima, the Holocaust, Armenian genocide, and the Vietnam war.

But what about the children? a survivor asks. *Must our children know of these terrible memories?* A survivor replies that she does not want her children to know because she does not want them to grow up learning to hate and feeling the desire to murder. More than a few survivors take the position that if we immerse ourselves in memories of ethnic cleansing, then it will inevitably lead to passing on hatreds and the desire for vengeance. Some other survivors speak in opposition. They say that if we had only had access to our past memories of ethnic killings from World War II, then our generation would have been better prepared for ethnic cleansing.

This dialogue starts sounding familiar. Next I expect the survivors to say that if we had only kept the memories of World War II alive, then we would have known that Serbs were murderers, and that we couldn't live together. But I am surprised; these survivors are really trying to say something different. They are not telling stories of atrocities just to demonize the Serbian people. Actually, they have not made up their minds that different peoples can't live together. They do not really know what the Bosnian future will be, but they are nonetheless able to struggle with some of the more difficult questions on the boundary between the self and history: Could we have done something different with our memories of ethnic nationalist aggression in World War II? And even more pressing, what are we now to do with our memories of ethnic cleansing? Comments like these inspire us to try to use the testimonies as a means of helping Bosnians and Bosnia come to new understandings of the dilemmas of memory that come of the personal and historical nightmares of ethnic cleansing.

Narratives of the Self's Historical Nightmare

Testimony work with survivors of state-sponsored violence, including both torture and genocide, has always been concerned with the relationship between the self and history. But in the case of ethnic cleansing in Bosnia, our experience using testimony finds self and history intertwined in new ways that deserve further exploration.

Survivors often begin their testimony by introducing their self as directly rooted in the context of history and its past nightmares. A. begins his testimony by saying: *I was born in Gacko in the war year of 1943. My father was killed when I was three months old. He fell victim of the same goal that is killing people today. My grandfather was also a victim of the same goal, but at a different time.*[15]

Survivors like A. who were old enough to have lived through World War II will often relate their direct, personal experiences of this history. Younger survivors (such as B., quoted in the Prologue of this volume), speaking what they know about Bosnian history in stories of their parents' or grandparents' lives, also portray a strong sense of the self in history.

A certain kind of historical awareness of the nightmare of World War II has been understandably heightened as a result of surviving ethnic cleansing. However, these historical memories of atrocity are deployed here not merely to justify today's desire for vengeance toward the other side (although that is an issue for some), but often enough to face the terrible price Bosnians have paid as a result of their wars. In their testimonies, survivors find themselves sharing thoughts about how World War II damaged their lives or their families' lives in ways they were unlikely to have discussed with anyone previously. Sometimes it can seem as if chronological time has collapsed and the struggle to live with the nightmares of World War II, though actually some fifty years old, dominates the realities of here and now. Ironically, it took the recent genocide and war to give Bosnians the unwelcome but invaluable chance to grasp from those old nightmarish memories some truths that could not be grasped before, given that communism had encouraged them to push those memories aside.

Survivors give testimony in which they share vignettes about unforgettable moments in their lives in Tito's Yugoslavia, emphasizing how, contrary to the ideology of Brotherhood and Unity, the links between personal and ethnic identities were made incredibly, and often painfully, clear to them. A. describes his years in the Yugoslav National Army.

My immediate squad commander . . . asked me after a whole year of service how it was possible that I was such a nice guy when the letters in my file were indicating the opposite. Then I realized what had been written about me in their files was really dark and awful. I was sort of "an enemy of the people." They believed that I came from an Ustasha family, because my father was killed in 1943 and he was not a Partisan. The Serbs were the ones who were creating the files, writing the characterizations. And if both my father and grandfather were killed by Serbs, I had to be a bad guy too. That has really hit me hard. It was in my head for years. . . .

In his head, but not in any kind of meaningful public discourse on the dangers of ethnic nationalism. No such dialogue existed in Tito's Yugoslavia.

Now in testimony, the survivors will often struggle over their memories of Tito. Their thoughts and feelings concerning Tito, who after all was primarily responsible for managing the struggles of national identity in Yugoslavia, are understandably intense and conflicted. A. wonders:

I don't know if it was good that he existed or not. Maybe it would have been better for us if he had never existed. I think about his responsibility in solving our problem: whether he was intentionally postponing the solving of our national problem or not; whether he had the power to change anything. For me, that is the most important question. I know how successful, or unsuccessful, he was in leading the country's economy. But for us Muslims, the solving of the problem of Muslim nationality and national identity was a very important one. And I don't know whether he had the power to solve it. And for us that was crucial.

In testimony, survivors are given permission to tell these stories of the memories and dreams that one kept in one's head, or maybe told only within one's family, during Tito's Yugoslavia. The testimony becomes a place for survivors to open up other difficult aspects of the complicated relationship between self and history. They struggle over how, probably without acknowledging it, they wagered their lives on the integrity of Tito's Brotherhood and Unity and lost. A. thinks back over the years of living together.

We lived in one system, and that was Tito's Yugoslavia, and that has reflected upon our lives everywhere, in schools, factories, offices, in our homes. He was speaking about this brotherhood and unity, pushing that idea, and we believed in it. I don't know why, but we believed in it. . . . But still, we believed. And we've been cheated. We've been cheated by the brotherhood and unity concept, that apparently only we believed in. We have been used by everybody. And we've been living fine and enjoying ourselves, hoping that the bad things would never happen again.

Sometimes survivors reach a point in their testimony beyond which they cannot pass. As with A., it can be the position that says we were cheated by "them"—politicians, communists, religious leaders, other ethnic groups. Far less often will the survivor implicate himself or herself—as an individual, family, culture, or way of life—for having held to a naïve view of history.

Sometimes survivors themselves can glimpse it, but even when they do not, the testimonies provide evidence of just how problematic is the place of memories of collective traumatization in relation to the imagined community of Bosnian life. Survivors' testimonies reveal that although survivors carried memories of aggression from World War II, and often the sense of the aggressor as an enemy, this was essentially not a part of a political understanding. The testimonies do not convey the sense that those memories of aggression have been linked with the idea that ethnic nationalism is a public enemy. Some survivors will note that some war criminals were punished by the state, and others went into exile, but the testimonies do not convey the sense of participating in a political culture that had a basic political understanding of what kept living together going, and what threatened its existence. Rather, in the testimonies they tend to idealize the experience of living together as a kind of dream, and reminisce nostalgically about the good old days. The more I listen to these testimonies, the more I feel that in order to consider what made ethnic cleansing in Bosnia possible, we have to listen not only for accounts of what the aggressors did, but also for the ways in which the survivors have been constructing and relating to memories of aggression in their narratives of historical nightmares.

The close relationship between self and history takes on an added dimension in our testimony work, given that the history of ethnic cleansing was far from finished when we were receiving testimonies in 1993, 1994, and 1995. We were giving survivors a chance to tell their version of this latest chapter in Balkan history before that history had been written, let alone finished. Survivors were telling stories that bore evidence of the historical events they had just lived through. Even if they had achieved a safe haven, their families and communities were still in the grip of the historical nightmare of which they spoke. What would happen with their own lives, let alone with history, was unknowable at the time they were giving their testimonies. It is only fitting that we have not been asking survivors to predict the future, or to analyze what has happened. What then do we want?

For mental health professionals like myself, as well as journalists, human rights activists, artists, and others who were committed to receiving survivors' stories, our desire to listen during the ethnic cleansing was in part motivated by an urgency to make the historical truth of genocide more widely known.[16] Many in the mass media and governments in the West had been complicit in spreading the perpetrators' message that spoke of ancient ethnic hatreds, civil wars, and Muslim fundamentalism. We operated under the belief that if more people were exposed to the truth contained in survivors' stories, it would be harder for people to be misled by leaders seeking to avoid taking responsibility or action. We endeavored to receive survivors' stories and to get those stories out, and we hoped they would mobilize others' concern and action on behalf of the Bosnian people and in opposition to genocide. We were trying to influence people's inaccurate historical perceptions in the hope that it would help to change the course of history and to save Bosnia.

Then in September 1995, President Clinton did what we had wanted done years earlier, and the military aggression against Bosnia-Herzegovina stopped. We were then forced to shift our approach in response to the demands of the post-Dayton era, with its imperatives of stopping the war and forging a lasting peace and democratic society in Bosnia. This immediately changed the whole context for testimony.

Testimony now has to serve the processes of recovery and of peacemaking in the post-Dayton milieu, with all its burdens of too much history. Our testimony work becomes an attempt to confront the dilemmas of memory of the post-war, post-ethnic cleansing, post-living together, post-communist era. Our aim now is to work with survivors to produce narratives that might lead to new understandings of the historical nightmares in Bosnian life, and importantly, a new public ethics regarding ethnic diversity. Our belief is that the transition to democracy requires new understandings of the experience of living together in Tito's Yugoslavia; these understandings must include reassessing the attitude that has been called merhamet.[17]

Reassessing Merhamet through Testimony

Because it has been at the center of the "Bosnian spirit" that inspired living together, one might think that merhamet would be a primary force in the evolutionary process of making peace and building solidarity in post-Dayton Bosnia-Herzegovina. However, as a woman in Grbavica said in her testimony, *The worst part is I used to be so open, now we all are so closed.*[18] This closedness, also associated with fear, mistrust, hatred, and extremism, is a truthful confession of what it is actually like to live in the aftermath of ethnic cleansing and its trauma to merhamet. The testimony offers a space where one can begin to reflect on what is left of the years of living together and merhamet after surviving the nightmare of ethnic cleansing. Listening to these testimonies, one gets the impression that merhamet is in real trouble.

As difficult as it is to speak of the nightmare of genocide, it can be even more painful for survivors to speak of this dream that once animated their lives. My belated discovery of merhamet in testimony with E. teaches me how important it is to assist survivors in putting the experience of living together into words. Sometimes, they are so understandably preoccupied by the memories of ethnic cleansing and the new mentalities it provokes that they may not spontaneously mention merhamet, or try to give any words at all to the multi-ethnic experience. Yet often enough, Bosnians show a strong desire to use testimony not only to name the traumas that have disrupted their lives but also to name what the years of living together mean to them.

A. spontaneously broaches the topic: *We Bosnians, we are different. We forget easier. That is Bosnian merhamet. It is deeply rooted in our culture.* And so you find that some who shared in the values of merhamet are still trying to evoke that mentality as a way of dealing with memories of ethnic cleansing. They say that they are ready to forgive the aggressors, to forget what they did, and to move on with life.

When faced with the awesome challenges of the Dayton peace accords—to develop common institutions; to hold democratic multiparty federal and municipal elections; to reconcile with former aggressors; to re-accept displaced persons—nationalist, nondemocratic, non-open mentalities are often provoked. In this context, merhamet is at risk of being abandoned, or of being submerged by the momentum toward an exclusive Muslim identity for Bosnians and their society. For some, merhamet is seen as a big part of the problem, not at all as a part of the solution.

For survivors occupying either of these positions, testimony is a chance to begin to reassess merhamet and to redefine its place in the new landscape of Bosnia-Herzegovina. What will the Bosnians now do with this element of their culture, these survivors are asked to wonder. Will merhamet overcome even what genocide has done? Will it survive? Or has merhamet become the genocide's greatest object of destruction? Was it actually responsible in part for the genocide?

In testimony, we ask survivors to share more than just their memories of aggression. We also want to know if they identify the aggressor as an enemy, and if so, in what sense. We are curious about what the survivors did or desired to do in response to the aggressors. Then we ask about their sense of merhamet toward the aggressor, be it benevolence, forgiveness, charity, mercy, or something else.

We would like to believe that the very act of speaking of merhamet in relation to memories of aggression can redeem it. That testimony stories regarding merhamet can provide narrative evidence of its centrality in the Bosnian experience. Through testimony those who say that merhamet is still alive and as strong as ever in their hearts and lives can be encouraged to talk about what they will do to make it work in the new Bosnia. But we know that that alone is not enough.

We ask them if there are contingencies associated with their sense of merhamet. Some, like A., say that we can have merhamet if a court of law prosecutes the real war criminals. Some say that we can have it if the Bosnian Serb leaders in Pale would admit their guilt in the genocide and commit to multiethnic living. Some say that we can have merhamet only if there is a strong enough army and police to protect us from ethnic nationalists. Thinking about contingencies is important because it serves to move merhamet in the direction of a more political approach to reality, something it has historically lacked.

Yet we find some survivors saying that after ethnic cleansing there is no contingency that is adequate to make merhamet work. Yet not even its strongest detractors would argue that merhamet has completely disappeared. We think that it can be valuable for Bosnians to know about the many ways merhamet will continue to influence their way of thinking about themselves and their world. We also believe that it is just as important that testimony be used to learn more about merhamet's problematics, revisiting the political culture of Tito's Yugoslavia and the place of memories of aggression from World War II.

After World War II, the moral community elevated the Partisans' defeat of fascism above all else. Though there was living together, the moral imperative of the day was not to look at how to reconcile the experiences of living together and memories of aggression from World War II. In that sense, we can say that merhamet was not really tested. Citizens of the Second Yugoslavia were never given the option to consider acting on behalf of their ethnic group and to reconcile the advantages of taking a pro-ethnic stance against the costs of mass violence and destruction. Because it was never tested, then, merhamet is something less than a moral attitude. Perhaps it is more a humanistic sentiment. That would account for the relatively plastic way many survivors react to a question about merhamet. *I don't have merhamet now, but maybe in two years, I will,* says one survivor.

But now, after ethnic cleansing, merhamet is being seriously tested. It cannot simply go dormant, then reappear unchanged. For one thing, too many survivors have said that merhamet let the Bosnian Muslims down, that it did not prevent nationalism and genocide in Bosnia. With such dramatic changes in the Bosnian landscape of memory, it is no exaggeration to say that ethnic cleansing has provoked a moral crisis concerning merhamet. How is it possible to face this moral crisis in the highly politicized atmosphere of Bosnia after Dayton? Now, merhamet is being subjected to far greater political pressure than it ever was in Tito's Yugoslavia.

We should not expect that testimony would simply purge survivors of nationalistic attitudes and strengthen merhamet, any more than it would magically purge them of their traumatic memories. But could it help them to contextualize their hatreds and vengeance, and to assist them in negotiating those attitudes—reconciling them with their opposites as a part of a moral struggle?

Testimony, with its insistence on honest personal accounts, is especially open to engaging the moral crisis, deepening and advancing the moral struggle. Testimony looks at the self's narrative constructions of these radically contradictory historical realities without totally subjecting them to the political order of the day and without overly privatizing or pathologizing them. It is not only that testimony takes place on the boundaries between the self and history; it is also that it encompasses four, if not more, distinct historical epochs: living together in Tito's Yugoslavia, the recent ethnic cleansing, the ethnic atrocities of World War II, and the post-Dayton period.

Listening to these testimony accounts of the mentality of multi-ethnic living suggests that merhamet was entirely apolitical in the sense discussed by the political theorist Carl Schmitt.[19] Schmitt wrote that the nature of the political centers on the distinctions a state and its people make between public "friends and enemies" (Schmitt, *The Political*, 26). The survival of a democracy depends in part upon its capacity to know its enemies and to combat them, forcefully if necessary. Liberalism is denounced as a "negation of the political" (p. 70) that throws a "smoke screen" (p. 84) over the realities of public friends and enemies, thereby endangering democracy. Although Yugoslavia was no liberal society, the ideology of Brotherhood and Unity created the illusion of liberalism amidst the totalitarian control of a political state and its culture. To Schmitt, there is nothing more dangerous than believing that you have no public enemies. Testimonies reveal that survivors really believed in Brotherhood and Unity and its sense of merhamet, which promised to deliver their historical dreams unto them. Schmitt implies that it was a shroud that kept them from seeing or attending to the very significant ethnic tensions and threats in Yugoslavian society. It also prevented them from attending to the haunting memories of ethnic nationalist violence, which would then eventually return with a vengeance, creating enemies anew.

Testimony seeks out two kinds of courage from survivors. The first is the courage that comes of surviving a genocide and enduring horrific physical and emotional hardship. The second is the courage that comes of the self facing the collision of two or more conflicting historical realities and figuring out who one is and what path one chooses. Testimony asks the self to struggle with that which cannot be reconciled, and to face the moral problems that come from that struggle. If merhamet is to be an element in the moral order of the new Bosnia, then it will surely have to survive this trial.

Toward a Civic Dialogue on Survivors' Remembrances

A. concludes his testimony:

I think the stories should be collected. This time we have to know our history, because otherwise, others will be falsifying the history, as they did before. All we have to do is to record the truth. We need to have our stories, our figures, and our statistics. That is why I am happy that my story has been documented.

The psychiatrist and scholar Jonathan Shay, who explored combat soldiers returning to civilian life in a fascinating reading of Vietnam against ancient Greece, cites the need for "new models of healing which emphasize communalization of the trauma."[20] Chilean testimony addressed this through collaborations between survivors, survivor groups, mental health professionals, human rights activists and organizations, and eventually, a government truth commission.[21] Conceptually, the Chilean mental health professionals thought of this as "to de-privatize their pain" (Agger and Jensen, *Trauma and Recovery*, 146), which they considered a necessary departure from the mainstream psychiatric approach toward psychotherapeutic work. Holocaust scholars have organized testimony projects in order to build a collective, historical memory out of the many particular experiences of survival.[22] Agger and Jensen report that a major goal of testimony work is to facilitate the "construction of social memory" (p. 228), a process that must accompany reconciliation.

In Bosnia-Herzegovina, this social processing of memory has suffered greatly not only from five years of genocide and war, but also as a consequence of communism and the failed transition to democracy. Bosnia in the post-Dayton era lacks the individual habits, the professional skills or ethics, the institutions, or the cultural understandings to adequately support this kind of memory work. Therefore, the successful transition to democracy and the forging of a lasting peace in Bosnia-Herzegovina will require new understandings and new initiatives concerning memory. Memories of aggression must be openly communicated and fundamentally linked to a moral understanding of the values of liberal democracy and to the identification of ethnic nationalism as its enemy. Further, the transition requires nurturance of a social dialogue where the democratic system of values and the peoples' memories of experiences have a chance to interconnect. This in turn requires that cultural elites and institutions prioritize working with remembrances, and integrate this work with democratization and with their other aims and tasks. At this moment in time, I see this work taking shape in three approaches in Bosnia-Herzegovina and its Diaspora: (1) establishing oral history projects in civic institutions; (2) facilitating interdisciplinary approaches to the study of traumatic memory in the university; and (3) developing curriculum on memories and reconciliation in elementary and secondary schools.

Oral history projects are needed in order to collect survivors' testimonies, both in Bosnia-Herzegovina and the Diaspora. In Chicago, we found that establishing testimony archives set a large group context that helped support the testimony work with individual survivors. All too often the survivor is silent, or speaks as a lone wolf. Testimony can give the individual survivor a voice that is empowering in and of itself. Many survivors would probably not tell their story if it was only "one to one" with a therapist, but because they know that their voice will be joined with many others, they suffer less fear and aloneness. Our work attempting to gather testimonies in Sarajevo and in Germany indicates that this will be equally true in Bosnia-Herzegovina.

What should these testimonies contain? First and foremost, they are to be the survivors' accounts of ethnic cleansing. Second, they are to be remembrances of living together. Third, there are the long-suppressed stories of World War II, as well as other prior episodes of historical violence that have lived on in memory, perhaps through the family and its elders. Fourth, they are to deal with the oppressive effects of the communist system, even though it was not the harshest of those seen in Europe. These testimonies must primarily focus on the dangers of ethnic nationalism and the values of multi-ethnic tolerance and understanding.

So far we have found that after telling their stories, survivors were very well aware that the testimonies they gave were something other than a deposition for legal proceedings, as necessary as that might be. They knew that their stories deserved a special reception that would somehow acknowledge and deal with them as rich and complicated historical narratives. At our Project in Chicago, we established a small archive where survivors' stories could be held. As with the Holocaust testimony projects, we sought to locate them in proximity to the Bosnian community and to the academic and professional communities. Our belief was that by better grounding the testimonies in these worlds, we could work against marginalization, and toward developing new understandings and new approaches.

When professionals and scholars, artists and writers, community leaders and educators, groups and institutions get involved in the process of giving, receiving, and working with survivors' testimonies, there is the possibility of opening the way for societies to develop a civic dialogue on survivors' memories. A testimony project brings a critical mass of survivors' stories into a special social context. The psychologist Daniel Schaecter points out that this kind of large-scale yet individualized approach offers some increased protection against the distortion and manipulation of testimony that comes when a very small number of stories, with all their potential for being nonrepresentative, are involved.[23] It allows for the development of an open, group dialogue on the critical issues of reconciling the memories of living together with those of ethnic atrocities. It creates a safe social space in which a community can struggle toward developing a collective narrative of historical memory, and can invite others into that dialogue.

However, there are many obstacles to the gathering of testimonies. The first set of obstacles are practical: those having to do with the daily hardships that make individual, family, and institutional life so difficult for most Bosnians. The second set has to do with the legacy of communism itself, which encourages people to silence memories of ethnic atrocities in order to promote living together; to disavow any collective memory because of the taint of mistrust associated with the collective forgetting of Brotherhood and Unity; to escape from history into private life and private memories. But fear is probably the biggest obstacle to testimony. It is all too obvious, with the provisions of Dayton, that this history is not over with. The perpetrators and criminals are still on the loose. Nobody really knows who or what entity will be in power in the years to come. There is also the all too real fear of exploitation of these testimonies by anyone who wants to seize on a memory and misuse it. The shattering of trust, so common in traumatized individuals, families, and communities, is pervasive in Bosnians.[24]

The establishment of testimony projects in Bosnia-Herzegovina and the

Diaspora would be a necessary step in developing a civic dialogue on survivors' memories there. That is why I have been calling for the establishment of testimony projects in Sarajevo, to start. To best reflect the multi-ethnic communality of Bosnia, these projects should include survivors of ethnic cleansing and war not only from the three major ethnic communities in Bosnia—Muslims, Orthodox, and Catholics—but also from the so-called "mixed" persons. Listening to the stories of Bosnian Orthodox and Catholics, which will undoubtedly contain some stories of persecution by Muslims, will be hard for some. But there is much more to be lost by not including their voices. It would send a clear signal that the new Bosnia has overtly nonpluralistic and nondemocratic designs.

The testimony projects in Bosnia-Herzegovina should be located in relation to institutions of higher education. This would keep the body of testimonies in contact with an interdisciplinary intellectual community of students and scholars, increasing the likelihood that the testimonies would become connected with their ongoing studies. I picture students in history, sociology, religion, literature, and psychology going to the testimony archives, using them in their papers and presentations, and growing up intellectually, morally, and politically in relation to them.

The testimonies are by no means primarily psychotherapy, and the phenomenon they bear is not exclusively psychiatric. An interdisciplinary approach will be needed to address the testimonies adequately, and especially the dilemmas of memory they contain. Psychiatrists must join with historians, anthropologists, sociologists, journalists, politicians, human rights activists, and artists. Interdisciplinary methodologies for receiving, collecting, studying, and transmitting survivors' testimonies must be developed. Yet such disciplinary boundaries are often not easy to breach. In Bosnia-Herzegovina, there is the added problem that the educational institutions are poor and depleted, and in the face of the shattering of their way of life, scholars and teachers may cling ever more tightly to that which they knew, and resist the new.

When Tvrtko Kulenovic and I presented a three-day seminar in Sarajevo, in October 1997, we hoped it would serve as a step in the interdisciplinary direction. We called it "Dilemmas of Collective Memory and History: A Workshop for Interdisciplinary Inquiry in Sarajevo."[25] The very title we chose caused some sparks to fly. *We are victims of collective memory*, said one physician, to which many heads nodded in agreement. He meant the collective memory of Serbian suffering, which had been associated with virulent ethnic nationalism and which stood behind ethnic cleansing. There was also the matter of the collective forgetting of communism's Brotherhood and Unity, by which they all felt duped. I don't want to be a part of any of these collectives, they seemed to be saying. Collective had left too bad a taste in their mouths. Fortunately, we were able to examine it together and not get stuck there.

The participants were researchers, scholars, professionals, writers, or artists, actively engaged in work that addressed survivors' remembrances. We chose not to present a highly structured research plan. Rather, we presented the totality of possibilities of interdisciplinary inquiry into memory with the explicit intent of impressing people with its difference from the accustomed ways of thinking about these things in contemporary Sarajevo. We taught current methodologies, approaches, and techniques concerning the interdisciplinary study of collective memory (with an emphasis on literary and psychological approaches). We shared the language, attitude, and approaches to understanding issues and problems of collective memory. We were aiming to develop an interdisciplinary community and dialogue interested in nonpartisan approaches to survivors' remembrances. I am not proclaiming that it was a success, because to know that I would have to see it translated into actual work, which it of course has not been as yet and probably won't be for some time. On the other hand, we think that this kind of international, interdisciplinary dialogue and collaboration is just what will be needed to develop new ways of thinking and working with memories.

Just saying these words, which look forward to successful ways of working, brings to mind their opposite. One clinician who attended the workshop professed total enthusiasm for what was discussed, then before parting, let slip, *I will soon have more opportunity for creative endeavors*. In other words, he had just lost his salary. It is awfully hard to think about history when day-to-day living is so impossibly hard.

Communalization of survivors' memories will certainly require more than scholarship and intellectual dialogue. Creative artworks are necessary to confront the experience of atrocity and to help facilitate the transmission of knowledge of genocide. The imaginative force that they bear can engage traumatic memories without letting fear, hatreds, and mistrust dominate. Art can show the possibility of creating narratives and images that do not intentionally or inadvertently succumb to the violence and nationalism that has shattered the way things were. Art can bridge the personal and the historical in the most believable ways. Jonathan Shay points out that in ancient Greece, theaters were actually located in healing centers.[26] With its rich cultural history, Bosnia could yet develop new kinds of working alliances between mental health professionals and creative artists.

The issue provoked by testimonies is not only the transmission of traumatic memories, understandably of interest to trauma clinicians, but also the transmission of the totality of value systems upon which a people's survival depends. How does a society treat its younger generation and transmit to them its collective memories and values?[27] The International Commission on the Balkans recommended the establishment of joint historical commissions to make new guidelines for writing textbooks that do not abuse history "for nationalist purposes."[28] What better way to approach the telling of history than through testimonies, which provide the best possible evidence of how history has been misunderstood and misused, but which also inspired and strengthened an open, democratic view. Survivors' testimonies should be at the center of innovative curricular approaches to teaching youths about Bosnian history. Such approaches have been developed in the West concerning the Holocaust, civil rights, human rights, and international identity.[29]

As A. says, we cannot afford to end the testimony, because the survivor's story has far to go on its journey into history.

Well, this story could last for years. I have no illusions that I told you everything because each and every day of that time is a whole story. Sometimes, one hour of a day was a story. But I am pleased at being able to tell you this whole story. And I will be happy if my story can help anyone. If it is recorded for history.

As for the survivor H., in a follow-up meeting we ask if we can read from his testimony at some presentations to professional groups. He says that he would be deeply honored. After each presentation, we'd call him up to let him know how people responded, and what they said. Most memorable was the time we invited him to present his story in person with us to a group of clergy, ethicists, and mental health professionals in Chicago. His story, more so than any published book or newspaper article, really communicates the truths of surviving ethnic cleansing. When he saw for himself that his voice was being heard and that something was being understood about Bosnia, the look on his face showed he felt something strong and good.

Finding New Ways of Being Professional

From the testimonies of several academic psychiatrists, I learn that in Tito's Yugoslavia psychiatrists by and large avoided addressing the post-traumatic psychological sequelae in civilian and military survivors of World War II. They report that some professionals heard survivors' stories, but these stories were not systematically collected, reflected upon, discussed, or analyzed. (Jovan Raskovic in Croatia is a notorious exception.) Only rarely did individual psychiatrists do trauma-oriented work with survivors. This kind of work was not taught, studied, or practiced. As late as the 1980s, the leading psychiatric textbooks in Yugoslavia did not even mention post-traumatic conditions related to war or genocide.[30]

Ethnic cleansing and war made abundantly clear the immense disadvantages of Bosnian psychiatrists' not having acquired the clinical skills to address war-trauma-related conditions. It also showed that Bosnian psychiatrists had no particular expertise regarding survivors' memories, no psychological or historical view that prioritized survivors' stories, and no more investment in a civic dialogue on survivors' memories than anyone else in Bosnia.

During the ethnic cleansing and siege, mental health professionals were drowning in survivors' stories, and they did what they could. There were scores of individual efforts to hear the stories, to relieve suffering, and more than a few efforts to gather testimonial evidence for the war crimes tribunal. But neither governmental nor nongovernmental mental health organizations developed anything resembling Holocaust or Chilean testimony. This was largely a consequence of the very real problems of enduring genocide, siege, and war. After all, they did not have the tape recorders, computers, money, time, institutional support, or safe space we did in the rich world. All they really wanted to do was survive. But it was probably also a consequence of the larger tendency to push aside memories of aggression, which was the norm in Yugoslav Bosnian society.

It would be wrong, though, to imply that international mental health professionals who trained the Bosnians in trauma work during the aggression, and the whole tradition of trauma mental health work, were not in some ways also implicated by this unpreparedness. During the ethnic cleansing and war, international mental health experts poured into Bosnia-Herzegovina and Croatia in order to teach them trauma mental health work and to organize programs to help survivors. In sharing their expertise on trauma with Bosnian professionals, who had a lot to learn about trauma work, the internationals did much good. During the siege of Sarajevo and the ethnic cleansing of Bosnia, the priority was on providing humanitarian assistance. International mental health professionals were caught up in the same bind as all humanitarian projects—you may help the sufferer, but not confront the aggressors. This severing of the humanitarian from the political may have discouraged international mental health professionals from adequately attending to survivors' memories and the ethical dilemmas they present.

But now, with the transition to a postcommunist, post-genocidal, postwar psychiatry and mental health system underway, professionals redefining their work with survivors and their memories cannot afford to ignore these issues. What is required is nothing short of a radical redefinition of the professional identity of the psychiatrist in Bosnia-Herzegovina, as well as the development of new understandings by the international psychiatrists who work with them.

For the internationals and Bosnians, this will require more than attention to treating PTSD, which presents a risk of overly privatizing and pathologizing the experience. It will require that the approach to trauma survivors be accompanied by a serious consideration of the ethics of professionals' relationship to genocide and to survivors' memories in Bosnia-Herzegovina. That will require a greater depth of understanding of the Bosnian landscape of memory than most internationals, not to mention most Bosnian mental health professionals, have thus far acquired.[31]

The new understandings that need to be reached are consistent with the point of view that the medical professional participates not only in a narrow biomedical role, but actually in a broader social, political, and cultural project, especially when it comes to social traumas.[32] The basic proposition that psychiatrists and other health care workers explicitly see their work with survivors in relationship with social and political processes is familiar to the evolving movement of mental health and human rights.[33]

The Chilean professionals spoke of the position of "ethical non-neutrality" and the "bond of commitment," which reflects an ideology according to which professionals are to make links between their patients' symptoms and sociopolitical processes, and to take positions (in therapy and in public) on the etiologically significant human rights violations.[34] Dori Laub spoke of the role of the physician as a "witness" to the trauma survivor in the sense that the physician must fill the void and be there to document the historical truth of social traumas.[35] Robert Jay Lifton has described the role of the "witnessing professional," deploying professional expertise within a carefully drawn ethical and historical framework to address both the individual survivors of traumatic situations and the communal and historical dislocations within which the traumas took place.[36] Supported by these ideological structures, mental health professionals receiving survivors' stories have been able to participate in larger processes of social and political change, in a number of different sociohistorical contexts.

Yet insights such as these into the relationship between the personal and the collective, the psychological and the sociopolitical, have never come easy. Even in the relatively privileged conditions of the West, the development of a human rights and mental health movement has taken a long, long time. We should also note that it was not until three or four decades after World War II that psychiatry started to pay more systematic attention to the struggles and stories of survivors of the Holocaust and that there have been similar time gaps concerning other instances of genocide, such as the Armenians and the Cambodians. To this day, there is still a tendency to see social and political traumas through privatizing or pathologizing approaches. The paradigm of PTSD, which frames the psychiatric approach to surviving trauma, dominates the mental health professionals' approach.[37] Is there another way?

Agger and Jensen identify the "wounded healer" as one who may be able to transcend such limitations, in spite but also because of the problems their condition also presents to them (*Trauma and Recovery*, 87–88). They quote Jung: "only the wounded physician heals." They believe that the personal suffering of a healer who has also been traumatized can enable that healer to develop greater empathy and understanding of trauma survivors. What's more, the healer's involvement in human rights work and engagement in a political project can in turn be spread to other survivors through prevention and clinical work, as well as interdisciplinary collaborations with other domains of human rights work.

Dori Laub makes the claim that psychiatrists can be witnesses, not because they themselves are necessarily survivors (which in his case was true), but because they are fundamentally engaged in transmitting survivors' stories in a way that may stimulate the survivor to tell the story in the first place.[38] Now in Bosnia, most if not all professionals have their own trauma experiences and memories to draw from. If Bosnian mental health professionals are to redefine themselves, then they may very well have to begin with the understandings and approaches they derive from their relationship with their own traumatic experiences, memories, and nightmares.

This is not to say that mental health professionals are the only people who can be witnesses. But their work as psychological trauma healers puts them in a likely position to receive survivors' stories, and gives them the means to interpret and transmit those stories. They have the skills of nuanced interviewing and listening that can help to establish the interpersonal conditions that make testimony possible. Their expertise with narrative approaches embraces a special commitment to eliciting, receiving, documenting, understanding, and communicating survivors' stories. Psychiatrists and other mental health professionals who work with survivors are in a privileged position for developing a civic dialogue on survivors' memories. It can be done with activities that are a part of many professionals' lives: teaching other professionals, educating the public, building and strengthening social networks, changing organizations and institutions.

Testimony work requires not only certain technical skills, but also an ethical knowing of survivors' memories and one's own relationship with them. Before doing testimony work, the professional must undergo a process of moral and psychological preparation in order to be positioned as a receiver of testimony. Little is known about the nature of this process or how to nurture it. We stand to learn a great deal from those Bosnian professionals who will chronicle their own journeys to redefine themselves as professionals in this time of great historical change.

Another important aspect of the possible transformation in professional work stems from how the testimonies open up new approaches to conducting research. As in the testimony itself, the primary commitment in the intellectual inquiry into testimonies is to survivors and their stories. The testimony researcher endeavors to avoid becoming merely an appendix to a diagnosis, a scale, or a theory. The researcher is as committed to questioning his or her own beliefs as to questioning the survivors in testimony. This may render the work nonobjective, in the sense that it does not follow a scientific methodology. However, that does not mean that it is without discipline. Nor is it without precedent: the emphasis upon intensive biographical interviewing, survivors' narratives, ethical commitment, and moral reading has also been evident in the "advocacy research" of Robert Jay Lifton, the "normative ethics" of Philip Hallie, and the testimony writings of Inger Agger and Soren Jensen, Dori Laub and Shoshana Felman, to name a few.[39]

The testimony sets up a comparatively egalitarian relationship between the survivor and the researcher.[40] The latter is there to listen and learn from the survivors. The survivor is encouraged to raise questions about the researcher and all that role represents to the survivor. This unique relationship then becomes a part of the researcher's intellectual inquiry in the form of a double confession. The survivor has given testimony to the researcher, who in turn gives testimony to the reader, with the same commitment to detailed, close, honest reflection. In doing so, the researcher, like the survivor, cannot stay removed from the stories. The professional must necessarily take sides.

Testimony translates into a kind of scholarship that is not necessarily about constructing a theory or testing a hypothesis. Testimony research yields a narrative that can be of use for survivors, educators, professionals, intellectuals, artists, and others. This narrative does not invite within only a narrow group of readers who share a common professional language or preoccupations. Like the testimonies themselves, this narrative of intellectual inquiry focuses us on major social issues, but also on the question of how we define ourselves.

The researcher seeks not so much to avoid the problems of nonobjectivity as to exploit its possible benefits. The inquiry seeks out encounters, collisions, conflicts, and confrontations between the different voices, different sides, including that which is known and that which is not. For survivors, professionals, and readers, the aims of entering into this narrative can be to become more aware of: how we listen and know; how we live with suffering in our midst; how we live with oppression and traumas in our midst; how we can make meaningful changes in the self that support taking action in the social and political realms.

And yet the inescapable fact of Bosnia-Herzegovina today is that there are far more suicides than testimonies. Isn't there a way in which each suicide says that taking one's life is a sensible response to the weight of living with too much history? The futility of their struggle was also anticipated by Joseph Roth. "The old revolver that Herr von Trotta had taken along pressed in his back pocket. What good was a revolver? They saw no bears and no wolves in the borderland. All they saw was the collapse of the world!"[41]

No countervailing narrative proposition exists in Bosnia-Herzegovina that can overcome all the loss, destruction, and misery. The search for memory cannot be readily resolved, despite the yearnings. Not tens of thousands of Schindler-inspired testimonies would be enough to contain much too much history to bear. Testimony work is based on the human desire to tell and to listen to stories no matter how difficult things are in reality. It could be said to "work" to the extent that it brings the survivor, the researcher, and the listeners into contact with the dilemmas of memory that are at the center of the struggles for individual and societal recovery. By no means should we ever consider the proposition of testimony to be some kind of solution to Bosnia's current and future dilemmas. It cannot guarantee healing or justice, at an individual or a collective level; but perhaps it can assist in the development of a better knowing, where many have their say, and the history that is learned is also more knowledgeable about memory processes and the significance of remembrances. Now, in the post-Dayton era, as Bosnians wake up from their nightmare, the time is right to begin.

Artists Witnessing Ethnic Cleansing

Chapter 8

Fantastic Reality

"Everything in the world exists to be turned into a book," wrote Danilo Kis, one of the great Yugoslav writers of the post-World War II generation.[1] Kis, whose father disappeared in World War II, was quite aware of what the twentieth century had included in this everything. Kis's piece, "The Gingerbread Heart," is considered one of the finest essays written against nationalism. Susan Sontag read from this essay at the 1993 New York PEN benefit for writers in Sarajevo, and though written a decade earlier, it still had the ring of truth.

In "Schizopsychology," a lesser-known essay found in a collection of his writings edited by Sontag, Kis confronts the destruction wrought by nationalistic violence. He applies Dostoyevsky's quote, "Nothing is more fantastic than reality" (Kis, *HomoPoeticus*, 52), to the atrocity-scarred twentieth century: "Hiroshima is the focal point of that fantastic world, whose contours could first be discerned at about the time of the First World War" (p. 53). Kis describes that fantastic reality as "the ghastly sight of a city resembling the moon's surface with two hundred thousand corpses and human bodies disfigured on a staggering scale" (p. 52).

How should the writer address this "fantastic reality"? "The writer has an obligation to put that paranoid reality on paper, to examine the absurd plexus of circumstance on the basis of documents, probes, investigations, and to avoid proffering personal, arbitrary diagnoses or prescribing medicines and cures" (p. 54).

Danilo Kis died of lung cancer on October 15, 1989, three weeks before the fall of the Berlin Wall. His friend Susan Sontag writes, "Happily—it is the only thing about his premature death which gives some consolation—he didn't live to see the collapse of the multi-confessional, multiethnic state of which he was a citizen" (p. viii).

Nor did Kis live to struggle with the problems of writers and artists during the years of ethnic cleansing, siege, and war, when creative artists were confronted by the most fantastic reality in their streets, schools, and homes. Most fantastic of all was the trauma being perpetrated upon a way of life, but also the people's struggles to resist, survive, and claim a future. Writing and art have been important tools in those struggles.

Unfortunately we will never know what Kis would have discovered had he lived and written in a Sarajevo like the surface of the moon. In this chapter I discuss the work of several other creative artists and writers who occupied the "fantastic reality" that was Sarajevo during the siege and wrote and made art of witness. This discussion is necessarily incomplete, because there are many artists whose works touch upon ethnic cleansing who will not be discussed, and because (it is hoped) many more creative artists will step up with artworks in years to come. Yet it is not too early to begin looking at art that bears witness to genocide and exploring what art has uniquely contributed to the confrontation with ethnic cleansing and its memories.

Diaries

The diary, a literary form in and of itself, was abundantly written by Sarajevans during the war, and these have been getting published and read.[2] Eventually there will be scores of diaries, written by Bosnians and internationals, politicians, journalists, doctors, writers, and even children.

Why should diaries be discussed here, in a chapter on creative artists? For one thing, diaries are mostly what was written in Sarajevo during the siege. The traumas of Sarajevo compelled non-creative writers and nonwriters to write about their horrific experiences. Even the amateur writer was also trying to fulfill Kis's mandate—to put that fantastic reality down on paper—although not necessarily equipped with the tools of expression a creative writer brings to the page.

I have chosen to look at two published diaries written by survivors who were not creative artists. One is the diary of an adolescent girl, the other of a professional journalist. Their texts allow us to consider: How can a diary confront the memories of ethnic cleansing and find meaning there? How does the desire to bear witness shape the very form of a diary? How may it succeed in the representation and transmission of the survivor's experience?

Nadja Halilbegovic's *Sarajevo's Childhood Wounded by War* was published in 1995 by the Turkish Ministry of Culture.[3] It is a physically slight book—consisting of multiple daily entries, from May 31, 1992 through March 21, 1994—that conveys the existential horrors of the siege. Many but not all of the entries begin "Dear Diary."

In her first entry, Nadja explains her reasons for writing. She says her writing is part of a public dialogue:

> I watched all those war images of Sarajevo on television and all the hard feelings I kept within myself I transferred onto the paper. My texts and rhymes were broadcast in the programs of radio and television of Bosnia and Herzegovina. (Halilbegovic, *Sarajevo's Childhood,* 9)

Her writing did not serve only a domestic public function. In that same entry she makes clear that her writing was also crucial psychological work for the young self struggling to survive a war:

> All that misfortune forced me to start with the writing of my war diary. The echoes of shells are taking me back to this war May Sunday and our reality. Watching them destroying my town, every time something breaks in my heart and thus, still not realizing why is this happening to us, I am gradually forgetting those quiet and so to say happiest days of my childhood. (p. 9)
> I am trying to find myself in this nightmare. (p. 9)

The public side of Halilbegovic's writing was ostensibly for those citizens remaining in Bosnia who listened to her stories on the radio or read of them in the papers. But in the third entry, June 2, 1992, Nadja makes it clear that she is also trying to communicate with those who have left Bosnia and are scattered around the globe: "I decided that my war Diary is not going to be my privacy and I hope that some of my friends who have gone 'far away' will read it and understand what was going on, when they read what a young soul felt and wrote" (p. 10).

The next entry finds her defending and ennobling her family's choice to stay: "We remained here, in our birthplace. We remained here because we have a right to love, help, live. Even sharing the last piece of bread in love and happiness" (p. 10).

Much of the diary reads as a rather straightforward account of the daily experience of remaining in Sarajevo. After Kis, we want to know, how does Nadja's diary attempt to capture that fantastic reality? And, how does her diary deal with merhamet?

Some passages, like that of July 4, 1992, have a narrative power that comes of using clear, simple imagery to describe something terrible that Nadja heard about or saw.

> It is a bloody day today. A massacre happened in an orchard, while children were collecting cherries. Maybe even unripe cherries but eagerly awaited as prime fruit and utmost joy for children. Seven innocents were killed only because they wanted to refresh with a few cherries. (p. 11)

Other strong passages occur where Nadja tells the story of something terrible that happened to her. The story of her injury from a shell explosion has an emotional intensity equal to any survivor's account of atrocity. She struggles with the survivor's dilemma: is it a nightmare or is it real? She worries about the other children she meets who appear worse off. Will she use up bandages and blood that could go to another in greater need?

Under the strain of war, she still has merhamet for her fellow Sarajevans: "Today I was given a gift-parcel with food, received from "Merhamet" as a wounded person. I am very grateful for such care although I know there are thousands of those who would need the same care" (p. 23).

She has no "merhamet" for the people who are shooting at her city, calling them "murderers, criminals, black birds" (p. 17), and "beasts" (p. 43). Survivors will endure their nightmare and rediscover their dreams, but as for those on the other side:

> Only you black bird,
> only you, will exist
> never again. (p. 17)

Many passages develop a narrative tension around the opposition between this war, many times called "nightmare," and peace. Running parallel is the narrative tension between Nadja's sense of her emerging adolescence and her vanishing childhood. On March 5, 1993, she wrote:

> I have almost forgotten how did the morning look when you were not awoken by the sound of shells, I have forgotten what was a quiet day and a peaceful sleep. I am getting used to this, I do not know how to call it, humiliated life. I do not go to school again, I do not play. I do not know. I again think that these days, weeks, years go by in vain. I do not know whether we are ever going to come out of this insane war. (p. 33)
>
> Sorry my dear Diary, because I am so sad today and even to myself I seem to be somehow grown up, mature as well as the other children. We have matured too early. (p. 33)

Nadja skillfully exploits these oppositions—the adolescent growing old on war/the child who knew not of war—in a way that gives the reader a handhold on the overwhelming experience of surviving genocide.

> On the steps near my school I see a body. It does not show any sign of life. It shocked me even more and later I found out it was a woman without a head. . . . If people who live in freedom hear about this, they will probably think about it and ask themselves as to how such monstrous words of experience may come out from the mind of a fourteen year old day dreamer and they are not going to be able to comprehend that such things happen and have happened at a, I say that with pride, cross-road of the BIG EUROPE. (pp. 64–65)

Ideas such as these were common parlance in Sarajevo. Young people heard their parents say these things all the time. All citizens feel the strain of massive historical dislocations, but adolescents are uncommonly open to their resonance with the changing developmental seasons of their own young lives. Nadja's child-hood corresponds to the years of living together in Bosnia; her adolescence cor-responds to the years of ethnic cleansing; and her adulthood corresponds to the post-Dayton Bosnian future. Those adolescents with gifts of self-expression, like Nadja, can communicate this synchronicity of experience with unusual clarity. This departure from the straight, chronological descriptive narrative makes Nadja's book something other than a diary and connects it with other writings and artworks of witnessing.

The diary was also used as a literary form by the professional writer. To date, the best-known example of this narrative is *Sarajevo: A War Journal*, written by Zlatko Dizdarevic. Dizdarevic is a journalist for Sarajevo's daily newspaper *Oslobodenje*. He lived in Sarajevo during the siege, and as a writer, bore witness to the genocide from the inside while it was happening. His *War Journal* con-sists of fifty-nine entries, each a few pages in length, written in the first year of the siege, from April 25, 1992, to August 18, 1993.[4]

Dizdarevic's writings on Sarajevo are not journalistic as that term is usually understood. Though he presents many facts, he is not primarily reporting fac-tual information. He is writing about the truth that has emerged out of his ex-perience as a survivor. He does not write with a journalist's "objective" voice. He is speaking to us with the fierceness and desperation of one who fears that he, and his city, may not survive. The cognitive tone, though very thoughtful, is not contemplative but "written in spontaneous reaction to what was happen-ing." This is what he says about his writing:

> These pieces are an attempt to tell what is happening to ordinary
> people, who find it incredible that such events can take place in plain
> view of the world, under the eyes of those who claim to respect justice,
> order, law, and liberty. (Dizdarevic, *Sarajevo*, 7)

Dizdarevic places the truth at the center of his writings. "The truth itself is 'occupied,'" he writes. "Instead of the truth of what is actually being done to our city, people will be told monstrous lies by those who have come to 'liberate' us" (p. 13). His work is "to strike out at the lies—the lie has slithered in amongst us—and to be the bearer of the truth" (p. 160). There is nothing sentimental about the deadeye accuracy with which Dizdarevic chronicles the strangeness and otherness of life in Sarajevo: "This is not a war. This is a horror that has no name. It is a black hole in the spectrum of all reasoned thought" (p. 172).

He tells many stories of people who are living in fear and desperation but deploy black humor to cope with the surreality of their situation. He animates their losses: "That's what this war is, nothing but a long good-bye. You say good-bye to your illusions and your past, your dreams, your habits, hopes and projects, all things great and small, and all the places inseparable from days gone by. You even say good-bye to the simple things that make up a life" (p. 61). And their existential bind: "As bad as things were, the emptiness is worse."[5]

He assaults the lies that obscure the harsh realities of genocide by saying, "It's an outbreak of sheer madness, and no one knows what it's all about. . . . It is a war in which everyone fights everyone else, and you can't make sense out of it" (p. 3). Dizdarevic employs a brutally ironic tone to make his points: "It's all right to shoot paramedics, kidnap children, 'arrest' entire villages, steal international humanitarian aid supplies; now it's even all right to turn around television transmitter" (pp. 13–14).

What kind of text is Dizdarevic's *Sarajevo: A War Journal?* How does it attempt to capture that fantastic reality? How does it deal with "merhamet"? Dizdarevic writes that the text is composed of "pieces" (p. 7) that were written during the siege, pieces that "tell what is happening to ordinary people in a city that refuses to die" (p. 7). He says that the text was written to "broadcast a warning" (p. 7). He says that his text is one of "witnessing: to a renaissance of Nazism and Fascism; to the abolition of all recognized human values" (p. 7).

On the one hand, his text is a journal, telling one man's story of life and death in his city. The journal gives close and detailed portraits of Sarajevans living during the siege. Story after story tells us what life was like in the "depths of human misery" (p. 179) for Sarajevans of all kinds.

In addition to being part journal, his text contains many elements of the essay. Each entry is dated, but also titled. The writings tell stories about the events of the day, but they are also full of thoughtful reflection, such as one might find in a newspaper's commentary section. Many of the stories are clearly shaped by ideas, and at times are trying to address a conceptual point or even prove a thesis—primarily to prove that "what is happening in Bosnia-Herzegovina is not a civil war" (p. 4) and to show that the Serbs have been committing genocide. A secondary purpose of most of the pieces is to implicate the passive bystanders of the world community for their lapses.

The text, in its commitment to telling stories, to relating subjective experience, is a purposeful rejection of the journalist's objectivity. By speaking in the survivor's voice, decidedly un-neutral, Dizdarevic offers something other, and tries to engage the reader in another paradigm: a survivor bearing witness.

This mixing of journal and essay is partly what accounts for the text's narrative force. It provides stories, journal-style, of experiencing the genocide. It also cuts with insight, essay-style, into the mentality of surviving and the mentality of passive bystanding. By combining these elements it is able to say: I mean to tell you that there is something happening that you must see, that I will show you (in the hope that some of you may then see), and at the very same time, I will condemn you for not seeing it, for a blindness that is certainly at risk of continuing.

Dizdarevic never mentions merhamet directly, but he is thinking about multi-ethnic living when he says: "Nothing is the way it used to be, and it never will be again" (p. 35). He speaks of a member of an old Sarajevan family, "a man who has built his whole life on the idea of tolerance, forgiveness, and a remarkably strong sense of attachment to his neighbors" (p. 33), who now openly wishes to fire the bullet that kills Radovan Karadzic. Then there is the entry of May 8, 1992, called "Dirty Politics," in which he discusses the father of a three-year-old child shot by snipers who "invites the assassin to a cup of coffee" (p. 16). This father does not seek revenge, but says, "One day her tears will catch up with him" (p. 15). Dizdarevic's response:

> There is absolutely nothing to be done for this nation. It will never attain justice and happiness if it cannot bring itself to recognize an executioner as an executioner, a murderer as a murderer, a criminal as a criminal. If the most barbaric act imaginable in this war, a sniper shooting at a three-year-old girl playing in front of her own home, elicits only an invitation to a cup of coffee and hope for forgiveness, then Bosnia-Herzegovina doesn't stand much chance to survive. (pp. 15–16)

Dizdarevic likens Sarajevo to a madhouse, and the United Nations to its doctors: "To put it bluntly: we will never find our way out of this madness in a madhouse where both the patients and the therapists are collaborating against sanity" (p. 17). For Dizdarevic, the merhamet Bosnians once knew is over, and feelings of vengeance are expectable and understandable. But the nightmare and madness will not be over until there is some form of internationally brokered justice. Then we shall see what will be the collective shape of one man's quickness to vengeance, or another's willingness to forgive.

Both diaries demonstrate that to endure this siege and ethnic cleansing, just writing a diary is not enough. The victim writes not only for the self, but in the context of a relationship to others, real and imagined, outside and inside the experience of survival. A diary can be a means of communication to these others, but like any other form of communication, it cannot be entirely trusted to convey the reality of the survival experience. The survivor/writer must double back on the diary's intent; introducing other formal elements into the diary; calling into question its ability to communicate the survivors' experience at the same time as it is expanding that experience.

Some conversations with Zlatko Dizdarevic help me to learn just how difficult it is to live and write within the dilemmas of this fantastic reality. In April 1994, between sessions at a conference on "War Crimes in Bosnia" at the Yale Law School, we have a few beers down the block at Naples Pizzeria in New Haven and talk together about his life and work.

At the time Dizdarevic is the celebrity journalistic witness of the moment. Upon the publication of his book just a few months previously, with introductory pieces by Joseph Brodsky and Robert Jay Lifton, he is invited to attend the PEN International Benefit for Sarajevo writers at the Symphony Space in New York City. I remember how visibly uncomfortable he seemed with celebrating Sarajevo writers in the bright lights of the New York literary scene.

Where this discomfort was coming from becomes clearer to me as we talk, six months later in New Haven.[6]

I'm writing really what I want to write. I'm writing from my gut. I don't care about reactions. I don't have nothing to lose. I don't work on the basis of any calculations. I just think that if I'm in a position to say something, or write something, I must say what I mean and write what I mean, and I don't care.

Dizdarevic cannot exclude himself and his celebrity from the clarity of this vision. He sees that despite his privileged position—being able to publish a book, present on TV and at fancy international conferences—there is the distinct possibility that *the real result of my working, my talking, my writing, strategically is zero. It's nothing.*

The writing itself is one thing. Dealing with people's reactions to the writing is another. He cannot help believing that he is being celebrated as a witness by politicians and intellectuals, in the same countries that are doing little or nothing to stop ethnic cleansing, so that these parties can flatter themselves that they are taking a stand. Dizdarevic is acutely aware that he was being used like a minstrel singing a sentimental song to create the illusion that the listeners actually felt for Bosnia, and that their governments were actually committed to saving Bosnia.

You know, in the end my book is translated into five different languages. It sold more than 70,000 copies. I don't know, maybe this 70,000 copies means that 70,000 people around the world today are thinking a little bit differently than yesterday. It's not easy to say. I'm personally very, very tired after all this.

He speaks from within the exhaustion that any survivor knows. It comes of trying exceptionally hard to make bystanders see truths that they do not want to see. But I have the distinct impression that he is also speaking as a writer of diaries who feels constrained by the limits of the diary in addressing ethnic cleansing's fantastic reality.

Take a Photograph

Ordinary Bosnians who were enduring ethnic cleansing wouldn't have had much time, if any, to pause to take a photograph; but Sarajevans living in a city under siege for several years did take out their cameras to put their experiences on film. Some videotapes were even shown at a competition organized by the Bosnia

PEN center in Sarajevo in 1993. It was one of many events in Sarajevo during the siege that celebrated the arts as a means of resistance to nationalistic violence.

Whether by their own cameras, or by another's, Sarajevans are probably the most photographed group of victims of genocide of all time. Photographers from the international press were a constant presence in the city. The attitude of many Sarajevans toward the international photographers is captured in a story told to me by a young Bosnian woman. A sniper shot her in the head while she was running across a bridge over the river Miljacka in Sarajevo. A photographer had set up a tripod there, on the site where sniper attacks were likely to occur, waiting for the next victim, which this time happened to be her. She said that she honestly hated the photographer more than she hated the one on the hill who put a bullet into her head.

Photographers such as the one waiting by the bridge were there to visually record history in photographic images for the mass media. The print journalists' stories needed pictures, and there were many great pictures to be had during the siege in Sarajevo. Early in the siege Bosnians wanted their experience to be photographed. There was a special belief in the photograph, that it could totally capture these all too unbelievable historical events and make their occurrence indisputable. Photographs could give better proof of an event's happening than a story. The journalists' photographs could be used to capture definitively the historical truth of ethnic cleansing and the siege. Individual Sarajevans, and the Bosnian government as well, encouraged the international photographers to keep taking pictures and to show them abroad.

But at some point a line was crossed, and the photographers' continued presence in the absence of meaningful responsive action by the international community became an unwanted parody of genuine witnessing, or even a grotesque exploitation. Sarajevans began to think and say, if nothing concrete comes of the transmission of this image, then who is it for? If it is only for you, then I want no part of it.

The photograph's power to convey the truth, and the difficulties that power imposes, were further underlined when it was revealed that the CIA had surveillance photographs of Serbian concentration camps from as early as 1993, but had reportedly suppressed them.[7] My main focus is not surveillance photographs, nor photojournalism, nor is it on the snapshots that remain at home. Here I am interested in the art photographer, who takes a photograph with a creative vision, intending to put that fantastic reality into the photograph.

The Bosnian art photographer Kemal Hadzic recorded the images of destruction in Bosnia and Sarajevo during the siege. When he escaped to Phoenix in early 1996 to start his life over, he brought with him more than 10,000 images on film that had not yet been developed. When he got enough money to set up a studio, he was able to develop them and see what he had. But in order to get money, he needed a job, and to get a job he needed to learn English. He might be an artist, but at the time, the more pressing reality was that he is also a refugee. In March 1996, the Villa Aurora of Pacific Palisades paid for his ticket to come and present as part of a symposium on "Writing in a Time of War: Surviving in Sarajevo." That is where we met.

Hadzic displayed a great many photographs of Sarajevo that showed what the destroyed city looked like. Many of the images seemed not too far removed from what you would find in your newspaper. They didn't say anything more to me than photojournalism, or for that matter, than my own memories of what Sarajevo looked like during my first visit. Yet some of the images were astonishingly different.

When Tvrtko Kulenovic spoke of these other photographs, he put some into the category of the "dramatic" and others into the "aesthetic."[8] Although any attempt at categorization is necessarily imperfect and limited, this seemed a reasonable place to start.

What makes some photos "dramatic" is a certain unusual human proposition. Most notably dramatic are the photographs of the double graves from the Sarajevo cemetery. Rows and rows of double graves, because Sarajevo under siege does not have enough free cemetery space to accommodate the war dead. The new marker, made of wood, is placed next to the old one made of stone. The double graves in Hadzic's photographs are marked by crosses, indicating that the dead are Christians; the Cyrillic lettering indicates that they are Bosnian Orthodox.

The photograph touches on truths that extend beyond the concrete images. Why are Bosnian Orthodox dying in Sarajevo? Were they killed? If so, then who killed them? You look on the cross for the dates to see if it was a young person, and likely an unnatural death. The visual truth, that Bosnian Orthodox were killed in Sarajevo, works against the false presupposition that only Muslims died there because Sarajevo was all Muslim. The dramatic statement made by this photo is that Sarajevo was home to Bosnian Orthodox too, many of whom remained in their city, fought for their city, and died for their city.[9]

These photos provide a view of a small, but not trivial, slice of Sarajevo that forces the reader to consider many questions. The double grave brings up many questions: Did the coupled dead know each other in life? Or were strangers belatedly doubled up? Were only Bosnian Orthodox doubled up, or were Bosnian Muslims and Bosnian Croats doubled up as well? Would you ever find a mixed doubling, or are the dead segregated? Your eyes strain to find evidence in the picture to answer these questions, but it cannot be found. These photos encourage questions about what has happened to the fantastic multi-ethnic proposition of Bosnia and its merhamet. They show us that even after Sarajevans died, there were still tremendous problems of multi-ethnicity to be attended to. They also have us wondering whether merhamet lives on or in fact died in these double graves.

The "aesthetic" photos consist of a small series of images. These are the first to grab my attention. Here the camera is pointed in the direction of a destroyed object, for example the National Library of Sarajevo. On the perimeters one can see traces of the physical objects as they once stood. An oriental façade. A third-floor row of windows. An old stone walk. Most of the visual field, though, is occupied by a blur. But there is a tautness to this blur. Lines pull or fall or swirl across the photo image. Something is happening here—what, we do not know, but surely something.

Hadzic spoke of the technical innovation in the photographs. *I used to work in this commercial photography business, and I had some pieces of glass left from there. I kept playing with it, until I got what I was looking* for.[10] Technically speaking, the blur comes from inserting an additional piece of glass between the lens and the object, disrupting the smooth passage of light into the camera. In ordinary circumstances, the blur might belong to that category of technical surprises that Roland Barthes says make the photographs "rare," but do not excite in the way of the "punctum."[11] But in the world of fantastic reality that is Sarajevo under siege, the blur takes on a different function.

Upon first seeing the aesthetic photo series, I ask Hadzic about the blur.

"Can you say what effect you were looking for?"

The realistic photos did not show what Sarajevo was really like. I needed to go to these to show what was the reality. In Sarajevo, the buildings and material objects carried a new energy. That is because at any second they could explode and kill. Like an egg that can hatch, except it brought danger and death.

In introducing Hadzic's photographs to the audience at the symposium organized by the Villa Aurora, Tvrtko Kulenovic offers another possibility. He says that the blur is like a waterfall in front of the destroyed object. Later he mentions to me that he forgot to say it is also like a curtain, as in the theater.

These arresting images can also be regarded as photos of witnessing. I propose to Hadzic: "Here you introduce the dilemma of the person who is the witness to such destruction. The blur makes you ask: Can you see it? Did it really happen? What has happened here? Do I want to see it? Can I erase it?"

Later I see that the blur is serving other functions. In the photograph of the destroyed National Library, the blur makes you want to go inside. Through the blur you can still see the sun from an opening on the other side, inviting you in. Is the building alive or dead? It should be dead, shouldn't it? But the blur makes it look as if something still lives. Another photograph presents a simple façade of a small building in Bascarsija. We see, at the top, a row of four windows with the creases of UNHCR foil instead of windowpanes, and on the

bottom, the walkway of old asymmetrical stones. The blur keeps you from seeing anything else—either that which has been grotesquely destroyed, or that
which has been strangely preserved. In this instance, the blur keeps you from
seeing too much.

The problem with so many of the ordinary photographs of a destroyed
Sarajevo, from an aesthetic and a psychological point of view, is precisely that
you see too much. The photographers' struggle becomes: How can you show
something, without making the viewer see too much? How can you show something about the seeing itself? The success of the blur was to find a way to keep
some of the objects of destruction in the photo but also to introduce "not seeing" into the photograph. The blur is one way, but of course there are others.

A subsequent series of photographs Hadzic made of Sarajevo are images looking downward at the streets, as if through the eyes of a person walking on foot.
You see no people, but the street itself has a human presence. It is as full of details as the skin of a human body, a shoulder, neck, or face. There is a sorrow in
looking down at the street, but also a pleasure in the taking in of so many fine,
small details. These photos are built around the prospect of looking away from
the more obvious scars of bombed-out buildings, shattered windows, and traumatized passersby. Here the looking away actually becomes a very powerful way
of looking. You can take in a lot by looking at the street. A pothole is all that's
left from a shell. A sewer cover reminds you of the lack of water. The light indicates daybreak, and a peacefulness that seems impossible—soon to be shattered. In this way, the street photos give you the war, if you want it, but they
don't abuse you. If you want to see traces of the war, you can. If you want to see
just a city street giving off its urban shine, then that is also there for you. It
depends on how you look.

This is opposite to the sense I get when flipping through the photographs I
myself took in Sarajevo. Mine are completely full of images intended to stun
the naive viewer. Surely, whatever power is in them is Sarajevo's, and does not
come from my camera or me. They were simply shots made as a record of what
a new visitor to the city under siege saw. When I saw something striking, I felt
the impulse to record, and pulled out my camera. I hardly ever took photographs
of people because I figured they'd been subjected to far too much of that already. I shot photos for family, friends, colleagues—Americans who had never
seen anything like that before. Insofar as they provide the visual information of
what a shell does to a sidewalk, or what UNHCR glass looks like, they are adequate. But where is the "fantastic reality," the "schizopsychology"? It is not there.
Merely showing destruction does not capture the terrifying madness, the redemp-
tive merhamet, or any struggles with the real.

My unsuccessful amateur photos remind me that in a way, the problem of
the photographer in wartime is much more difficult than that of the writer. The

photograph is completely dependent upon what is seen. The photographer in Sarajevo must start with the images of the siege on the street. In its fantastic reality, the city itself has become a surrealist image. Shot after shot of the strange is possible, or even necessary in some perverse way, but not sufficient as art. In this context, photographers must take care not to be shocked entirely out of their aesthetic sense, though some shock is unavoidable. They must take care not to lazily record simply what can be seen because the images are so intimidating, but to use what the streets give to produce some aesthetic image that captures Kis's madness.

Art photos like Hadzic's work because they make you see how the physical, the material has changed its very nature, from peace to war. They make you see how looking and knowing has also been changed. You don't just see Sarajevo, as in my photos. You see what a Sarajevan sees, and how a Sarajevan sees, and at the moment a Sarajevan sees. You see how the seeing of a Sarajevan siege differs from the seeing of American peace. Once Sarajevan physical and perceptual realities have gotten inside you, punctured your soul, as Roland Barthes has said in his famous essay, they are there forever. By seeing and entering into the complexities of seeing, you have become a kind of witness.

Witnesses of Existence

The works of eight visual artists from Bosnia-Herzegovina were combined for a group exhibition entitled "Witnesses of Existence," produced in Sarajevo during 1993. The artists were Nusret Pasic, Zoran Bogdanovic, Ante Juric, Petar Waldegg, Mustafa Skopljak, Edin Numankadic, Sanjin Jukic, and Radoslav Tadic. The group exhibit was intended to represent Bosnia-Herzegovina at the 45th Venice Biennial but was unable to get out of the besieged city. It was subsequently exhibited internationally in Europe and even in New York, where I saw it in winter 1994 at the Kunsthalle.[12]

The artworks were made during the first year of the siege, from November 1992 to April 1993, when the first exhibit took place in the destroyed Obala Gallery space in Sarajevo. These artists had been invited by Mirsad Purivatra, the Obala Gallery director, to create individual exhibitions during the course of the first siege year. The space where the exhibition was held, though destroyed, provided relatively safe passage through a dangerous sniper area, so every day scores of Sarajevans passed through the exhibition. In that strange and terrifying reality, the artists and their viewers both believed, and rediscovered, that art is necessary for survival.

The title "Witnesses of Existence," taken from Nusret Pasic's contribution, is the exhibit's central organizing theme. "Witness" is not interpreted narrowly, but as an existential proposition. The exhibit is surprisingly free of references to politics, ethnicity, religion, and nationalities. The viewer is not expected to bear witness to the siege of Sarajevo or ethnic cleansing in Bosnia in any strictly literal sense. The images are not horrific, not in any way like the images of Bosnia seen in the newspaper or the television news. Your eyes are not asked to see too much of that which has been destroyed. The exhibit steers away from this most concrete level of witnessing—your seeing evidence of atrocities. To the contrary, one of the most haunting aspects of the exhibit is how many eyes are staring out at you.

So, what is witnessed? And who witnesses whom? And what is it to witness? In these artworks, witnessing is treated straightforwardly, but not simplistically. This is truly remarkable, given the fact that all the artworks, and the exhibit as a whole, were made within the besieged city, during a time when its citizens desperately wanted the world to know what was really going on. The artists' ability to avoid literalism under these conditions is itself a kind of aesthetic and human triumph.[13]

Witnessing is not just the subject; it is itself what is being reclaimed via the art. To claim the mantle of witness without fully engaging in its complexities would, of course, be utter contradiction and thoroughly unsatisfying. But much of what passes for "witnessing" is nothing more than that. We are sometimes too quick to use the label. We think we are bearing witness when all we offer is literal representation of graphic images of destruction. (That may be to witnessing as pornography is to love.) The very title of the Sarajevo artists' exhibition accurately conveys the existential dimensions to witnessing that each artist expresses, in his or her own way. Although each of the artists' works certainly merits a full discussion, I will talk here about only three.

Zoran Bogdanovic's "Memory of People" presents a collage of minute faces cut from yellowing newspaper pages, eight feet long and several inches high. From a distance, the work's simplicity, elegance, and yellow hue remind one of Viennese Secessionist art of the once dominant Austro-Hungarian Empire.[14] Establishing a pictorial link with central European high culture is to say that we in Bosnia are not Balkan savages, but civilized people. Looking closer, you can see that the collage is composed of scores of formal photos, from weddings, graduations, or other such occasions, that then became obituary photos in the Sarajevo papers.

The work's title, in English, is traced in big black letters over the portraits. Not a people, but people, of many different peoples—or one people, as Bosnia once was. An empty chair sits before the wall, begging you to sit and look. A soundtrack from Bosnian radio plays messages that citizens sent to their family or loved ones, separated, missing, or feared dead.

A photo from living has become an obituary photo. Obituary photos of many people together become an obituary for people. These are still people. What do the dead want from us? What do they expect of us? They want to be remembered. But how can we remember them? What do we do with the memory of a people? How do we construct the memory of people, writ large, from the deaths of many, many persons? What people is this? What does it mean to remember them? Again, there is resistance to presenting a unifying national concept.

The dead also look out at us from the ground of Mustafa Skopljak's "Sarajevo '91, '92, '93, '94." A smooth pile of soil covers part of the gallery floor, and embedded behind small glass windows in the earth are the heads of some simply painted folk-art figures. Some are buried alone, some together. Simple, majestic lamp-lit pyramidal towers made of piles of broken glass shimmer and rise from behind the small graves.

Skopljak's work keeps the dead in relationship with the living. These dead are rendered in a furtively personal style. Once again, these dead are people. The work insists that the relationship be both with the individual dead, and with the larger group of dead. No preference is offered, nor is there any simple way of resolving the tensions between individual and collective dead. Skopljak's work is replete with small details that bear the traces of the artist using his own hands, carefully piling up the glass, painting the faces, sweeping the soil off the window. This memorialization is most definitely marked by the identity of the one who made it, the artist/witness.

This work also manages to balance the tensions between the individual and the collective. Here attention paid to a collective killing does not come at the cost of that paid to the individual dead. The person, even in death, has not been dehumanized. Neither death, nor life, is reduced to a cause. Nor has the sorrow or the haunting been drained off in favor of some easier emotion. These works give us a chance to simply be with Bosnia's dead daughters and sons.

One of the exhibit's other artists, Sanjin Jukic, engages in the art of witnessing, but in an entirely different way. Because Jukic was in New York to install the exhibit and was open to talking with me about his art and life, I can report on our conversations. Had circumstances not prevented the others from attending the exhibit at the New York Kunsthalle, I expect that I would have had as much to say about them, the more senior artists of the group, as about Sanjin. But here again, the realities of the siege intrude.

Sanjin Jukic was educated in philosophy and comparative literature and has worked in the theater and with video.[15] He defines his aesthetic approach as "conceptual," and cites as major influences Joseph Beuys, John Cage, Robert Wilson, and the Dadaists. By conceptual, Jukic means the idea is given a prominent role in shaping his artworks. The function of the concept is to concentrate the experience of the viewer upon the experiential world defined by the concept and to isolate the viewer, the artists, and their interactions through the artwork from most other things. Joseph Beuys's own description of his method in "Coyote, I Like America and America Likes Me" comes to mind: "I wanted to isolate myself, insulate myself, see nothing of America other than the Coyote."[16] This approach works very well for Jukic's effort to make art that emerges from the extremely chaotic and disorienting environment of genocide and war. It can be said that the fragmenting and disconnecting effect of this fantastic reality begs for a strong conceptual frame.

What Jukic wants the viewer to see is driven by what he saw happening to his world in Sarajevo and Bosnia-Herzegovina. When war came to Bosnia, Jukic found himself asking about its origins.

I tried to find a reason, a real reason for the war, for this stupid aggression. Because we were living together, and I'm thinking about the power, a very specific kind of power, to brainwash people, to brainwash and to put them in the position to fight against each other.

Jukic was struck by the appeal to the Serbian people of the Serbian "nationalistic epic myth," which led to a mentality fertile for ethnic cleansing toward the end of a "Greater Serbia." Jukic also focused his attention on the West's failure to notice and effectively intervene in response to the genocide or its mentality. His view of Bosnia as essentially a Western European country further implicates the West for having abandoned Bosnia to extreme nationalists. When it comes to the issue of *how does the outside world think about us?* Jukic specifically implicated the Western media for failing to represent adequately the genocide and war in Bosnia and for failing to present the tragic situation in a manner that would offer a serious challenge to the values, ethics, and norms of Western democratic society. Jukic's work may be seen as an attempt to provoke and engage Westerners, and specifically Americans, into reassessing and reworking their relationships as complacent bystanders to genocide and war in Sarajevo and Bosnia.[17]

Though he comes to us from a position inside ethnic cleansing and siege, Jukic's works, like the other works in the exhibition, are not primarily organized around the presentation of brutal images of genocide intended to convince the bystander that genocide is occurring. Jukic is not primarily using his art to transform the viewer into an outside witness by forced exposure to traumatic images. Instead, his art draws attention to the possibility of the outside bystander as a witness, and to how one's capacity for witnessing is mitigated by certain forces or factions such as the media, culture, politics, ideology, and trauma.

Jukic considers "The Meal" to be his most powerful work from the war. It consists of a plate, knife, fork, and spoon; on the plate there are pieces of shrapnel and broken glass. Jukic presents us with what the Bosnian people have had to live on for the past few years through the metaphor of a meal waiting to be consumed (and the visual pun of a clean plate). Jukic wants you to see it, smell it, taste it too. What shrapnel and broken glass do to human flesh is not shown, but left to be portrayed in the viewer's imagination. The work also suggests the media diet of war images provided daily to Westerners in the morning paper and the nightly news. In this sense, "The Meal" is working on two levels—the ethnic cleansing that Bosnians have had to live on and the media images of that experience that Americans have lived on—and on the tensions between these two disparate images.

Jukic's other war works explore the tension in this relationship even more explicitly. "Sarajevo Spectacle" presents audio and visual tracks above a Hollywood-style track-lighted "SARAJEVO." Jukic evokes the mentality of Hollywood to raise questions about the power of the media to create distorting illusions and fantasies. The video track consists of images drawn entirely from TV news clips assembled in a collage that evokes the terror and confusion of being enveloped by genocide and war. Simultaneously, Jukic projects a word poem consisting of seventy terms commonly used to describe the events in Bosnia. It has the effect of drawing attention to the distancing effect of "big" words and "profound" concepts. The audio track consists of selections from operas that evoke high culture and its function of defining European national identity. The viewer becomes subject to the competition of mass-media images, sociopolitical definitions, nationalist culture, and pop culture, and gains an awareness of how these various sensoricultural channels impact on the witnessing. The deceptively simple experience of knowing the terror of genocide is complicated by the knowing about these other factors that frame and shape one's witnessing experience, factors that have certainly been very active in outsiders' collective witnessing of genocide in Bosnia.

Jukic's "Sarajevo Likes America and America Likes Sarajevo" juxtaposes flags of the two nations and two maps (the fifty states and the Olympic map of Sarajevo) above an oriental-style table upon which rests an American Coca-Cola, a pack of Marlboros, and a Bosnian Turkish coffee server. On one level, these everyday objects bear witness to the Bosnians' struggle for basic survival as well as to the fight to maintain and strengthen their culture through the production of creative artworks. On another level, the viewer is asked to bear witness to the more superficial images of the relationship between America and Bosnia—the American utopian vision of multi-ethnic coexistence in Bosnia, and the Bosnian utopian vision of Western consumer capitalism. On a deeper level, the viewer is invited to reflect upon America's interest in Bosnia and Bosnia's interest in America—and to discover the common principles and values and ethics that define the relationship, or that must be reworked at this moment of crisis in the relationship.

Jukic's approach is theatrical in that it centers on performance. Each work sets forth an experiential space that invites or demands the viewer's interactive participation. You are asked or even required to become a player on the stage he has set. To illustrate what this might be like, I offer an account of my encounter with Jukic and his work one day in New York.

On my second visit to the "Witnesses of Existence" exhibit at the New York Kunsthalle, Jukic and I meet for an interview. We stand in the empty gallery and watch his film "Sarajevo Spectacle." I expect that he will be bored by yet another viewing, but he watches intently with me, as if he is seeing the film for the first time. After the short film is over, we stand together in the darkness, and then he leads me across the empty gallery space and has us sit down inside his work "Sarajevo Likes America and America Likes Sarajevo" as if it is a table at the Jaffa cafe down the street. At first I feel uncomfortable, as if I have touched something I am not supposed to touch. Will the gallery workers come over and say that we cannot sit there? No one comes to bother us. The longer we sit there the more I realize that the discomfort was not due to violating another's boundaries, but precisely the opposite. After all, I have allowed Sanjin to escort me out of my world and into his—a world in which familiar objects are now rearranged as "signs" in accordance with the artist's conceptual scheme to yield a startling new experience.

He says, *I wanted it to be like a cafe in New York or Sarajevo. A place for sitting and talking like you and I.* And indeed it is. Sanjin sits under the "Sarajevo Likes America," and I sit beneath the "America Likes Sarajevo." We continue to sit there for an hour after the gallery has opened, and guests filter in, eyeing us as if we are a part of the exhibit—which in fact we are. It is a performance for others to see—of an American and a Bosnian making a real interpersonal connection.

Our conversation would not have been the same had it taken place anywhere else. I feel incredibly moved by the clarity in Sanjin's method of focusing on the relationship between that which is Bosnian and that which is American. In that moment, we share an acute awareness of our roles as participants in larger dialogues—across geopolitical boundaries, across cultural boundaries, across traumatic boundaries. We are also able to experience the quiet tenderness and respect of two brothers.

The meeting with Jukic stirs my memories of the many Bosnian refugees I have sat with in testimony encounters. His artwork seems rooted in the basic assumption that it is possible for two people to connect, meaningfully and satisfyingly, and in the simplicity of the method of questioning, listening, and framing inherent in the testimony encounters. The work also seems to validate not only that we are just two people talking in a cafe, but also that immense complexities surround such an encounter—cultural, political, social, psychological, historical and ethical.

The meeting with Jukic in the gallery is, in part, evidence of the theatrical performative element that does not require the artist's physical presence but is actually present in the artworks themselves. This element accounts in part for the power of Jukic's artworks to engage the viewer. Viewers see the artworks as objects and are also asked to see themselves as objects operating within the world defined by the artwork, as well as subjects. You may have the experience of being a witness to the content of the artwork, a witness to yourself within the experience of being a witness to the content of the artwork, a witness to yourself within the experience of the artwork, a witness to your actions in the world that have been highlighted by the artwork, and as a witness to the situation to which the artwork has drawn your focus.[18]

What Jukic gives us may be considered a refracted witnessing. Here the act of straightforward witnessing (the direct giving and receiving of a testimony from one to another) is complicated by the juxtaposition of other phenomenological aspects of witnessing. Jukic's works set a frame that invites you into the role of a witness but primarily directs your attention to other determinants of your witnessing. You are asked to bear witness to the experience of witnessing itself, and to experience all its possibilities and limitations.

Your experience as a viewer is centered less upon the precise situation being witnessed and more on the multiple intersubjective phenomenological layers of the witnessing process and its bearing on what you are seeing. You emerge from Jukic's world more knowledgeable about the possibilities and pitfalls of witnessing encounters. What you do with that knowledge and experience is left up to you. No specific limitation or guidelines are imposed.

The History of an Illness

An excerpt from Tvrtko Kulenovic's *History of an Illness* appeared in a London literary magazine in spring 1996.[19] Kulenovic wrote about the fantastic reality in Sarajevo in a new form that contained both faction and fiction, as his mentor Kis had prescribed. One part of the text, titled "Zeko's Diary," consists of brief, terse, curious entries describing some of the day's events.

> Sunday 1st March
> The bro' and I went to see Aisa Fazlic, to Mother on Ilidza and then to the Popadici
> Monday 2nd March
> Didn't go to work because of the demonstrations in town.
> Wednesday 4th March
> Five years since we lost Father.
> Saturday 5th March
> Went for a walk.
> Saturday 25th
> Went with the bro' and Lida to 30 Djure Salaja to fetch some of my

things and some food, and then to "Danny's" with the bro' for a haircut and a shave. I told the bro' I would always go to "Danny's" from now on, and then drop in to his place before I went home, and he began to cry and said that his place was my home now.
Wednesday 29th
Lida and I to Mother in the Kosevo hospital, then to Lida's work mates, Rada and Emina.
Sunday 17th
Told that Mother had died.
Monday 18th
Heard Mother to be buried at the Lion cemetery near the hospital tomorrow at 12.
Mother buried at the Bare cemetery, where Father is. (Kulenovic, History, 38–39)

Zeko's cognitive impairment acts as an odd sieve for daily experience—sometimes his observations on the trivial and the eventful come out the same, and sometimes they don't.

Another part of the text is somebody else's diary, spoken in a very different voice:

Mother was lying in a room with three beds, the head of her bed was right in the corner, between two load-bearing walls, and along one of the walls, towards the window, there was a large wardrobe. "I'm well protected," she said. "But why have you come today, in this lunacy?" I said that it was Sunday, visiting day, that it was my turn, that I hadn't been for a long time, ever since the last time when I did in my back running, when Zeko and I came under crossfire. It hadn't occurred to me that I would soon be running every day, for months on end, and that my spine would have stopped hurting, probably because it was carrying so much less body weight.

"I've got you with me, engraved in my heart," said Mother, and asked me to bring her a bedpan as she needed to pee. She avoided asking me to help her with the other thing, since she had concluded that it disgusted me, although I had got used to it. I told her I was in a hurry, that I had just come to bring her some food and that the shooting could start up at any time. (p. 40)

Two diaries with two voices tell two stories. One voice, "Zeko's," constricted; the other voice, "bro's," expansive, each one's personality in a way generously permitting the other to be himself. These are not just multiple subjectivities; the two brothers' voices are in relationship with one another—and with their dying mother, and their dead father, and Sarajevo under siege, and many others who live or lived there.

Why take us into a hospital with a dying old lady? Why clumsily emptying bedpans and why soiled shirts? Tvrtko Kulenovic has brought the text this close to dirty Sarajevan siege life—a part not seen on television. Television has preferred the shooting, blood, and instantaneous deaths. Horrible, but in a way, clean. Not the plodding, unheroic deterioration of an old lady.

Tvrtko explains why "clean" didn't get through:

> The world has not heard that sound of shrieking, running, and that appalling shouting when a shell falls on a courtyard full of children. Still, the cameras and microphones have done their job honestly, journalists have risked and lost their lives, the television and radio stations have broadcast the material they taped. Almost everything could be seen and heard, but now unfortunately it appears that very little was seen or heard: why? Let us remember what Hamlet said to the queen: "I see him in my mind's eye." The world sees with its eye, hears with its ear, but its mind is calm, fed, relaxed, washed before bed, deadened. And a deadened mind is the vestibule to the death of the mind, and the death of the mind leads to the death of civilization. (p. 43)

In contrast to the media's clean rendering of ethnic cleansing, *History of an Illness* gives us bodies cancerous and soiled; minds confused and broken. These bodies and minds are very much a part of the siege in Sarajevo. Zeko and bro' are honest to the truths writ from the wet beds of the ill and fearful citizens of Sarajevo.[20]

The book tells the stories of the sick, not the well. It reminds us that during the siege, people got sick just as before; but lacking the basic supports the sick usually receive, they did not fare as well. If war was not good for the young and healthy, it was even worse for the sick and the elderly. *History of an Illness* is a testimony to this unfortunate reality.

Having dead and dying persons as the subject provides the desired effect of bringing loss and grieving and memorialization into the text. Often, the stories are dealing with one person taking leave of someone they loved. The text gives us the psychological realities of these relationships being strained by illness, dying, and death. How do you live amid death and dying? When so much is dying, what's left for the survivors?

History of an Illness reads as if it were written in part to be the book that would put an end to Sarajevo war diaries. It essentially contains two diaries that provide two distinct close, detailed readings of the daily experience of the Sarajevo siege. The way Tvrtko has used the diary form in his text has us questioning diaries in ways not prompted by the actual diaries discussed earlier. Zeko's diary, giving us just facts, many of which seem incredibly trivial, has one wondering: why should we want to know what the diarist knows? Does it have any meaning for us beyond the obvious truth that it happened to the person who then wrote it down?

Other Sarajevo writers have written against the diary form: "The diaries of Sarajevo are more or less worthless heaps of notes, because in them is written down mostly what will be forgotten first."[21] Rather than condemn, Tvrtko's text contains, embraces, and transcends. Zeko's diary grounds the overall text, and without ever being condescended to, creates an inviting milieu for "bro's" more literary voice.

Tvrtko's text is a piece of creative writing that tries to pass itself off as part diary, but the force of this narrative lies in its clever combination of forms. It gives us diary in a way that doesn't disrespect, but makes us want more. The literary flourishes could not exist without the diary, but neither could the diary without the literary voice.

Tvrtko has used an odd combination of forms to meet his aim of awakening minds to the nightmare of history in Bosnia. There is diary, mystery, travelogue, memoir, history, anthropology. As a result, for all its preoccupation with dying, this text is extraordinarily alive.

It's fiction and faction, Tvrtko explained:[22]

Life made it. But life made it in such a way that you feel the form. For example, there is the story of how he couldn't go to bury his mother on the other side of Sarajevo. By telephone he made arrangements to pay a young man to bury her. That young man was later killed in the bread line massacre. His mother, a refugee in Ankara, found out he died when she recognized his body on television. One son, one mother. Another son, another mother. In the middle becomes a kind of emotional volcano of what happened. It's almost completely fictional, but the faction has given the form to the fiction.

The book *turns and turns and turns* with stories and ideas of *many facets*. A carriage driver from Montenegro who accidentally kills a young man, and has his family contemplating vengeance. A memoir of the people who helped Tvrtko on his travels to India. A mourning for the France that was supposed to be a symbol of freedom. A mystery about a Muslim engineer from Kashmir who becomes the lover of the narrator's wife. A professor and a student discuss what kind of books should be written. Many, many facets.

Another turn brings it back to Danilo Kis:

> In this history of an illness, this history of death which was conceived with the death of my mother, and which begins with Ranko's and my father's death, or perhaps with the death of Cedo Minderovic, the next in line was Danilo. I had been in America in January, in sunny Florida, which I had chosen so I had no one to blame, when I heard from people in New York that Danilo had been there in November, and they had found that he had lung cancer ("A real smoker's cancer, sir!"), and that he had gone back to Paris, where they had already removed half his lung. We agreed that he had never seen a man of such steely strength as his and he would certainly get over it. But a memory was awakened in

me then which had oppressed me before, for quite different reasons, I admit, but now it became a drill boring into my mind.

We had known each other for years already, I had been visiting them for years, when one evening I asked Danilo whether his mother was still alive. He looked at me, this time not even with that harsh look of his, the way he looked at you when he wanted to hit you, but quite simply with contempt. Luckily Mira came to my rescue, by saying: "You must mean his aunt," whom we used to visit and often mentioned. His mother died long ago, in great pain, from cancer, like my father.

First there was that earlier question, an earlier pressure on my consciousness which simply had no connection with my stupidity: was it possible that I had not known, I had seen her picture so often, the picture of a very beautiful and over-serious woman, and if I knew what I meant by asking that question, what layer of my conscious or subconscious mind could have produced it? But, what I certainly had not known was that she had died of cancer, and it was that fact that had created the drill which gave me no peace, by asking: "Is there any connection, is there any connection, is there any connection?" (p. 41)

Two more sons, two more mothers. Too many cancers, far too many deaths. Much too much violence and loss, leading to too much forgetting. It is our fortune that the creative imagination is uniquely able to bring forth not only the marks of destruction in that fantastic reality, but also that generosity of spirit and knowing that has long been a central part of the Bosnian experience, and is so needed for making peace and trust anew.

Chapter 9　　The Bosnian Awakening

Some Awakening

The awakening of Bosnia after ethnic cleansing is not associated with much celebration. Although Bosnian society is crawling out from under two recent disastrous political paradigms—ethnic nationalism and communism—this is no revolutionary or heroic time. Bosnians generally have greeted this latest transition with reserve, despite Bosnian state television rerunning Rambo-like scenes of Bosnian troops patrolling forests and crossing rivers hoisting their machine guns high over their heads, or sweeping victoriously into another town, as if they hope to perk Bosnia up by repeating these video images of victory over and over.

The spirit of these days is more darkness than light. The most telling gesture is not a fist in the air or a leap, but a shrug, a smiling grimace, or a faraway look in the eyes. This is not to say that people aren't trying to enjoy themselves. Young lovers walk hand in hand and sit in the cafes laughing, and children bound up and down the streets.[1] But the reminders of hard times and hard feelings are never very far away. Bosnians need only look at their streets, their families, or themselves.

When you awaken from a nightmare, you do not bounce out of bed to greet the new day. You sit up slowly, put your feet on the floor, and pause while you slowly rub your palm across your forehead. You stand up tentatively, and you may sit back down for a few more minutes before trying again to get up. Should you trust the day? You are not so sure. The nightmare image that remains with you radiates too strongly to be forgotten. Still, you have no real choice but to get up and get on with things. It's time to get busy. Aren't you supposed to be somewhere now? These feelings seem to be everywhere I go in Bosnia-Herzegovina and the Diaspora.

This Bosnian awakening has been made possible by a series of events that began with the Dayton Peace Accord in November 1995. That accord lifted the siege of Sarajevo, ended the fighting (at a time when the Bosnian-Croat Federation had actually been tallying a series of victories over the beleaguered Bosnian Serb forces), and at least for the time being, ended the war. Then came the longed for departure of UNPROFOR and the subsequent arrival of a large contingent of IFOR soldiers. In September 1996, federal elections were held throughout Bosnia-Herzegovina, resulting in the reelection of Alija Izetbegovic as president of Bosnia and as the overall head of the tripartite presidency composed of the heads of the Muslim, Croat, and Serb entities in Bosnia-Herzegovina. Municipal elections, delayed several months due to widespread voting fraud by the Bosnian Serbs, were then held in 1997. There will be, Bosnians and others hope, more elections and political restructuring as a part of the processes of democratization and peacemaking.

This Bosnian awakening is approached yet more warily given that postwar life comes with its own set of nightmares. Bosnia-Herzegovina remains sandwiched between a Croatia and a Serbia still in the grip of nationalistic leaders who continue to threaten Bosnia's territorial integrity, and who also contribute to a fearful atmosphere within Bosnia that further erodes multi-ethnic coexistence. With its destroyed infrastructure and economy, its shattered communality, and its ethnocultural isolation from Europe, there is a great fear that Bosnia-Herzegovina is now poised to become a lasting open wound in the heart of Europe. These conditions, combining with other factors, have produced a threat from the inside: Muslim nationalism, which is becoming a growing cultural and political paradigm in the wake of the disintegration of the prior communal order. Talking with Bosnians to get their sense of this awakening—some awakening!—I also remember to ask about merhamet.

The Librarian and the Hagaddah

At the Philosophy Faculty of the University of Sarajevo, Kemal Bakarsic the librarian has the office next to Tvrtko Kulenovic, who is working with us back in Chicago. Tvrtko's name is still on the door, as if he is on sabbatical for a semester ("When is Tvrtko coming back?" his students kept asking me).[2] It was Tvrtko who told me to meet with the librarian.[3]

Like most Sarajevans I meet on that visit in October 1996, the librarian is extraordinarily busy, but tries to make some time to see me. Two things have come up all of a sudden. He was told to prepare a lecture for UNESCO regarding cultural preservation. Never mind that he was asked to substitute for another presenter at the last moment or that the two most important international sponsors would probably not even show. It is still up to him to try and sell something to the international funders. The Bosnian government needs the money to support their cultural programs. For the librarian, this is just one more in a neverending sequence of *small humiliations*. On top of that, he has just been invited to the White House by Hillary Rodham Clinton for a Rose Garden ceremony honoring some cultural redevelopment programs for children in Bosnia (such as a comic book that warns children not to play with land mines). He is thrilled, but he also dreads the time and energy it will cost him and his family. Just to get the proper visa will take a week of sprinting through a bureaucratic maze.

Postwar life, as it turns out, has its own set of hardships. The salaries are nonexistent or laughable. Physical ruin is everywhere, with no money for reparations. There is no adequate housing for scores of Bosnians, especially in Sarajevo. For professionals and academics, the worst is the humiliation that comes of constantly begging for money from international agencies. Since the shelling and sniping stopped, there is no longer the fear for daily survival. But in a way, these struggles are worse. They seem far less dignified (if that can be believed), and it is much harder to sustain the same commitment and asceticism that got you through years of siege.

When the first mortar explodes in your garden, the intellectual forms of your mind fall apart. From that moment nothing is important except carpe diem. What's important is survival. Minimal survival.

After wartime in Bosnia, the main problem for individuals and institutions is *the pocketbook*.

The librarian says that his life used to center on being with his family, but also on being with his books. *Unrealistic and meditative. That's what comes of a life with books all around.* As the librarian, he was one of those responsible for taking care of the famous Sarajevo *Hagaddah*.[4] When the siege came to Sarajevo, he continued to do his job as best as he could, like so many others who tried desperately to maintain some semblance of normalcy amidst madness.

After the siege started, he began to reflect on the meaning of the experience of surviving ethnic cleansing in relationship to the Jews' experience of surviving the Holocaust. This may have been due to his self-described *dreamy nature*, to his *bookish lifestyle*, or to the special place of the *Hagaddah* in his life. It came to be that for the librarian, survival meant not only getting enough water for his family, or keeping his books safe and dry, but also resolving some particular problems of historical memory. *How to survive also meant to recollect if there is any historical parallel between besieged Sarajevo and the Jewish Sephardic population in the city.*

Just before the war broke out, the librarian had been preparing a small article on the Sarajevo *Hagaddah*. In this article, finally published during the siege, he wrote about how this writing took on new meanings and a new purpose in the siege:

At the *"Sefarad '92" Convention, held on September 11, 1992, in Sarajevo's Holiday Inn Hotel, we were talking about the half-millennium tradition of our peaceful neighborhoods in Sarajevo, called "Jerusalajim Ketana" (Little Jerusalem), watching the mighty artillery demolishing the front lines of Sarajevo—the old Jewish cemetery, just opposite the Hotel. We talked about Sarajevo's "Korizo" dating from 1581; it was never a Jewish ghetto, just a city zone in the middle of the Old Town.*[5]

The librarian said to me: *In order to protect yourself from the two contradictory ideas, you have to find another parallel to solve this problem.*

He wrote: "More and more parallels have occurred as time passes—in particular, a tragic similarity in the historical experience between the Bosnian Muslim population in 1992 and the Jewish population in 1941. . . . Should we conclude that nothing can be learned from the world's historical experience?"

The librarian asked me if I could tell him what meaning could possibly emerge from the harsh facts of his victimization. *I was a home dinosaur. I didn't do anything wrong. What is my fault?* That same dreamy and bookish nature assisted him in finding something else there with which he could combat nihilism. *It is not the reality that matters. It is a matter of the story.*

The actual story that preoccupied the librarian, that came to be so important to him during and after the siege, concerned the legendary tales of the protection of the *Hagaddah* during World War II. This was not only a story about a famous book, but a human story about Muslims and Jews in the city, and about two experiences of survival from two wars. What the librarian discovered is that his own relationship to the story was complex, and that his telling it would have to involve a new and unfamiliar kind of historical and personal narrative. He recalls:

As an author, I failed. I was writing a simple historical article and I failed to be a historian. I could not avoid it. I could not talk as a scientist, a historian, as an ice-cold man on a subject that presents an interest. This is an amalgam story. There is a piece of history. And a mystery story. And a confession by the author who wrote the story. I was lucky. I found documents that illustrated a different kind of approach. In writing I was aware that I could be wrong. The question is, is there any possibility of writing objective history without the involvement of the one who writes. It's about the use and misuse of history.

In his published article, "Rare Books: The Story of the Sarajevo *Hagaddah*," the librarian tells the following story. The *Hagaddah*, world renowned as a masterpiece, came to Sarajevo in the sixteenth century. There are two *Hagaddah* rescue stories told in parallel, from 1941 and from 1992. Both stories turned out to be shrouded in myth. The legends about the rescue in 1941 celebrate the heroic activity of a museum director named Petrovic. The librarian discovered documentation indicating that it was not Petrovic, but another named Korkut, who was the actual rescuer of the *Hagaddah*.

Then the *Hagaddah* had to be saved again in 1992. Although this operation was contemporaneous, myth and legend again intervened. The librarian quotes a few accounts that fictionalized and dramatized the rescue. He does not directly criticize, but more seems to be pointing a finger at the human tendency to construct *a horizon of stories that fill a gap*. The librarian writes against the mystification of reality. But then what does he write for?

The problem explored is that of personal responsibility. When the war is over someone will ask me: OK, you were the chief librarian of the museum. What did you do to protect the museum and the Hagaddah? If the Hagaddah disappears, what would be my responsibility?

It is not my intention to be a famous researcher, though I am proud that my paper is being published in the U.S. It is not really an article, but a confession. Something that I had to tell. What I did identifies me in a position that is the opposite of the people in the article. Then, the museum was not in a mess. They saved the Hagaddah without complication, simply. After the war was over, they developed a story. After Tito came, the town was liberated, and life returned to normal, someone asked a question, who are you and what did you do, and they invented a story. All the people in that mystery were sentenced for collaboration with the Germans.

The librarian wants to tell a story that provides an accurate rendering of the *Hagaddah* episode from World War II, but also the more recent history. He wants to address the stories told about the *Hagaddah* in this war, which he says were nasty and accusatory toward the Bosnian government.

On May 14, 1994, The New Republic reported that they had evidence that the Bosnian government had sold the Hagaddah for one million dollars for weapons. My government does not have the energy to respond to each and every humiliation. Then four or five Hagaddah hunters showed up in Sarajevo, searching through their channels. We wrote a letter to the editor, but it was never published. We scheduled for it to be shown, out of the blue, on Passover.

The Bosnian government absolves itself of the humiliating accusations regarding the *Hagaddah*. And the librarian clears himself. Each has done the job that was expected of them.

But for the librarian it does not end there. He confesses, *I am also a mouse in the mousetrap that I built.* I understand this to mean that he has not succeeded in entirely avoiding mystification, nor heroism. He has become another teller of stories (and a semi-famous one at that). There is no doubt that the librarian seeks more than *partial historical reconstruction of the past events*. He too is a teller of a history that draws a connection between Bosnian Muslims and European Jews. What kind of history was he trying to tell?

The *Hagaddah* signifies the unique historical link between Bosnia and its Jews. Sarajevans like to recall that Sarajevo was the only place where Sephardic and Ashkenazi Jews had long lived together. Let the truth be told about Sarajevo and its Jews, says the librarian. Do not tell lies. There is something more to the struggle to establish this link. The librarian wants to say that the Jews and Muslims share the same plights: Holocaust and ethnic cleansing. The librarian wants to know: how can the Jewish experience of surviving the Holocaust give meaning to the Bosnian experience of surviving ethnic cleansing?

This question is raised also when the French filmmaker Claude Lanzman visits Sarajevo just a few weeks before the librarian and I meet. The city's intellectuals are still buzzing with the energy of his visit. His Holocaust film, *Shoah*, is screened and there are numerous public dialogues. Judging by the comments of the Sarajevan intellectuals who conversed with Lanzman, there are attempts to find parallels between the experience of the Holocaust and ethnic cleansing in Bosnia. They speak of how Muslims and Jews had shared the position of the "other" in European civilization. They speak of common themes in what motivated the aggressors: ideology and thievery. In talking with Bosnians, I wonder if those who talked with Lanzman or saw his film got the other part of his film's message.

What distinguishes *Shoah* from the mountains of works on the Holocaust is that it is "a quest, a search for truth."[6] Lanzman made the film against untruthful renderings of the Holocaust experience, false attempts at knowing, be they apologistic, positivistic, heroic, or sentimental. There is a gap of believability and knowing that separates us from the Holocaust, and Lanzman knows very well that he cannot bridge it. He cannot explain why the Holocaust happened and he does not try to. Rather, his task is to stick with description, minute by minute, of the facts of genocide. "The real problem is to transmit" (Lanzman, "Obscenity," 211), not to understand, which Lanzman believes too often amounts to an escape from history.

Lanzman and *Shoah* are a superb provocation for Bosnians, but what truths will they find in his method? In the liberal democracies of the West, the idea of probing the silences strongly resonates with postmodern critiques against positivism. Yet this message has a very different audience in Eastern and Central European postcommunist nations, including Yugoslavia, than in the liberal democracies of the West. Postcommunist Bosnia-Herzegovina is still heavily draped in silences, distortions, and untruths concerning the memories of World War II, often far more so than its own citizens believe. Without a critical knowing of those silences and untruths in public and personal life, how is Lanzman's *Shoah* to be understood? Without the habits or the institutions that would support a greater public dialogue and openness, how will Bosnians make use of any new insights? Amongst Bosnians, I often find a certain knee-jerk response to understanding history. It seems like an old communist habit, reflecting the need to rapidly recalibrate oneself to fit with the perceived social and institutional milieu. This is the opposite of what Shoshana Felman claims regarding Lanzman's film: "the process of the revelation of truth takes time and cannot really take place without taking time" (Lanzman, 202–203).

The librarian's gripes against *Hagaddah* revisionism are, you might say, a distant cousin of Lanzman's critiques of Holocaust representations. There are no heroes. The librarian was simply doing his job. And the Bosnian government was fulfilling its responsibility to protect an object of Bosnian and Jewish cultural value.

Mystification of the victim experience is an unwelcome guest, both for Lanzman and for the librarian. Too much is at risk of being misunderstood. The librarian insists that Bosnians be as clear-minded as possible about the consequences of their having misread history in the past. The misreadings of World War II and communism, and the legacies of ethnic nationalisms, were part of what made ethnic cleansing possible. He also asks, what forthcoming disasters do we court if we escape from the historical truths of this ethnic cleansing? if we do not allow ourselves to recognize our own shortcomings in facing the history around us?

The librarian gave the example of the failure to realize a non-nationalistic agenda for Bosnia-Herzegovina:

We failed to create an iconography, and a social propaganda, in comparison with the Croats and Serbs. We failed to create anything that would give us a background ideological framework for the future. Brigades with Islamic titles, funny salutes of one another, it's totally ridiculous. If Muslims were the good guys preserving multi-ethnic living, OK, but they failed to be distinctive and energetic in stating that we live together.

This problem creeps up again when it comes to securing international funds.

The international community is hesitant to give a Marshall Plan. Because they don't want to give money to the ruling political parties, too claustrophobic and nationalistic.

Of course, these processes feed on each other. The people in a country with nothing have more reason to fear and to be impatient and intolerant and ungenerous with one another. Such is the shape of their new lives in the new history, according to the librarian:

Now everything will be an issue. War will be magnificent compared to postwar. We have a saying: "Let God give you plenty, and then take it all away." Nothing will be the same and everything will be a problem. The people are still afraid. Still, it gives us hope that we will be different from Serbia and Croatia.

"Will there be merhamet?"

My opinion is not political. It is based on the basic issue of the mentality of the people here. No matter who you are, what your political orientation is, or nationality, we all have a piece of Bosnia in our hearts. But it took fifty years for Spain to change. It took Germany fifty years to be what they are today. I will not be witnessing the rise of the Bosnian nation in my lifetime. I am forty and my main problem is the home budget.

Regarding the temporary nightmare that our city is passing through: we have to understand that this city will be the most important city in Europe for the next five years. Will it become 100 percent fundamentalist or will it become what it really is— a decent place for living where everyone can find a small place for playing, without the glamour, without one main frame of living, but lots of different, various, part worlds?

The more I listen to the librarian, the more I feel his fear. He never fully articulates it, but this fear of his appears to differentiate the Muslims and their Bosnia from the Jews and their Israel. Was Sarajevo, and the whole of Bosnia, about to become the ghetto for its Muslims that it claimed it never was for its Jews? A little place in Europe for the "other" to reside? A dirty, run-down place that feeds on its own misery and survives on the occasional handouts it gets from the rich world? Yet you have to be impressed by this librarian, and other like-minded souls, who are so totally committed to finding a new path for Bosnia.

The Teacher

I visit with teachers at several schools to inquire about what youths are being taught after ethnic cleansing. One such meeting seems to best represent what I hear from many of them. A few chairs are quickly improvised around a coffee table for my meeting with the teacher.[7]

He begins with the unsolicited statement, *When we face a subject, we face it like nothing has happened.* The conversation is cordial, though less so when I press for a response to the question preoccupying me. Several times I ask, "How has the memory of that which has happened to Bosnians and Muslims entered into that which you give to students, either formally or informally?"

Each time he insists, not at all. Then finally, he confronts me with a question that makes me more than a little uncomfortable:

What if I take a scissors and cut off your hair and tear up your clothes? Can you be content that if I did this to you that it would not change your psychology or your approach at all?

I tell him about how important the Holocaust was in my Jewish education. But he will not say that anything has changed at the school. After we part, I decide that his response to this questioning reveals something more valuable than the answer I was looking for. It reflects one of the most powerful binds in

the Bosnian awakening. There is at one and the same time the absolute recognition that everything has changed, and the stubborn insistence that it remain
completely the same.

To the teacher I am yet another international expert ready to condemn
Bosnian Muslims for Islamic fundamentalism. Because he sees me as prepared
to redescribe him and to see something false, there is essentially no way for him
to answer truthfully the question I pose. So he refuses to engage it.

Instead, he tells me that he is primarily engaged in teaching young persons
to value the *spiritual* over the *material*.

*Let's raise a young person who will be conscious and moral and everything will
be OK.*

He values interfaith activities and education, to protect agains the "virus"
that came to Bosnia from the outside.

*We didn't produce that virus here. It looks like we were a very suitable host for
that virus so it stuck to us. You as a doctor must know about that. If we didn't have
the virus imported, then we would be OK. I am happy that the students are going in
the direction of confronting the virus.*

But for the crimes that have already been committed in Bosnia, another
approach is needed:

*There is one thing we appreciate and care for: justice. Society has the right to
look for justice.*

This justice cannot be individual, he says, but must be systematically delivered by a court.

A moral education is the best guarantee for the future of Bosnia, but it alone
will not suffice:

*We are now raising 90 percent of them in the moral way. And the rest, it will be
easier to keep them in some kind of ghetto.*

Did the teacher really mean ghetto? I don't know. But I do not think that
the solution to one ghetto in Bosnia is to produce another. On the other hand,
the teacher knows very well that there are fundamental problems with this peace.
Bosnia has been forced to remain neighbors with those who committed aggression against it, and to remake a living together when nationalistic mentalities
are so pervasive within its borders. What the teacher means by "ghetto" may be
what the international community calls "partition." Each is an admission that
what has changed is that living together under the old formula is no longer possible.

The Women of the Mixed Marriage Association

In October 1996, I am sitting in the windowless basement office of the Mixed
Marriage Association in Zenica, for coffee, cigarettes, and conversation. The

three women who are the group's leaders tell me about their association and about themselves.[8]

We are in a big dilemma. Bosnia is divided into camps, with the majority of each nation in each one. This is a consequence of ethnic cleansing. It's especially a problem for the children. We do not want them to get educated just in the church or the mosque, but multi-ethnically, multiculturally. We try to teach the children not to look at a person by their nationality, but by whether they are good or evil.

The reality these women describe is a Bosnia in which most are still dependent on humanitarian assistance provided through the NGOs, even in postwar life. The problem they confront is that the two major NGOs in Zenica, Caritas and Merhamet, are not providing the other mixed-marriage families with any humanitarian assistance.

My husband is Muslim and I am Croat. When he went to Merhamet, they asked him, "Why did you mix yourself?" And in Caritas, they asked me if my children are baptized and did I marry in a church. You must understand that forty years ago we didn't ever think to marry in a church or baptize our children. That was not the way it was. At Caritas they told us we are on our own.[9]

Facing this threat to their basic survival, thirty families in the same predicament joined together to form the Mixed Marriage Association. They approached Merhamet hoping for the best, but did not even get a reply. Caritas told them that they already had too many members of their own kind, and did not have any spare food for them. *We were rejected.*

The women estimate that in October 1996 there are 5,500 mixed families in Zenica. Assuming the minimum of one child per couple, that means 17,000 individuals at the very least. Of course the number before the war was much greater, they explain, but many mixed families left Zenica and Bosnia to resettle elsewhere. *The worst is that mixed families are still leaving.* This is particularly hard to swallow because Zenica, in comparison with many other Bosnian cities, did not suffer much in the way of direct military assault during the war. But the assault on the Bosnian way of life was very strong. It came not from the outside, but from the inside, in the form of Islamicization. The recent elections, which national parties won by wide margins, were yet another marker of the Muslim nationalists' domination of this internal battleground over identity and communality in Bosnia-Herzegovina.

The biggest disaster is the victory of the national parties in this election. It is the legalization of the tearing apart of Bosnia-Herzegovina. Nobody wants to stand up and say, what we really have is a divided country. Serbs go there. Croats go there. Muslims go there. And then try to solve the problem of mixed marriages, which are unwelcome in every part. So we have a choice to divide, and divide children amongst themselves and each side.

For the adults and children in a mixed marriage, politics reaches down into the family and threatens to divide brothers, sisters, and couples.

My son is fifteen. He learned to speak Serbo-Croatian in school. Now he is supposed to speak Bosnian. In three years he will go to the army. Which army? In that case the child is supposed to kill someone from the father's or the mother's side.

I cannot be a Bosnian of Catholic religion. I am supposed to be Croat. I am considered to be from a foreign country. There are only Bosniaks and not Bosnians. We cannot be Bosnian.

There are lots of Mujahedeen in Zenica. You can find them everywhere. They come from Afghanistan and Iran. They now have Bosnian citizenship. When the U.S. asked them to leave, they just changed over to being a humanitarian organization. If they marry a Bosnian, they receive citizenship. This morning one spit at me on the street. My skirt was too short.

The Danish psychologist Inger Agger, well known for her writings on testimony psychotherapy, has worked for more than four years in the former Yugoslavia. She tells me, "In *The Blue Room*, I found that humiliation was so important. So I started with thinking about what is humiliating for these people here."[10] She found herself drawn to the problem of mixed marriage, and did extensive field research. The women put it very succinctly: *Everybody has their own pocket. We don't fit in any pocket.*

Reflecting on her knowledge of humanitarian work in Bosnia-Herzegovina, Agger notes how unfortunate it is that mental health, human rights, advocacy, and women's groups are often working separately from one another. Her vision is that individual and communal healing are inseparable, therefore interventions must also link these different realms. Agger concludes a paper on this subject: "One could hope that the millions of people in mixed marriages and children of these marriages would unite in a human rights 'Movement for Mixed Marriage' converting shame to pride. In this way, they could become living proofs of the absurd thinking underlying ethnic nationalism."[11]

Agger visits the Mixed Marriage Association the week before I do. She arranges for a public meeting of the association, at which she will give a talk and dialogue with the group. Zenica TV comes out. Agger wants to assist the women in making their voices heard. So, after she says a few words, the women are to tell their stories. But as soon as she finishes talking, the crew stops filming and packs up their cameras. The only mention on television that night is that the international psychologist Inger Agger has visited Zenica. For the women, it is yet another humiliation. *They all treat us like an anonymous organization. Not to be shown in public.* The women recall how, on another occasion, a local journalist interviewed them for three hours but did not publish a word. They tried to reach him but he would not answer their calls. *Probably he is ashamed because I know that he too is from a mixed marriage.*

Zenica is the opposite of Sarajevo in many ways. Whereas Sarajevo is known for its multi-ethnic spirit, Zenica has become known for its strong Islamic presence. Alija Izetbegovic's government has nurtured Zenica's Islamic community so as to make it a kind of Islamic capital of Bosnia. It is not the kind of place you would expect to be hospitable to a Mixed Marriage Association. Then again, it is probably for that very reason that such a group had to come into existence there. However, the conditions that gave rise to its birth are also threatening to destroy it.

The association is housed in a basement apartment near the center of town. They were evicted from their last premises after they celebrated Christmas 1995 with a Santa. *So they threw us out onto the street.* The group has not received any money from the municipality. Nor have they gotten any verbal recognition or assistance. Now, they have a small coffee bar and a meeting room with seven or eight tables. It's a place for people to socialize, especially the elderly. *Merhamet and Caritas founded public kitchens for the elderly. One is just around the corner. But the older people living in mixed marriages do not have the right to eat there. So they can come here instead.* They play cards and drink coffee. Members come to talk about their problems. *We talk but there is very little we can do to solve the problems.*

All that we have achieved is survival. That's all. Nothing more. We can only be proud because of our existence. And also that our families are connected to one another. They are wanted by someone. By some organization.

Humanitarian assistance with food and shelter is essential, but so is community. The association manages to provide a communal space where mixed-marriage families can feel that they belong. These women awoke to find that they were activists fighting for social change. No one would say that they came anywhere close, but they were able to make things better for many of the mixed-marriage families in Zenica.

We are the only such organization in any city in Bosnia. It would be completely impossible in villages. We wonder how will we continue? You have to have strength. We have hope for a better tomorrow.

Nobody bothers us. Nobody is throwing us out. Nobody is chasing us. Nobody threatens us. That is the good part. But the reality is, survive on your own if you can. The best way for you is to leave. Even then, Europe is too small for you. That is our life. We feel like we are in Kuwait. But we don't have salaries like Kuwait.

As long as the current leaders are in the government, and the national consciousness of the people is being awakened, we do not have a future here. I don't know why the international community does not do something about this.

Their struggle is still for basic survival. They will consider themselves fortunate if their group survives another six months. Walking out of their bunkerlike space, I wonder if the Mixed Marriage Association will still be around the next time I come to Zenica.

When I tell other Bosnians about the Mixed Marriage Associations most think it "cute" that this group exists at all, let alone in Zenica. I think, maybe they will be able to keep themselves fed, but it does not seem likely that they will succeed in widening their struggle against Islamicization in Bosnia.[12] In the Bosnian awakening, it looks as if they woke up on the wrong side of the bed.

Yet the women cannot simply step away from these ideas, being that they are inscribed in the lives of their families. It is not because they are interested in politics. *Politics disgust us*, they say. Their activism comes out of their love for their husbands and children. They are trying to find some way to keep their marriages together and to raise and educate their children. Their will to survive necessarily gives rise to an activism on behalf of diversity, and in opposition to narrowing ideologies and mentalities. Their political struggles are indivisible from their family struggles. For mixed-marriage families in Bosnia, the stakes of these struggles are very high. They cannot survive by remaining quiet and accepting that which is swirling around them. If they are to stay, they must make themselves heard and fight for a space in the newly emerging order.

While other organizations are building hate, we are building love. My friend told me, "Either you will be the first to unite Bosnia, or you will be in prison because of that."

Because they were in love, they married. But when Bosnia changed, they were rejected precisely because of those marriages. Those marriages that aren't already broken still have that love. It is this ordinary but impossible love that characterizes these mixed marriages in Bosnia-Herzegovina. The women of the Mixed Marriage Association know of that love, but they also know that it isn't easy, that love is not all they need to get by in the new Bosnia-Herzegovina. I leave our meeting wondering if they manage to keep pushing. Will it ever be understood?

I return one year later, in October 1997. Only one of the women is still there. One went to the United States, and the other no longer comes. Money is still a huge problem for the Association, but certainly not the only worry.

With this kind of policy, there is no future for mixed marriage in Bosnia.

It will be sad if this kind of association fails, because it is a place where we can socialize.

I will try to somehow keep this association going. But my husband lost his job and is unemployed. We will go to Nebraska.

The most important reason to do this is for my children. They have no future here.

As in so many other conversations I have had in Bosnia, the sense of mutual understanding is suddenly punctured. Forty-five minutes of knowing are thus instantly rendered nearly meaningless because of what is now being said. Announced with the casualness of a change in the weather, it speaks either to my own obliviousness or to the absolute impermanence of reality. In any case, once spoken, it makes so much sense that reality cannot be imagined in any other way.

The Imam and the Reis

The staff at the Refugee Mental Health program of the Chicago Health Outreach invite the Mufti of the Bosnian Community in North America to come and speak as a part of their seminar on cross-cultural mental health. The American staff asks him, "Can you tell us about the Islamic view of mental health problems?" They hear him say:

Good Muslims do not have mental health problems. I was away in Bosnia, and could not attend the meeting. Later, I sit with the Imam, repeat this claim to him, and ask if that was what he really meant.

Yes. If we really apply Islam in our lives then we shouldn't have mental problems. Or the teachings of any religion properly. But today it is probably impossible to devote yourself to the cause of Islam as it was possible a long time ago, because society is more and more secular, and people are leaving the straight path, the path of faith. And that means more problems, more doctors and more medications.

This answer comes from an idealistic position. But how does he address the realities of having lived through ethnic cleansing?

If you eat something, and you don't feel well, then you can vomit and relieve yourself from what bothers you. But when you see or hear something, you cannot simply make it go out. It is in you, and people have to deal with that, and psychiatry can help a lot to deal with what is inside them. This healing is more complicated than healing people physically. And of course, religion can help too.

The Imam has actually been very supportive of mental health work for Bosnian refugees, and is collaborating with our new Coffee and Family Education and Support (CAFES) project for Bosnian families in Chicago.

A member of his Mosque gives me a text the Imam had presented at an international Islamicist meeting, "The Reality of the Genocide Against Bosnian Muslims."[13] It reads:

Allah, Most Glorified, Most High says in the Qur'an in Sura Ra'ad:
"Allah will not change the situation of a people until they change
themselves." . . . It must be clearly stated and conveyed that very often
(if not always) the essence of suffering lies within the Muslims themselves. In the same way or manner the exit from such a state depends on
their willingness and ability to change themselves in accordance with
the teachings of Islam about the straight path.

If we don't analyze our weaknesses and if we don't build possibilities
for everlasting, strong, solid defense through the process of permanent

self-improvement and correction, then we can expect the situation in Bosnia to be repeated elsewhere, even at the places where the tragedy would be much greater. Allah commands us to have a program of strong, active self-defense in the Holy Qur'an.

But what precisely is the nature of that weakness and how is it to be remedied?

Considering what I know of the situation of the Muslim communities in both the United States and Bosnia and due to the bitter experience Bosnian Muslims have suffered, we have no other choice but to move, with a strong initiative, following appropriate and well-coordinated actions, to form a Muslim community which will serve Allah Almighty and not his enemies and which will be strong in body, in spirit, and will be unified; such a community will be honored firstly by ourselves and then by others. It depends only on us (as Muslims) whether we will have a powerful united community based on Qur'an and Sunnah. As long as we don't accomplish this goal, it will be in vain to accuse others for our mishaps. We must hold onto the faith and commands of Allah, they are like a rope that attaches us to Heaven.

The Imam claims that new paths are to be found through transforming the Muslim self and Muslim community. Others have carried this to an extreme, calling for a totally new Islamic social and moral order. For example, the women of the Mixed Marriage Association are quick to show me a newspaper clipping from a local Muslim cleric enthusiastically denouncing mixed marriages.

There was a time when part of me really did not want to believe that this could be so. Americans asked me what I found on my first trips to Sarajevo, and I responded that there were more miniskirts than veils. Because I was clearly partial to the Bosnian Muslims, so accustomed to defending them and justifying their position to outsiders, I was reluctant to criticize them. As Islamicization spreads, and extremism appears in Bosnia and in the Diaspora, I open my eyes a little bit wider and see more than I have before. There is a widening gap between the multiculturalists and the Islamicists.

But I do not want to be too quick to judge the Islamicists. I go to the Imam to ask him about his text. He says it sounds strong because it was a presentation given at an international meeting of Muslims. He stresses that he is not closed or intolerant to other religions. Were he meeting with other religious leaders or groups, he would convey a very different message, and try to achieve different goals.

We need to meet together and to respect each other and to find solutions how to work together and then to teach our subordinates how to apply universal moral teachings in their communities, because the moral teachings of all religions are pretty much the same.

"Is that anywhere near happening in Chicago?"

I don't think that will be ever possible. Maybe some sporadic cases will be pos-

sible, but not on a larger scale. Because in Chicago, there are large numbers of highly nationalistic Serbs and Croatians.

This is one of many instances where the Bosnian Muslims' capacity to live according to their historical traditions of tolerance and openness is being diminished by the extremism of its neighboring groups.

I learn more about the Bosnian Muslims' positions on these matters when the head Muslim cleric of Bosnia-Herzegovina, Mustafa Efendi Ceric, visits Chicago in November 1998 to meet with the Bosnian community. My colleague B. made sure to be at all of his talks, and took in all of the Reis's words. I ask B. to tell me everything.[14]

He said that the situation in Bosnia is still difficult, but it is better every day. He told us that he is not the happiest person because there are many refugees outside of Bosnia. He would like people to come home. If people can stay out and be a success, then they should stay. If people cannot be successful, then maybe they will come back to Bosnia and find a position there.

B. is still trying to make it in this country, working and studying.

He said that we learned something from this genocide. We can't think first about others and then about ourselves. We must take care of ourselves, think of ourselves. We have learned who we were and who we are. It was they who gave us the name Muslim with a capital M. But then we lost our country. We have been forced to be a part of the worldwide Muslim community, but it was not our prior national identity. So what we learned is that we are Bosniaks. Think of it this way: your first name is Muslim and your last name is Bosniak.

The Reis said that a mixed Bosnian asked him if he was a Bosniak or what? And the Reis answered I don't care whether you see yourself in that, but you will not confuse me with questions like that. It is important for me to learn who I am and who we are. Who you are you must find out for yourself.

"How did people respond to this message?"

It was a big success. Nobody gave any objections. We all believe in that. I know what you might be thinking, that it sounds extreme. But the Reis is not extreme. He even said, we have our extremists and we have our "multi-multi's." As a leader he is trying to work with them both to make a kind of balance.

"What do you think?"

I think he says Bosniaks are Muslims. We are Bosniaks. Who they are, I don't care. I feel like they can't be Bosniaks, but I'm not sure. In Switzerland, you have Germans and French and Italians. In Malaysia, you have the Mulgars, Hindus, Pakistanis. In Bosnia, we will have to make something like that.

The Reis is also asked about forgiveness.

The Reis told us that when he is asked, he says to himself, "I am ready for forgiveness." But I don't answer immediately. I want to go home and think about it. I think of Tito who said, "Truth, justice, and forgiveness." I go back and tell them, justice and then forgiveness. It may take a hundred years and it may never finish, but something may be done.

"Only the victims have the right to forgive," wrote Timothy Garton Ash.[15] To the Reis, forgiveness must be tied to certain other conditions. The Reis is teaching Bosnians to put a check on their merhamet, not to leap to forgiveness, as they have been conditioned to do. I ask B. what he thinks of this.

I think it is very wise. We can forgive. But first we need justice. We can have merhamet. But first we must be in a position of security and strength. That is something that we can only get through knowing that we are Muslim.

I accept B.'s answer, but want to know more. Again, I ask the Imam. He says:

The door of Bosniak identity is open to everyone. We believe that once we were all Bosniaks. With the split of Christian church in 1054, those who declared themselves as Orthodox became Serbs, and those who declared themselves as Roman Catholics became Croats. But before they were all Bosniaks. We didn't accept Catholic or Orthodox Christianity. We stuck to the Bogumil religion until the Turks came, and then we accepted Islam. We stayed Bosniaks. I think that our religion didn't change us as much as it has changed our neighbors. They look down at Muslims, and they think that they are superior. But the door of this nationality is open, as far as I am concerned. We want coexistence, after all that has happened, we are ready to forgive, not to forget, but to forgive, and to live in coexistence with others. Bosnian religion and culture teaches us that Bosnia is for everybody who can accept the Bosnian way of living, which is multi-ethnic living.

"So you can be a Catholic Bosniak or an Orthodox Bosniak as well as a Muslim Bosniak."

Yes.

"And what of mixed marriages?"

I always approach every issue from the Islamic point of view, being an Imam. The Koran is the Constitution for me. It teaches us and prescribes that Muslim ladies cannot marry non-Muslims, and that Muslim men are allowed to marry non-Muslim ladies as long as they believe in one God and as long as they can commit themselves to raise children in Islam. God's order is my opinion.

I also ask him about merhamet.

As an Imam, somebody who knows Koran and the tradition of Prophet Muhammad, this concept applies only to Muslims, because Koran teaches us that it should be exercised among Muslims, and for non-Muslims, with caution. The problem is that Muslims didn't understand this concept properly, so they opened their heart to everybody and they applied this concept to everybody. That's why President Izetbegovic said in his book "Islamic Declaration" that during the Second World War Chetniks and Ustashas became wolves because we were sheep.[16] When you are sheep then it causes others to become wolves, to eat you. So we have to for the sake of our future and survival, we shouldn't give another chance to our hostile neighbors to attempt another genocide, because this is too much. The Koran teaches us that a Muslim should not let himself be bitten twice by a snake from the same hole. And this is the same snake that is attacking us for the tenth time. So we have really to change some things, and this concept of merhamet is one of many things that we have to change.

As we are leaving, I ask B. if he has learned something new today.

Yes, absolutely.

He is learning a new history for the new Bosnia.

Heretics

Conversations with other Bosnians in the post-Dayton milieu find them curiously dipping into medieval history to develop a sense of who they are now. *We have always been heretics. It is a part of our history since the middle ages.*[17] I cannot remember them saying this before as sharply or as often as they now are. When they go into this particular well of historical memory, what are they reaching for? What are they trying to say about their current sense of themselves in history? These are the Bosnians who are trying to reawaken in a Bosnia where all the people lived together.

Now, as in medieval times, they find their society precipitously and dangerously balancing on the cusp between Eastern and Western civilizations.

When Germany was united, there was celebration. But now, we are again drawing the borders of Europe. It is an ethnic line right down the middle of Bosnia. Now it is the Drina River, which really separates East and West. This border divides my bed because my wife is Catholic. If I accept your idea of where Christian Europe ends, then I will have to divorce my wife. On the other hand, if the U.S. establishes Milosevic as a hero of peace negotiations, then maybe the border is between Russia and Serbia.[18]

This man does not know precisely where the East/West line will be drawn, nor does anyone else. What he does know is that it will be drawn, either just to the east, just to the west, or right down the middle of Bosnia as he knew it. And he knows that the drawing of that line will determine how the world relates to Bosnia-Herzegovina, which will in turn shape his community, his family, and his life. When he turns to medieval Bosnia, he is looking for a reason to believe that their current geopolitical position is familiar to Bosnians, and that they can weather it.

Now, as in medieval times, Bosnia struggles to find a third way between the Catholic and Orthodox traditions. Then, there was the Bosnian Church, which somehow managed to cut a third path. In this regard, the peace activist Ibrahim Spahic says, *Bosnia is a scandal in the heart of Europe.*[19] But will Bosnia be able to resist the nationalistic mentalities that threaten it? When Spahic turns to medieval Bosnia, he is looking for a historical precedent for a third path, and he finds one in the example of the heretics who broke from international Catholicism.

The history they seem to be telling is one that is, understandably enough, reassuring to them in their present historical struggles toward a new era of living together in Bosnia-Herzegovina. It turns out that it is not so far from the truth of the historical record, as discussed by the historian John Fine.[20]

The shape of society in medieval Bosnia was, in part, geographically determined. Bosnia's imposing mountains complicated any outsiders' attempt at conquering, and led toward the development of a localism. Bosnia's Catholic Church was significantly free from the control of Rome, Croatia, and Hungary, and had its own distinct local characteristics, but also some Manichean elements. It apparently accepted "an omnipotent God, the Trinity, church buildings, the cross, the cult of the saints, religious art, and at least part of the Old Testament."[21] In the mid-thirteenth century, the Bosnian church became completely independent of Catholicism abroad. In the mid-fourteenth century, the Franciscans, responding to the heresy, came to Bosnia as missionaries and built convents, and the kings of Bosnia again became Catholic. The Bosnian church, never a state institution or a political body, dwindled and finally was terminated in 1459 through papal intervention, as the Catholic Church flexed its muscle on the eve of Ottoman invasion.

It is commonly assumed that the Bosnian church was both more differentiated from international Catholicism and more dominant within Bosnia than historians now accept. Modern historians would say that the image of heretical Bosnia, which lives on in Bosnia today, is part historical truth and part fiction. Still this heretical Medieval Bosnia is an inspiring proposition to any Bosnian who desires an open and pluralistic society today.

However, the forces and institutions bearing down on Bosnia in medieval times were religious, whereas in the current situation they are nationalistic and political. Multiculturalist Bosnians do not seek to protect a religion so much as a way of life. The external forces have not sought to promote religion (although they have certainly used religion for political purposes) so much as an ethnically clean nation-state. Bosnians do not depend upon religious institutions so much as on governments to protect them.

Another difference is that one of the keys to Bosnia's heretical character was its relative isolation from the world, largely geographically determined. Bosnia is hardly isolated now, in the communication age, with hordes of international soldiers, government officials, journalists, doctors, Mujahedeen, and humanitarian workers present, not to mention the more than one million Bosnian refugees now living in exile.

It is ironic to be trotting out the image of the heretic now, given the new conditions. However, to draw upon a usable history is a human need. Certainly, the Serbian nationalists drew upon a history, highly exaggerated and imagined (though in part real), in order to justify their nationalistic ambitions. Those Bosnians who want to awaken into a new era of living together, when they look for a history to draw from, have been choosing heretical Bosnia. In a way, it is not a bad fit. They feel every bit the heretic: unique, isolated, precious, and endangered.

When Bosnians look at the recent past, it looks as if history is closing in on them. Where there once was living together, along came ethno-nationalism. Where there was peace, along came war. Their friends in Europe stood by until it was done. Their friends in the Arab world said "come over to our side." Their country was destroyed and then divided. For those Bosnians who remained committed to the multi-ethnic paradigm, hearkening back to the image of heretical Bosnia brings some comfort. A visit to that time, to the possibility of Bosnians again finding a third path, is understandably reassuring.

To imagine is absolutely necessary in order to awaken into a new history. But to imagine is not enough. What they really want to know is how to make living together work again.

Voices for Unity in Diversity

Dr. T. is a psychiatrist not so beholden to the academy, and very open to the international mental health professionals who came to help address the war realities in Bosnia-Herzegovina and Croatia.

I am an optimist. Because we have been in Bosnia for many many years, Bosnia has many levels of history. We were heretics in the early middle ages. Genocides have been organized against us before. Always, we struggled to survive, to be independent. We have had many different nationalities in Bosnia for many years. I think that Bosnia will become something new and better. We are open. We are open to receiving the best things. Many international visitors come. Communication with the whole world is important to us.

However, this view has not always endeared Dr. T. to many of his colleagues, often leaving him standing alone.

I am also stressing the relationship between mental health and human rights. It's important to promote this idea. I have some support, but some are very reluctant. Many people in psychiatry here do not understand this connection. Some of my colleagues are very suspicious and resistant to change.

What we as psychiatrists should do, must do, now in Bosnia is first, we must be active on a professional level, as psychiatrists. Second, we must confront genocide and victims from a moral perspective. I don't mean just trying all war criminals in the Hague. The project of genocide itself must be sentenced. We must discuss this openly. After the wounds become colder we must put things on the table to discuss them openly.

Not with the aim of creating more legends for the Bosnian people. We must accept that in the second generation it can happen, that Bosnians would kill innocent people and children too. But first those responsible must be identified. Not just Mladic and Karadzic, but also the people in Belgrade.

Over the past few years, Dr. T. has cooperated with several of the international organizations that have been overseeing mental health work in Bosnia-Herzegovina, such as the World Health Organization and the U.S. Agency for International Development. He attends their seminars and reads their papers. The internationalists seem to have inspired and supported him to make his psychiatric work more socially and community oriented, and to think about the psychology of peacemaking.

Many Bosnians and Croats say all Serbs are the same. It's not true. We must recognize who created this and put away the responsibility of a whole nation. For Serbs this is especially important. It is important to distinguish between individual and collective guilt. Many Serbs were involved, but many were deeply against this. All Serbs are not responsible. They are victims in some sense. I will go to visit the Serbs in Banja Luka. I will talk to them and see what they say.

It is interesting for me to hear Dr. T. and other mental health professionals give examples where they, as individuals, are more willing than their institutions to reach out to those on the other side. To them it is a logical extension of their work as psychiatric professionals committed to addressing survivors. Being empathic toward their former colleagues and establishing a dialogue with the other side is another facet of their new work. One professional, who has worked to help the Serb families resettling in Sarajevo after Dayton, reported:[22]

I called one man who was my supervisor at the clinic where I used to work. I had tried to have contact with him six months ago but he resisted. Each month I sent him the newsletter of the NGO where I work, so he could know of our work. Then we talked. We talked like in therapy. I told him my experience, and he told me his. Before, during, and after the war.

"Did he know what happened in Sarajevo?"

I think he tried not to know. Before the meeting with me the government met with him and told him what to say and what not to say. He said that we should let our governments arrange for the next meeting. But I said, if we leave it up to them, who knows if it will ever happen. We have to do this ourselves, one to one. We must go step by step. I think it will take a long time.

One of the intentions of the international community in the post-Dayton period is to create common institutions within Bosnia-Herzegovina, between the Bosnian Muslims, Bosnian Croats, and Bosnian Serbs. Nobody expects that it will proceed in a linear fashion. But the mental health professional, full of empathic capabilities, may feel the desire to push things along through their individual efforts. Their capacity for empathy, even with those on the other side, and their tolerance of the psychosocial complexities that could explain the perpetrators' motivations, are associated with psychiatry's humanistic task. Some mental health professionals, like Dr. T., are finding they can try to lead their institutions and society in a new direction focused on openness, forgiveness, and human rights.

If one of the intended consequences of the nationalists' aggression against Bosnia was to drive it in a more Muslim direction, then one of the unintended consequences would have been to internationalize Bosnia. By traveling to international conferences, meeting with international colleagues, collaborating in research projects, the mental health professionals in Bosnia are exposed to a whole new world. Back in Bosnia, they become more active community voices for a Western-style liberal democracy, denouncing intolerance and fundamentalism. But it will take a lot more than a few trips abroad to really change professionals, and a whole lot more than that to change institutions and policies. It is important to remember that not only individuals, but also institutions are in distress as a result of ethnic cleansing and war, including the institutions where professionals work. Ultimately, it is these institutions, with their cultures and policies, that will also have to change.[23]

Tvrtko Kulenovic also sent me to see Ibrahim Spahic, a Sarajevan who holds four different leadership positions. He is the Director of the International Center for Peace, founded in 1991 during the war between Croatia and Serbia, which does publishing and organizing on peace issues. He also founded and directs the Winter Festival in Sarajevo, an international celebration of performing arts, visual arts, and literature. He is the president of the Citizens' Democratic Party, which is a leftist, multicultural party in coalition with Izetbegovic's SDA party. He is also the president of the Bosnian Lions Club, which has brought large amounts of humanitarian aid to Sarajevo's citizens and to hospitals.

Tvrtko says of Spahic, *His voice is always idealistic, but he is enormously practical.*[24] In our meeting, Spahic expounds on the visionary side of his leadership, speaking feverishly for several hours about the struggle for the Bosnian future, which he believes must stay committed to merhamet.[25]

Only with merhamet can we survive that which has happened. We can see that those who suffered the most are forgiving the most. It is characteristic of the Bosnian spirit. We say that Bosnians have a wide chest.

Spahic knows that this vision is enormously complicated by the terms of the Dayton peace accord, which forces Bosnians to live right next to their aggressors.

We have a partial solution of the Bosnian situation. Victims and victimizers are still in the same basket.

Yet he insists that the solution is still to be found in living together and merhamet. He tells the story of his recent mission to Banja Luka, the largest city in Republika Srpska, and his efforts to open a dialogue.

Two months ago I spoke on Banja Luka TV. This is merhamet. Forgiveness but with the knowledge that we should live together. It is the best investment for our future.

Spahic's claims are made with such a combination of passion and confidence, practicality and vision, that you actually begin to believe that it can indeed be done.

I get a different sense of Bosnia and its future from the Sarajevan intellectual Rusmir Mahmutchajic, who confesses to me in our conversation:[26]

I am very worried about Bosnia.

He is one of the Sarajevan intellectuals who speaks with Claude Lanzman. When he learns that I am Jewish, he asks me to tell him what the difference is between the Holocaust against European Jews and ethnic cleansing of European Muslims. Then he tells me what matters most:

The Jews found a way to work with the West and to be present among the West. The Muslims lost their presence among Christians. They didn't develop a way of speaking to the Western people to explain their destiny. There was a boundary line.

Yet the Muslim experience in Bosnia was unique.

Bosnia has been a place of refuge throughout history. Heretics found refuge in Bosnia. A place for others has always been developed in Bosnian history. We accepted the right of the other to have a different belief.

But what will now come to be after the destruction of Yugoslavia, the ethnic cleansing of Bosnia, and an unjust peace: "How can you speak of doing good in Bosnia if the victim is forced to recognize the Republika Srpska?"[27]

I wrote this book trying to fill an empty space.

In his *Living Bosnia* Mahmutchajic claims, "The idea of a section of Bosnia for the Muslims, to be thrown to them after the carve-up of their country, is part and parcel of the overall plan for our annihilation" (Mahmutchajic, *Living Bosnia*, 202). Bosnians must resist the impulse to organize around a politics to exclusively "save her Muslims" (p. 200). He offers an argument against a reactive extremism in Bosnia in the wake of ethnic cleansing: "In defending her, we run the risk that, for the sake of defending the form, the substance may be forgotten. . . . Our response to the forces of evil cannot just be a reflection of the acts of our enemies. Faith in the struggle for good must lie at the heart of the Bosnian State. Our politics must not lose its moral basis and its devotion to human rights" (p. 208).

He offers a moral argument: "The future of Bosnia depends largely on an awareness of a higher principle—why we are put into this world" (p. 157).

This moral argument is rooted in the lives of Bosnians. "Bosnia belongs to the people who live there. There is no freedom for just one people without freedom for the others. Those who speak of such freedom are driven by a warped awareness and only encourage violence. The underlying division within Bosnia should be seen, today and in the future, as a division between the true warriors for justice and freedom on the one hand, and those who deny justice and freedom on the other" (p. 198).

Those lives are rooted in the history of Bosnia-Herzegovina. "The ethnic identity of the Bosnian Muslims cannot be separated from Bosnian history. This means that Bosnia's lasting unity in diversity has shaped this people's distinctive spiritual and cultural features" (p. 141).

But the challenge for a Mahmutćhajic is how to reinvigorate such a moral vision of Bosnia when those Bosnian lives and history have been so tragically altered by recent experiences.

The challenge now is to try to rebuild the powerful structure of people accepting the Bosnian formula, or unity and diversity, to organize them as a power, a powerful cultural and political structure, it is the most complicated way in Bosnia. We are intending to establish a democratic alliance of the Bosnian people.

FAR FROM THE ACADEMIES and the corridors of power in Sarajevo, there is a small civic organization called the Democratic Circle of Bihac. I find them listed in the OSCE pamphlet on local organizations working for democratization. There I encounter another strong individual who has somehow managed to speak with a different voice. S. meets with me on a few hours' notice and tells her story and the group's agenda for Bosnia.[28]

The Serbian and Croatian national identity was formed on the basis of a strict animosity to the collective to which they belonged. Bosnian Muslims did not form themselves as a nation until this war. This war offered the opportunity for national unity of Bosnian Muslims. Unfortunately it opened up the opportunity for all the sick aspects of that idea. A nationally integrating mentality for Bosnian Muslims was offered to us in this war. The role of the victims was brought to its full potential. In that sense the victims are manipulated and abused. The repercussions of this have an expressly morbid character. Bloody victims from a bloody conflict. The development of hatred between two or more ethnic communities. A closed Bosnian community is created. Closed to the world.

Because of the fact that a community has gone to war, each and every citizen has suffered, and each and every citizen is a victim. Some in a material sense. Families broke apart. People lost family members. There are traumas. Media propaganda and political indoctrination is another kind of trauma. Applying pressure to one's free thinking, forced narrowing of thoughts has its own consequences. People are more prepared to rationalize the state's authority. Less prepared to accept other ways of thinking or behaving.

War crimes were committed by individuals. Every shell was fired by one person. But we are brought to the problem of collective guilt, because the criminals are nameless.

So the guilt gets placed on the whole community. At one point in this war I felt this personally. I succeeded in overcoming this. This was my most difficult war experience, this moral struggle.

I used frequent contact with representatives of the local Serb community to receive for myself that not all think the same, nor do they all want the same things. And I tried to show by my own example that we do not all think the same. This was exclusively private; keeping in mind that any more social project would have been impossible. The group consciousness was overwhelming.

During the war the overwhelming majority of the people with whom I connected never spoke of the enemy Serb army. They spoke of the Serb enemy.

"What can you say about merhamet?"

Merhamet is being mystified today. Merhamet is now being presented as this endless preparedness for forgiveness, which can be compared to fatalism. I don't accept this revision.

S. believes merhamet is not a suicidal mentality to be discarded, but something that still offers a basis for a way of life in the new Bosnia.

Near the end of our conversation, I ask her if she has any thing more to say about the Bosnian future.

Do you want my wishes or the reality?

"I believe that you just gave your answer."

There are not a lot of people here.

In Bosnia-Herzegovina after ethnic cleansing, the circle of peace and democracy is not empty, but neither is it anywhere near full. Bosnia's awakening from a history that is a nightmare is truly a struggle for our times.

Epilogue

It is January 1996 in Varazdin, two hours west of Zagreb. A dilapidated compound by the railway station serves as a camp for 800 Bosnian refugees. I am standing in a muddy square that is framed by four long buildings where they stay, three or more families to a room. The refugee boys make that square their playfield, as they have for the past several years. For them, history is that bleak compound, their youth a single soccer match of scoring goal after goal on one another without keeping count. People are still talking about what happened the week before; dozens of families got on buses for Bosnia, the first to be repatriated after Dayton. I watch the boys' spirited play, their bodies quickening to the whirling ball in the frozen mud. Someday they too will get on the buses along with their mothers and sisters. Where to? What will they find? What kind of life?

It is June 16, 1904 in James Joyce's *Ulysses*. Stephen Dedalus stands in a classroom beside his elder boss, Mr. Deasley, as their students romp outside.

History, Stephen said, is a nightmare from which I am trying to awake.[1]

All trauma mental health professionals must feel the pull toward Bosnia, with its epidemic of trauma and the need for effective interventions. As one of these professionals, I am concerned about PTSD and its treatment, especially for those Bosnians right here in Chicago. Yet it is not through the prism of PTSD work that I make contact with the Bosnia that matters most to me. Something else has me in its tow. Is it that I want to work for them in the face of the crime of genocide perpetrated against them and the overwhelming suffering they face? Yes, call this advocacy. But still there is something more.

Is it that through Bosnia, I am able to make contact with my Eastern European grandmother Kate and what she asked of me at twenty-three? Then I was so preoccupied with medical studies, New York, and my desire to do something and become someone. Did she really believe that I had forgotten? I would not have disagreed, but there was never enough time in my busy life to worry about all that. And we did not really talk enough of it in my family to help me know. Yet now, a truth is evident in the very fact of my having chosen to work with Bosnians. It tells me that my grandmother's question remains a central part of my life. Although I have not really answered it, neither have I forgotten.

WHAT SO INTRIGUES ME about Bosnia is that it is a landscape so palpably alive with memories and with intense dilemmas over how to live with memories.[2] Here I can pursue the practical and moral questions that fascinated me as a student of history and literature: How does one live after disaster? How does one find meaning, goodness, and "the milk of human kindness" in the wake of evil and tragedy? In Bosnia today, one finds the totally confounding juxtaposition of the overwhelming failure of governments and collectives to live in peace, but also the utter strength and courage of individuals who survive and continue to nourish a sense of humanity.

And one finds families trying to find a way to absorb historical change and transcend generational boundaries. B.'s parents taught him that he could be his own man and did not need to worry about history. It's what I too was taught, half a world away. Yet somewhere in each of our backgrounds, there is another message, one that says this history must not be forgotten. For B. and his generation in Bosnia it took visitation and ruin from the nightmare of genocide and war to wake them out of their slumber and to teach them about this other history. My family has had the immense good fortune to be spared such catastrophe, and I the extraordinary privilege to be able to learn through entering into the Bosnian historical tragedy from the outside—to help them and to study and write about it.

IN THE CLASSROOM Stephen Dedalus daydreams.

> From the playfield the boys raised a shout. A whirring whistle: goal.
> What if that nightmare gave you a back kick? (p. 35)

IT WAS IRISH HISTORY that bogged Stephen Dedalus down; however, his instantaneous reflection illuminates a historical truth about the Balkans and postcommunist Europe. Ethnic cleansing in Bosnia is the back kick to Europe at the end of the twentieth century. Just when the continent was looking up, with the total collapse of Soviet communism, and the progressive development of the European Community, came this unexpected blow. Just a few short years after the streets of Prague rang with the jingling keys and merriment of the Velvet Revolution, the streets of Sarajevo shuddered under snipers' bullets and rocket shells, and several million Bosnian people were forced from their homes.[3]

The Balkan Peninsula clenched and snapped, delivering a swift kick to the underbelly of Western civilization just before the end of the millennium. History had supposedly been preparing us for something else. Not for a nightmare's back kick, but for celebration when communism fell. Longstanding dreams of Western-style democracy and a market-driven economy were finally to come true across all of Europe. It seemed history had taught us to think that we would never again be caught as passive bystanders to a European genocide. It was even said to signal "the end of history."[4] But back kicks don't hit you when or where you expect them. Such is the melancholy of history.

A<small>T</small> V<small>RACE</small>, the memorial for World War II dead in Sarajevo, there was a theater where citizens came to watch the state's films of that war. No one visits there any more. Bosnian Serb forces held it throughout the siege, taking advantage of its lofty perch over the city to launch shells and snipe on the people below. They left behind their shells, tin cans, and magazines. They even put up two basketball hoops, turning one of the courtyards into a full court (for shooting hoops after shooting Sarajevans?). Stone walls once adorned by small stone letters spelling the names of thousands of the prior war's dead are partially or completely stripped. The force of the explosions and vandalism knocked many of the letters down to the ground, where they lie in small piles. A place where memory was once tenderly enshrined is now all fragments, garbage, and scatter. Still, there is a beauty to it. I come often with my camera to take photos.

This time someone has cleared away some debris and I find it is possible to make my way up the stairs and to enter the theater itself, with its fire-charred rows of auditorium seats. Hard to believe that this was once the state's hallowed space, where countless schoolchildren and weekend strollers came to view the films that gave them the official Titoist view of World War II. That history is now in total ruin. This Vrace Memorial is itself a victim of the history it tried to conceal behind the historical myths that marched across its screen. Being here feels like standing inside an Anselm Keifer canvas.[5] I have the sense that a new history is written all over this place. But what immense work it will take to piece it together and to tell it! This book is barely a beginning. I hear the Bosnian kids playing soccer on the ruined promenade just below.

T<small>HE LIST OF</small> what Bosnia needs to move on is far too long. In 1995, the Carnegie Endowment sponsored the Second International Commission on the Balkans and published its report in a book, *Unfinished Peace.*[6] The commission recommends against partitioning Bosnia-Herzegovina, which it fears is likely to result in annexations to Serbia and Croatia, and a nonviable state for Bosniaks. Rather, the commission argues for "promoting re-integration of a truly multi-ethnic Bosnia" (p. xx), and calls for all the measures that they deem necessary toward that end. They argue that the international community must put forth sufficient will and means for security, reconstruction and development, democratization, and protection of minorities. They call for the European Union to sponsor trade and economic agreements that aim toward the long-term goal of cooperation among Balkan states. They recommend that the international community make both Croatia's and Serbia's desire for normalization of relations and full integration into the international community absolutely contingent upon compliance with Dayton provisions—including return of refugees, arrest of war criminals, rights of ethnic minorities, and democratic elections. I do not think that they nor anyone involved harbors any illusions that this will be an easy struggle or a linear path. All are discovering that it is far easier to destroy a society than it is to rebuild one.[7]

What I have been wanting to know is what new sense of history is needed to support the project of making a new multi-ethnic Bosnian state? Eventually this new Bosnia will create new theaters of memory where it will teach its citizens their history.[8] The project of building peace, openness, and democracy in Bosnia-Herzegovina will need a new history that supports this system of values. However, this new history has no choice but to be born out of current conditions, and it must meaningfully address the difficult new realities. It is the presence of those realities that I feel in Vrace, as well as the immense difficulties of transcending them. And yet Bosnians have no choice but to evolve and redefine their sense of themselves in history.

TITO'S COMMUNISM structured the Bosnians' way of awakening from the nightmare of World War II into the Second Yugoslavia. But retrospectively we see that Yugoslav communism did not prevent, and may have even nurtured, the back kick of ethnic cleansing. The new Bosnian history must not repeat the mistakes of the historical remembrances of the past. It must endeavor to avoid the Titoist approach toward memories of aggression that pushed aside personal and family remembrances and forcibly imposed a state-scripted public memory of history. It must also not submit so completely to the ahistorical and nonpolitical cultural attitude of merhamet, which tends to forget rather than remember. These were systems that worked in one historical space, but are totally unworkable in the present and the foreseeable future.

The version of history shown in the theater must not be a history only for Bosnian Muslims, or those ready and willing to empathize with them as Muslims. It should not simply replace the value system of communism with that of Islam. It should be a history that is about the totality of the Bosnian experience. This new kind of history calls for Bosnian Muslims to have empathy not only for themselves as survivors of a recent genocide, but for numerous other dimensions. That must include their neighbors, Croat and Serb, who also suffered as ethnic minorities, recently and in the past.

As the prior system favored a history of forgetting, this one must favor remembering. This history must be fundamentally based upon the acknowledgment of individual and familial remembrances of aggression, and their relationship to a collective memory. What was so problematic about the approach to remembrances in Tito's Bosnia was the disjunction between public and private memorialization. This was in part symptomatic of the even greater problem of the distortions communist societies impose upon the relationship between public and private life.[9] In this history, individual and family remembrances must be respected, and allowed to gel into a collective memory, rather than suppressed by a totalitarian state's public memory. In place of an imposed moral code must come the fruition of a genuine sense of public and private ethics concerning ethnic diversity in Bosnian society. To thus tell history will be even more painful than the straightforward survivors' history of victimization. Painful because it calls for an inquiry that requires self-criticism. The Bosnian Muslims must examine their possible roles in: advocating Muslim nationalism; perpetrating human rights violations against Serbs or Croats during the recent war; perpetrating abuses and violence against Serbs in World War II and before; and supporting an inadequate reconciliation with the memories of World War II. These Bosnian Muslims so identified as the victims of the nightmare must even be prepared to see in themselves the maker of historical nightmares, the ethnic cleanser.

For B., who told the story of his grandfather's killing, that would mean taking a whole new look at this and other family accounts of history. The story that said that Serbs were killers, and the story that said that we lived together, though contradictory, cannot simply be kept split apart from one another. It is precisely in such contradictions that we must search for deeper truths. One other story that must be discovered is the story that describes what actually happened between Muslims, Serbs, and Croats in World War II in Foča.[10] This is a story about which neither B. nor I were sufficiently curious. But these histories will be of greatest use to Bosnia's present and future struggles only when there is this kind of fuller account of the complexities of remembrances of historical events.

This new history will clearly have to involve the generations finding a different way of talking with one another. B.'s father told me that he had taught his children differently from the way his mother had taught him. Unlike her, he had sincerely believed that with urbanization, the other history of ethnic aggression was over with. Now, both he and B. agree that they can no longer let themselves believe as such, but it is by no means clear to them—or, I hazard to guess, to most Bosnians—what the children and grandchildren should be taught now.

Bosnians today are justifiably worried about survival in the face of military, economic, and cultural threats. Unfortunately, it is in this desperate moment that they are being required to clarify for themselves and for the world who they are and what they are for. And at this point in time, the Bosnian Muslims may be the only group in ex-Yugoslavia who can meaningfully open up this new historical telling. Their lives' journey through history has exposed them to World War II, to communism, to living together, to ethnic atrocities, to nationalism, and to exile. They have truly seen it all. But more than that, they are in possession of a mentality that offers the only possible way out of the mentality of ethnic nationalism. It is the Bosnian Muslims, not Bosnian Croats or Bosnian Serbs, who had the largest investment in multi-ethnic living before the war. It is the Bosnian Muslims who have the cultural value of merhamet, which for all its problems is still something of value to build upon. It is the Bosnian Muslims' experience of surviving ethnic cleansing that taught them the hardest lesson of all concerning the costs of ethnic nationalism and genocidal violence in terms of the destruction of peoples' lives. Finally, it is only the Bosnian Muslims who can begin to offer forgiveness.

HISTORICAL REMEMBERING is not only a Bosnian, but a transnational undertaking. The multitudes of Bosnian survivors in exile have stories to tell. Like those in Bosnia, they are understandably preoccupied with rebuilding their lives. But despite such immense disadvantages, exile offers an outsideness from Bosnian society that might actually confer advantages for historical inquiry and struggle.[11]

However, Bosnia and its exiles will not be able to manage this historical remembering of ethnic cleansing alone. The region is still dominated by nationalistic leaders and governments in Serbia, Republika Srpska, and Croatia that will tolerate only those histories that support them. If the day ever arrives when more moderate regimes come to power, there may be a possibility for them to conduct a public examination of this dark period in their histories.

Presently, neither in Serbia nor in the Republika Srpska is there a process or structure to facilitate the Bosnian Serbs' and Serbs' taking account of their roles in ethnic cleansing. Because neither have been militarily defeated, they are not subject to the will of their victors, as were the Nazis. Nor have they been squarely defeated by their own people's political will, as was the case in the 1989 anticommunist revolutions in Europe, or the overthrow of apartheid in South Africa or of Latin American dictatorships. The Dayton accord neither made them confess to their aggression, nor seriously punished them for it. The prospect of any domestic process doing the same is not presently foreseeable. Slobodan Milosevic is still in power in Serbia. Radovan Karadzic stepped down in July 1996, but he and General Mladic still loom large as political figures in the Republika Srpska. All international sanctions against Serbia were lifted, and in the summer of 1996, the Yugoslav national Olympic team marched proudly around the field in the parade of athletes from hundreds of other nations at the Centennial Olympics in Atlanta. Nonetheless, within the Republika Srpska and Serbia, as well as in Croatia, democratic and non-nationalistic elements could play an important, albeit difficult role, as tellers of non-nationalistic historical truths.[12]

THE HISTORICAL lessons of the nightmare of ethnic cleansing are not just for Bosnia-Herzegovina and its people, but for all of us. It is important to acknowledge that the view of history that was taught to the generations after World War II as something linear that travels predictably forward did not assist in anticipating the collapse of Yugoslavia or ethnic cleansing in Bosnia. This historical view did not take adequate account of the ability of the incredible power of personal and historical memories of trauma and suffering to stimulate individual and collective changes and actions. Nor did it understand how mighty is the need to forget, nor the likelihood of not drawing the necessary links between the occurrence of different social traumas.

Ethnic cleansing in Bosnia-Herzegovina has compelled so many to reconsider the post-Holocaust anthem, "never again."[13] It was a modernist dream, where we believed ourselves to be in possession of the truth, and to have our hands on the reins of social progress. We dreamt that, after World War II, we could put this world into some kind of new order; that when we awoke from the Holocaust, we could make the nightmares of genocide in Europe disappear. This "never again" did not stop ethnic cleansing in Bosnia-Herzegovina.

Walter Benjamin has satirized the historical view centered on "progress" in his tale of the angel of history.[14] The angel is caught by a storm that spins him around and "irresistibly propels him into the future to which his back is turned, while the pile of debris before him grows skyward." The angel's face is turned toward the past. It is the memories of past traumas and suffering that drive this history and take it in the opposite direction of progress.

But there is also risk in giving oneself over to the belief that history is to blame, and that historical memories of collective traumatization can only serve to extend the cycles of violence. Experiencing a history that is a nightmare inevitably brings up dreams for that history. The suffering that comes of social evils can stimulate us to see what a history was, could have been, or now must be. Although they are no consolation for that which was destroyed, in dreams we find possibilities for social change that can bring remarkable new meanings and structures to survivors and their communities.[15]

It is a wave of collective memory from the history of the Jews that pushes me to engage other peoples' traumatization in different times and places. My personal search for one people's history propels me into another historical space, that of Bosnia-Herzegovina. It is there that I can help the survivors, but also reflect and write upon the totality of that history, in the tradition of literary documentary work.[16] I explore a historical landscape that is full of nightmares of atrocities, but also the years of living together, and endeavor to learn from intensive immersion into their collisions and connectedness.

This work becomes a testimony to the fact that the nightmares of history bring terrible suffering, but also to the faith that these nightmares actually contain gifts of great knowing, and can stimulate the necessary desire to receive and deal responsibly with such cruel and awesome stories.

Notes

Preface

1. All sides made aggression and committed human rights violations, but by no means were these equal in size or scope. This book focuses on the ethnic cleansing of Bosnia-Herzegovina by Serbian and Bosnian Serb forces, which was far and away the primary, the largest, and the most criminal act of aggression that took place in the collapse of the Second Yugoslavia. It does not address the war between Serbia and Croatia, the Croatian aggression against Bosnia-Herzegovina, nor the war between the Bosnian-Croat Federation and the Serb forces. These topics are addressed in many of the historical source materials on Yugoslavia and Bosnia-Herzegovina that are mentioned in the notes.

2. For a listing of many of these projects, see *Working for Peace in the Balkans: A Guide to U.S. Organizations* (New York: AFSC, 1996).

3. This sense is well captured in Judith Herman, *Trauma and Recovery* (New York: Basic Books, 1992); and Inger Agger and Soren Jensen, *Trauma and Recovery Under State Terrorism* (London: Zed Books, 1996).

4. For examples of several trauma scholars who have addressed this theme see Cathy Caruth, *Trauma: Explorations in Memory* (Baltimore: Johns Hopkins University Press, 1995); Robert Jay Lifton, *The Protean Self: Human Resilience in an Age of Fragmentation* (New York: Basic Books, 1993); and Fred Turner, *Echoes of Combat: The Vietnam War in American Memory* (New York: Anchor Books, 1996).

5. Descriptions of this kind of interviewing are to be found in the trauma scholars Robert Jay Lifton, *Death in Life* (New York: Touchstone Books, 1976), 3–12; Lifton, *The Protean Self: Human Resilience in an Age of Fragmentation* (New York: Basic Books, 1993), 1–31; and Inger Agger, *The Blue Room: Trauma and Testimony among Refugee Women: A Psychosocial Exploration* (London: Zed Books, 1992), 1–19. See also Robert Coles, *Doing Documentary Work* (New York and Oxford: Oxford University Press, 1997); Daniel Levinson, *The Seasons of a Man's Life* (New York: Alfred A. Knopf, 1978), 7–17; Levinson, *The Seasons of a Woman's Life* (New York: Alfred A. Knopf, 1996), 7–10; and Alessandro Portelli, *The Death of Luigi Trastulli and Other Stories* (Albany: State University of New York Press, 1991), 29–58.

6. Bosnian survivors directly quoted in this text gave informed consent in concordance with the Institutional Review Boards at the University of Illinois at Chicago and Yale University.

7. Several book reviews offer overviews of recent publications. These include Mark Danner's several articles in *The New York Review*, including "The U.S. and the Yugoslav Catastrophe," 20 November 1997; "America and the Bosnia Genocide," 4 December 1997; "Clinton, the U.N., and the Bosnian Disaster," 18 December 1997; "Bosnia: The Turning Point," 5 February 1998; "Bosnia: Breaking the Machine," 19 February 1998; and "Slouching Toward Dayton," 23 April 1998. See also Norman Stone, "History with a Vengeance," *Times Literary Supplement*, 14 May 1993, 10–11; Foaud Ajami, "In Europe's Shadows," *The New Republic*, 21 November 1994, 29–37. For World Wide Web sources, see the Bosnet website *http://www.bosnet.org/bosnet_nf.html* and its many links.

8. See Dori Laub and Nanette Auerhahn, "Knowing and Not Knowing Massive Psychic Trauma: Forms of Traumatic Memory," *International Journal of Psychoanalysis* 74, no. 2 (April 1993), 287–302; and Shoshana Felman and Dori Laub, *Testimony: Crises of Witnessing in Literature, Psychoanalysis and History* (New York and London: Routledge, 1992), 57–92.

9. See also Lawrence Langer, *Holocaust Testimonies: The Ruins of Memory* (New Haven and London: Yale University Press, 1991); Geoffrey Hartman, *The Longest Shadow: In the Aftermath of the Holocaust* (Bloomington: Indiana University Press, 1996); and Herbert Hirsch, *Genocide and the Politics of Memory: Studying Death to Preserve Life* (Chapel Hill and London: The University of North Carolina Press, 1995). See also Cathy Caruth, *Unclaimed Experience* (Baltimore: Johns Hopkins University Press, 1996); and Carolyn Forché, *Against Forgetting: Twentieth Century Poetry of Witness* (New York and London: W. W. Norton, 1993), 29–47.

10. Dialogism is brilliantly described by the Russian literary critic Mikhail Bakhtin as presented and analyzed in two excellent works on Bahktin's writings: Michael Holquist, *Dialogism: Bakhtin and His World* (London and New York: Routledge, 1990), and Caryl Emerson, *The First Hundred Years of Mikhail Bakhtin* (Princeton, N.J.: Princeton University Press, 1997), 127–161.

Prologue

1. The interconnectedness of these two realms is a major theme that has been explored by many of the writers referenced in this book, from the viewpoints of history, mental health, and art.

2. Zlatko Dizdarevic, *Sarajevo: A War Journal* (New York: Fromm International, 1993), 48.

3. Kai Erikson, "Notes on Trauma and Community," in *Trauma: Explorations in Memory*, ed. Cathy Caruth (Baltimore and London: The Johns Hopkins University Press, 1995), 183–199.

4. Robert Jay Lifton, *The Protean Self: Human Resilience in an Age of Fragmentation* (New York: Basic Books, 1993), 14.

5. Robert Jay Lifton, *The Future of Immortality and Other Essays for a Nuclear Age* (New York: Basic Books, 1987), 112.

6. See Daniel Jonah Goldhagen, *Hitler's Willing Executioners: Ordinary Germans and the Holocaust* (New York: Alfred A. Knopf, 1996).

7. See Edward A. Tiryakian, "The Wild Cards of Modernity," *Daedalus: Journal of the American Academy of Arts and Sciences* 126, no. 2 (Spring 1997, "Human Diversity"), 147–182

8. See Benedict Anderson, *Imagined Communities: Reflections on the Origin and Spread of Nationalism* (London and New York: Verso, 1983), 6. On the topic of nationalism see also Ernest Gellner, *Nations and Nationalism* (Ithaca, N.Y.: Cornell University Press, 1983); and Julia Kristeva, *Nations Without Nationalism* (New York: Columbia University, 1993).

9. Geoffrey Hartman, *The Longest Shadow: In the Aftermath of the Holocaust* (Bloomington: Indiana University Press, 1996), 28.

10. James Young, *The Texture of Memory: Holocaust Memorials and Meaning* (New Haven and London: Yale University Press, 1993), x–xi.

11. Claude Lévi-Strauss, *Conversations with Claude Lévi-Strauss* (Chicago and London: University of Chicago Press, 1991), 159–160.

12. Gerda Lerner, *Why History Matters: Life and Thought* (New York and Oxford: Oxford University Press, 1997), 199–211.

13. Carl Schmitt, *The Concept of the Political* (Chicago and London: University of Chicago Press, 1996).

14. Robert Jay Lifton undertook such a project in his studies of several "mass psychohistorical dislocations" of the cold-war era. His major theoretical treatise is *The Broken Connection* (New York: Simon and Schuster, 1979). See also Lifton, *The Life of the Self: Towards a New Psychology* (New York: Basic Books, 1984).

15. See Patricia Forestier, *Bosnia: The Minds Behind Purification* (Paris: Citizens Commission on Human Rights, 1994). The Citizens Commission on Human Rights is a unit of Scientology that describes itself as "Investigating and Exposing Psychiatric Violations of Human Rights Since 1969." See also Forestier, *War of Aggression in Ex-Yugoslavia* (Paris: Citizens Commission on Human Rights, 1993), and "Genocide: How the Barbarities of 'Ethnic Cleansing' Were Spawned by Psychiatry," *Freedom*, May 1993, 6–36.

16. For a discussion of a psychiatrist's involvement with Nazi genocide, see the chapter on Eduard Wirths in Robert Jay Lifton, *The Nazi Doctors: Medical Killing and the Psychology of Genocide* (New York: Basic Books, 1986), 384–414. See also Walter Reich, "Human Rights Violations Should Concern Psychiatry," *Psychiatric News*, Commentary, 18 May 1990, 8.

17. Yael Danieli, Nigel S. Rodley, and Lars Wesaeth, eds., *International Responses to Traumatic Stress: Humanitarian, Human Rights, Justice, Peace and Development Contributions, Collaborative Actions, and Future Initiatives* (Amityville, N.Y.: Baywood Publishing, 1996).

18. Hartman, *Longest Shadow*, 142.

Part I *Listening to History*

1. Bosnians receive specialized community mental health services through the Bosnian Mental Health Program of the Chicago Health Outreach, a collaboration of the Heartland Alliance with the State of Illinois Department of Human Services, and The University of Illinois at Chicago Department of Psychiatry.

2. B. [pseud.], interviews by author, tape recording, March 1995, Bosnian Survivors Oral History Archives, Project on Genocide, Psychiatry and Witnessing, University of Illinois at Chicago.

3. Bajram is the holiday that marks the end of Ramadan, the month of fasting.

4. In World War II, the city of Foča was the site of fierce fighting and horrific massacres by the Chetniks and Ustasha. See Noel Malcolm, *Bosnia: A Short History* (New York: New York University Press, 1994), 188; and Richard West, *Tito and the Rise and Fall of Yugoslavia* (New York: Carroll and Graff, 1995), 117–118.

5. Chetniks were the Serbian nationalist fighters in World War II led by Draza Mihailovic. See West, *Tito*.

Chapter 1 *We All Lived Together*

1. E. [pseud.], interview by author, tape recording, April 1995, Bosnian Survivors Oral History Archives, Project on Genocide, Psychiatry and Witnessing, University of Illinois at Chicago.

2. Abdulah Skaljic, *Turcizmi srpskohrvatskog jezika*, 4th edition (Sarajevo: Svjetlost, 1979), 460.

3. Tone Bringa, *Being Muslim the Bosnian Way* (Princeton, N.J. and Chichester: Princeton University Press, 1995), 32.

4. See chapters by Mark Pinson and Ivo Banac in Mark Pinson (ed.), *The Muslims of Bosnia-Herzegovina* (Cambridge: Harvard University Press, 1994), 84–128 and 129–154.

5. Selections from various survivor interviews conducted by Alma Dzubur, M.D. and by author, tape recordings, 1995 to 1998, Bosnian Survivors Oral History Archives, Project on Genocide, Psychiatry and Witnessing, University of Illinois at Chicago. All subsequent survivor quotes in this chapter not otherwise attributed come from this same source.

6. Ales Debeljak, *Twilight of the Idols: Recollections of a Lost Yugoslavia* (New York: White Pine Press, 1994), 35.

7. See Ante Markotic, Ejub Sijericic, and Asim Abdurahmanovic, "Ethnic Map of Bosnia-Herzegovina," *Why* (Sarajevo, February 1997), reprinted in Tim Judah, *The Serbs: History, Myth & the Destruction of Yugoslavia* (New Haven and London: Yale University Press, 1997), 317.

8. See Noel Malcolm, *Bosnia: A Short History* (New York: New York University Press, 1994), 156–173; Richard West, *Tito and the Rise and Fall of Yugoslavia* (New York: Carroll and Graff, 1995); and Christopher Bennet, *Yugoslavia's Bloody Collapse: Causes, Course and Consequences* (New York: New York University Press, 1995).

9. See Malcolm, *Bosnia*, 174–192; West, *Tito*.

10. Tom Gjelten summarizes data on intermarriage from the Bosnian Government's Institute of Statistics. In 1991, 34 percent of marriages in Sarajevo were mixed, as compared with 29 percent in urban municipalities and 9 percent in rural areas. Tom Gjelten, *Sarajevo Daily: A City and Its Newspaper Under Siege* (New York: Harper-Collins, 1995).

11. Roger Cohen, "A War in the Family," *New York Times*, 6 August 1995, Section 6, 32.

12. Inger Agger, *Mixed Marriages: Voices from a Psycho-Social Workshop Held in Zagreb, Croatia* (Brussels: European Community Humanitarian Office, 1996), 90. Agger estimates that in all Yugoslavia, from 1962 to 1982, the number of people living in households headed by mixed marriages was approximately 2 million.

13. Dzevad Karahasan, *Sarajevo, Exodus of a City* (New York, Tokyo, London: Kodansha International, 1993), 3.

14. Karahasan states it well: "Every member of a dramatic cultural system needs the Other as proof of his or her own identity, because one's own particularity is being proven and articulated in relationship to the particularities of the Other" (pp. 6–7).

15. *Manhattan*, directed by Woody Allen. Produced by Charles H. Joffe and Robert Greenhut, screenplay by Woody Allen and Marshall Brickman, 1979.

16. Malcolm, *Bosnia*, 240.

17. Debeljak, *Twilight*, 65–66.

18. Richard Rorty, *Contingency, Irony, and Solidarity* (Cambridge: Cambridge University Press, 1989).

19. Malcolm, *Bosnia*, 251.

20. N. [pseud.], interview by author, handwritten notes, 1996, Bosnian Survivors Oral History Archives, Project on Genocide, Psychiatry and Witnessing, University of Illinois at Chicago.

21. Stevan Pavlowitch, *The Improbable Survivor: Yugoslavia, 1918–1988* (London: C. Hurst, 1989), 132.

22. These matters are also taken up in Bogdan Denitch, *Ethnic Nationalism: The Tragic Death of Yugoslavia* (Minneapolis and London: University of Minnesota Press, 1994), 30–42.

23. Debeljak, *Twilight*, 70.
24. Pavlowitch, *Improbable Survivor*, 141.
25. See Drakulic's "Afterword" to Karahasan, *Sarajevo*, 119. See also her piece on nationalism in Croatia, "Nazis Among Us," *New York Review of Books*, 27 May 1993, 21–22.

Chapter 2   *Living Through Ethnic Cleansing*

1. H. [pseud.], interview by author, tape recording, March 1995, Bosnian Survivors Oral History Archives, Project on Genocide, Psychiatry and Witnessing, University of Illinois at Chicago. For other published interviews with survivors see Božica Ercegovac-Jambrović, ed., *Genocide: Ethnic Cleansing in Northwest Bosnia* (Zagreb: Croatian Information Centre, 1993); Alijah Gordon, ed., *Bosnia: Testament to War Crimes as Told by Survivors* (Kuala Lumpur: Malaysian Sociological Research Institute, 1993); *War Crimes in Bosnia-Herzegovina* (New York: Helsinki Watch, 1992); *War Crimes in Bosnia-Herzegovina, Volume II* (New York: Helsinki Watch, 1993); and Rezak Hukanovic, "The Evil at Omarska," *The New Republic*, 12 February 1996, 24–29.
2. See the first Holocaust survivor interviews published in English in David Boder, *I Did Not Interview the Dead* (Urbana: University of Illinois Press, 1949).
3. See Laura Silber and Allen Little, *Yugoslavia: Death of a Nation* (New York: TV Books, 1995); and Noel Malcolm, *Bosnia: A Short History* (New York: New York University Press, 1994).
4. See Silber and Little, *Yugoslavia*, 226–227.
5. For more information on Jews in Sarajevo see Dr. Moric Levy, *Sefardi u Bosni* (Sarajevo: bosanska biblioteka, 1997); and *Jewish Community, Sarajevo* (Sarajevo: Jewish Community, 1984).
6. See Daniel Jonah Goldhagen, *Hitler's Willing Executioners: Ordinary Germans and the Holocaust* (New York: Alfred A. Knopf, 1996).
7. Ibid.
8. There are many chronicles of ethnic cleansing. See Norman Cigar, *Genocide in Bosnia* (College Station: Texas A&M University Press, 1995); Laura Silber and Allen Little, *Yugoslavia: Death of a Nation* (New York: TV Books, 1995); Christopher Bennett, *Yugoslavia's Bloody Collapse: Causes, Course and Consequences* (New York: New York University Press, 1995); Bogdan Denitch, *Ethnic Nationalism: The Tragic Death of Yugoslavia* (Minneapolis and London: University of Minnesota Press, 1994); Nader Mousavizadeh, *The Black Book of Bosnia* (New York: Basic Books, 1996); David Rieff, "Original Virtue, Original Sin," *New Yorker*, 23 November 1992, 82–95; Andrew Bell-Fialkoff, "A Brief History of Ethnic Cleansing," *Foreign Affairs* 72, no. 3 (1993), 110–121; and Ed Vulliamy, *Seasons in Hell: Understanding Bosnia's War* (New York: Simon and Schuster, 1993).
9. *Genocide: Ethnic Cleansing in Northwest Bosnia*, 80.
10. "Serb Describes War Atrocities," *Dallas Morning News*, 17 December 1992, 1A.
11. The organized rape of Muslim and Croat women by Serbian forces has been the most publicly discussed of all the atrocities of ethnic cleansing. Understandably, it has also been extraordinarily difficult for survivors to talk about. Some writings on the subject include Alexandra Stiglmayer, *Mass Rape: The War Against Women in Bosnia-Herzegovina* (Lincoln and London: University of Nebraska Press, 1994); Beverly Allen, *Rape Warfare* (Minneapolis and London: University of Minnesota Press, 1996); and especially Seada Vranic, *Breaking the Wall of Silence: The Voices of Raped Bosnia* (Zagreb: AntiBarbarus, 1996); Catherine McKinnon, "Turning Rape into Pornography: Postmodern Genocide," *Ms.*, July/August 1993, 24–30; and Catherine McKinnon, "Crimes of War, Crimes of Peace," in *On Human Rights: The Oxford Amnesty Lectures*, edited by S. Lukes, J. Rawls, C. MacKinnon et al. (New York: Basic Books,

1993). Vranic describes several patterns to rape: "urban," where women in occupied cities were kidnapped and detained, raped, then murdered or released; "rural," where rapes were committed by military or paramilitary soldiers or locals as they cleansed; and rape in detention or "rape camps."

12. *Genocide: Ethnic Cleansing in Northwest Bosnia*, 77.
13. Chuck Sudetic, "More Bosnians Give Up Homes to Their Enemies," *New York Times*, 22 May 1993, A4.
14. For descriptions of concentration camps, see Roy Gutman, *Witness to Genocide* (New York: Macmillan, 1993); David Rhodes, *Endgame* (New York: Farrar, Straus and Giroux, 1997). See oral history sources from note 2, this chapter. See also *Calling the Ghosts*, a film by Mandy Jacobson and Karmen Jelincic, Bowery Productions, 1997.
15. *Genocide: Ethnic Cleansing in Northwest Bosnia*, 88.
16. See Gutman, *Witness*. See also an interview with Roy Gutman in Sherry Ricchiardi, "Exposing Genocide," *American Journalism Review* (June 1993), 32–36.
17. *Genocide: Ethnic Cleansing in Northwest Bosnia*, 81.
18. Gordon, *Bosnia: Testament*, 64.
19. See Rhodes, *Endgame*; Silber and Little, *Yugoslavia*, 265–275; and James Gow, *Triumph of the Lack of Will* (New York: Columbia University Press, 1997).
20. Zlatko Dizdarevic, *Sarajevo: A War Journal* (New York: Fromm International, 1993), 128.
21. See Rhodes, *Endgame*; also Jan Willem Honig, *Srebrenica: Record of a War Crime* (New York and London: Penguin, 1996).
22. Robert Jay Lifton, *The Nazi Doctors: Medical Killing and the Psychology of Genocide* (New York: Basic Books, 1986).
23. *Genocide: Ethnic Cleansing in Northwest Bosnia*, 101.
24. See *Urbicide—Sarajevo*, (Sarajevo: Association of Architects of DAS-SABIH, 1994).
25. See Tom Gjelten, *Sarajevo Daily: A City and Its Newspaper Under Siege* (New York: HarperCollins, 1995).
26. Lecture delivered by Dr. Enes Kujundzic, Beineke Library, Yale University, 1994. See "Destruction of Libraries in Croatia and Bosnia-Herzegovina," *International Leads* 7, no. 2 (1993), 1–2.
27. *Wararchitecture* (Sarajevo: Association of Architects DAS-SABIH, 1994). See also *Wararchitecture: A Special Issue of ARH Magazine for Architecture, Town Planning, and Design* 24 (June 1993). 28. *Wararchitecture* [special issue], 22.
29. *Genocide: Ethnic Cleansing in Northwest Bosnia*, 43.
30. Walter Reich, "Erasing the Holocaust," *New York Times Book Review*, 11 July 1993, 1.

Chapter 3　　*The Experience of the Bosnian Refugees*

1. Karen Malpede wrote and directed *The Beekeeper's Daughter*, which tells the story of a Bosnian woman survivor of mass rape. I was the dramaturge for the New York and Italian productions of this play from 1995 to 1997. See Karen Malpede, "Theatre at 2000: A Witnessing Project," in Charles B. Strozier and Michael Flynn, eds., *The Year 2000: Essays on the End* (New York: New York University Press, 1997).
2. See Arif Smajkic, ed., *Health and Social Consequences of the War in Bosnia-Herzegovina*, 4th edition (Sarajevo: Svjetlost and Institute of Public Health of Bosnia-Herzegovina, 1996), 72. Smajkic estimates that 1.25 million Bosnians are refugees living abroad.
3. The World Wide Web has provided a much-used channel for communication: the Bosnet website *http://www.bosnet.org/bosnet_nf.html*.
4. Those who maintain that the refugees are simply suffering from PTSD are themselves the victims of an impairment in time sense. For considerations of this change in time sense see the discussion of belatedness in the "Introduction" to Cathy Caruth, *Trauma:*

Explorations in Memory (Baltimore: Johns Hopkins University Press, 1995). See also David Becker, "The Deficiency of the Concept of Post Traumatic Stress Disorder When Dealing with Victims of Human Rights Violations," in R. J. Kleber, C. R. Figley, and P. R. Gersons, eds., *Beyond Trauma: Cultural and Social Dynamics* (New York: Plenum Press, 1995), 99–110.

5. Refugees in Europe never had that luxury, being far closer to Bosnia, geographically and emotionally. In many European countries, Bosnians were given only temporary refugee status. For a description of the 350,000 Bosnian refugees in Germany, see Alan Cowall, "For Bosnian Refugees, Return May Be an Illusion," *New York Times*, 8 December 1995, A6.

6. For discussions on the media and its relation to knowing and action see Johanna Neuman, *Lights, Camera, War* (New York: St. Martin's Press, 1996); James Gow, Richard Paterson, and Alison Preston, eds., *Bosnia by Television* (London: British Film Institute, 1996); Thomas Cushman and Stjepan G. Mestrovic, eds., *This Time We Knew: Western Responses to Genocide in Bosnia* (New York and London: New York University Press, 1996); Robert I. Rotberg and Thomas G. Weiss, eds., *From Massacres to Genocide* (Cambridge: The World Peace Foundation, 1996); Nader Mousavizadeh, *The Black Book of Bosnia* (New York: Basic Books, 1996); and Robert Jay Lifton, *The Protean Self: Human Resilience in an Age of Fragmentation* (New York: Basic Books, 1993), 17–21.

7. Zlatko Dizdarevic, *Sarajevo: A War Journal* (New York: Fromm International, 1993), and *Portraits of Sarajevo* (New York: Fromm International, 1994), 8.

8. See Prologue, notes 5 and 6.

9. See discussions on definitions of genocide in Leo Kupfer, *Genocide: Its Political Uses in the Twentieth Century* (New Haven and London: Yale University Press, 1981); and definition of refugee in Daniel E. Valentine and John Chr. Knudsen, eds., *Mistrusting Refugees* (Berkeley and Los Angeles: University of Califronia Press, 1995).

10. Simon Schama, *Landscape and Memory* (New York: Alfred A. Knopf, 1995), 478–490.

11. Ales Debeljak, *Twilight of the Idols: Recollections of a Lost Yugoslavia* (New York: White Pine Press, 1994), 54.

12. After Dayton, this changed—at least on paper. Still, few believed they would ever again live in their former homes.

13. Gordon, *Bosnia: Testament*, 67.

14. See text and reference list of Dan Bar-On, "Attempting to Overcome the Intergenerational Transmission of Trauma: Dialogue Between Descendants of Victims and of Perpetrators," in Roberta J. Apfel and Bennet Simo, eds., *Minefield in Their Hearts: The Mental Health of Children in War and Communal Violence* (New Haven and London: Yale University Press, 1996). See Yael Danieli, ed., *International Handbook of Multigenerational Legacies of Trauma* (New York: Plenum, 1998).

15. This is an allusion to Daniel Levinson, *The Seasons of a Man's Life* (New York: Alfred Knopf, 1978).

16. See Arthur Miller as quoted in Levinson, *Seasons*, 47. Concerning the relationship between man and society, Miller wrote, "The fish is in the water and the water is in the fish."

17. To rape a woman indelibly marks her life as inhabited by a memory that tells her again and again that she is not fit to participate in the life around her. A woman's ties with other generations can be severed, as are her ties to her husband, family, and friends. In this way, rape destroys not only the woman, but the community around her. Merhamet may also be a victim, because the woman, her family, and her community are likely to lose the capacity or the will to continue to participate in it. Mandy Jacobson's 1996 film, *Calling the Ghosts: A Story about Rape, War and Women*,

presents the stories of two women, Jadranka Cigelj and Nusreta Sivac, who have shown great courage and strength in telling their stories, in seeking social justice, and in doing humanitarian work for women survivors of rape.

18. Dizdarevic, *Sarajevo*, 61.

19. Dizdarevic, *Sarajevo*, 134.

20. See *Unfinished Peace: Report of the International Commission on the Balkans* (Washington, D.C.: Carnegie Endowment for International Peace, 1996), 86; Chris Hedges, "Islam Bent into Ideology: Vengeful Vision of Hope," *New York Times*, 23 October 1994, Section E, 3.

21. Robert Jay Lifton, "Dreaming Well: On Death and History," in Deirdre Barrett, ed., *Trauma and Dreams* (Cambridge and London: Harvard University Press, 1996), 125–140; Ernest Hartmann, *The Nightmare: The Psychology and Biology of Terrifying Dreams* (New York: Basic Books, 1984).

22. See Leonard Shengold, *Soul Murder: The Effects of Childhood Abuse and Deprivation* (New York: Guilford Press, 1989). Shengold explores the rat image as it appears in associations and imagery of trauma survivors. A fascinating exploration of the nature of suffering after torture can be found in Elaine Scarry, *The Body in Pain* (New York and Oxford: Oxford University Press, 1985).

23. For a discussion of exile, see John Simpson, ed., *The Oxford Book of Exile* (Oxford and New York: Oxford University Press, 1995); Julie Mertus, Jasmina Tesanovic, Habiba Metikos, and Rada Boric, eds., *The Suitcase: Refugee Voices from Bosnia and Croatia* (Berkeley: University of California Press, 1996); Rolf Kleber and Berhold Gersons, *Beyond Trauma: Cultural and Social Dynamics* (New York and London: Plenum Press, 1993); Anna Cataldi, ed., *Letters from Sarajevo* (Shaftesbury: Element, 1993); Zdenki Lesic, ed., *Children of Atlantis: Voices from the Former Yugoslavia* (Budapest: Central European University Press, 1995); Daniel E. Valentine and John Chr. Knudsen, eds., *Mistrusting Refugees* (Berkeley and Los Angeles: University of California Press, 1995). See also Monica McGoldrick, "Ethnicity and the Family Life Cycle," in *The Changing Family Life Cycle*, ed. Betty Carter and Monica McGoldrick (Boston: Allyn and Bacon, 1989).

Part II   *Psychiatrists Colliding with History*

1. Vaso Cubrilovic, "The Expulsion of the Arnauts," unpublished translated manuscript. The original of this paper is stored in No. 2, folder 4, box 69, Archive of the Yugoslavian Kingdom Army, Military Historian Institute of the YPA, in Belgrade, Serbia. See also *Roots of Serbian Aggression*, ed. Boze Covic (Zagreb: Centar za strane jezike, 1992), 106–124. There the Cubrilovic quote is translated as, "To cause the massive emigration the first prerequisite is to generate fear."

2. Robert Jay Lifton, *The Nazi Doctors: Medical Killing and the Psychology of Genocide* (New York: Basic Books, 1986). For example, the German psychiatrist Alfred Hoche coauthored a text that featured the concept of "life unworthy of life" and the approach of using "rigid medical criteria" to determine "incurability" with absolute certainty. Psychiatrists led the Nazis' "euthanasia" program, which provided direct medical killing of children and adults who had "Serious Hereditary and Congenital Diseases."

3. See Prologue, note 16. This was not the first time psychiatrists had been involved in addressing the clinical conditions of survivors of genocide. Kurt Eissler's classic paper, "Perverted Psychiatry?" describes the German Consulate's psychiatric experts, who assessed Holocaust survivors in response to their application for war reparations and failed to make the link between their traumatic experiences and psychopathologic outcome. These experts dismissed survivors' symptoms as being of "constitu-

tional etiology." See Kurt Eissler, "Perverted Psychiatry," *American Journal of Psychiatry* 123 (1987), 1352–1358.

4. For discussion of physicians' involvement in perpetrating torture and oppression, see U. Cilasun, "Torture and the Participation of Doctors," *Journal of Medical Ethics* 17 (1991), 21–22; G. Martirena, "The Medical Profession and Torture," *Journal of Medical Ethics* 17 (1991), 23–25.

5. The Council on International Affairs Report, Eugene Feigelson, M.D., Chairperson. *American Journal of Psychiatry*, February 1994.

6. L. [pseud.], interviews with author, handwritten notes, January 1996, Bosnian Survivors Oral History Archives, Project on Genocide, Psychiatry and Witnessing, University of Illinois at Chicago.

Chapter 4 *Jovan Raskovic's Fall and the Ascendance of Serbian Nationalism*

1. *Vjesnik*, Jovan Raskovic, 24 January 1992.

2. Personal communication, Charles Strozier.

3. Jovan Raskovic, *Luda zemlja* (Belgrade: Akvarius, 1990). Tvrtko Kulenovic translated the Raskovic texts for me.

4. From Alexandra Milenov, a review of Jovan Raskovic's *Luda zemlja* for Professor Cherif Bassiouni, 13 July 1993, unpublished manuscript. My first introduction to Raskovic's writings came from Milenov's scholarly discussion of them for Professor Bassiouni of the United Nations Commission of Experts for the War Crimes Tribunal in the Former Yugoslavia.

5. See Laura Silber and Allen Little, *Yugoslavia: Death of a Nation* (New York: TV Books, 1995), 97.

6. Concerning the Ustasha's brutality, see Richard West, *Tito and the Rise and Fall of Yugoslavia* (New York: Carroll and Graff, 1995); and Tim Judah, *The Serbs: History, Myth & the Destruction of Yugoslavia* (New Haven and London: Yale University Press, 1997).

7. Dusan Kecmanovic, *Vjesnik*, 10 September 1991.

8. Zarko Trebjesanin, *Vjesnik*, September 10, 1991.

9. An English translation of the complete Memorandum appears in Boze Covic (ed.), *Roots of Serbian Aggression* (Zagreb: Centar za strane jezike I Omladinski kulturni centar, 1993), 289–337.

10. See Silber and Little, *Yugoslavia*, 31–36. 11. This translation is quoted in Tim Judah, *The Serbs: History, Myth & the Destruction of Yugoslavia* (New Haven and London: Yale University Press, 1997), 160.

12. See Silber and Little, *Yugoslavia*, 37–47.

13. Silber and Little, *Yugoslavia*, 38.

14. Phillip J. Cohen, *Serbia's Secret War: Propaganda and the Deceit of History* (College Station: Texas A & M University Press, 1996), 3–27. See also Judah, *The Serbs*, 48–72.

15. See Judah, *The Serbs*, 168.

Chapter 5 *Radovan Karadzic and the Metaphors of Terror*

1. Richard West, *Tito and the Rise and Fall of Yugoslavia* (New York: Carroll and Graff, 1995).

2. See criticisms of the psychological approach to understanding terrorism in Joseba Zulaika and William A Douglas, *Terror and Taboo* (New York and London: Routledge, 1996).

3. Claude Lanzman, "The Obscenity of Understanding: An Evening with Claude

Lanzman," in Cathy Caruth, *Trauma: Explorations in Memory* (Baltimore: Johns Hopkins University Press, 1995), 200–220.

4. Some journalists have written profiles of Karadzic—most notably Mark Danner, who quotes several of the people I interviewed. See Mark Danner, "Bosnia: The Turning Point," *New York Review of Books* 45, no. 2, 34–40.

5. Marko Vesovic, interview with author, tape recording, January 1996, Bosnian Survivors Oral History Archives, Project on Genocide, Psychiatry and Witnessing, University of Illinois at Chicago.

6. The four people Marko alluded to were apparently Svetozar Koljevic (a professor of English literature), Nikolai Koljevic (his brother, a professor of comparative literature), Radovan Vukovic (a professor of Yugoslav literature), and Nenad Kecmanovic (a professor of political science, and the brother of another Sarajevan psychiatrist). All were Bosnian Serbs except Vukovic, a Serbian Serb from Kosovo.

7. Certainly the idea that it had to be a psychiatrist drew strength from the stigma associated with the profession—that psychiatrists are crazy and that they can control people's minds. Marko's comment was unsettling in other ways. If Karadzic was not the first choice, then we must of course wonder: how much differently would history have been had any one of the four others been chosen? Was the project structured in such a way that nearly anyone placed there would have served the overall genocide? This is a subject for historical study, but something that many survivors, especially those who knew Karadzic personally, puzzle over. Those who repeat to themselves: *If I had only known . . . .*

8. Petar II Petrovic-Njegos, a prince-bishop of Montenegro, published "The Mountain Wreath" in 1847, considered one of the most influential Serbian epic poems. It celebrates Milos Obilic, a hero of Kosovo who assassinated the Sultan, and is considered by Tim Judah to be "a paean to ethnic cleansing." See Tim Judah, *The Serbs: History, Myth & the Destruction of Yugoslavia* (New Haven and London: Yale University Press, 1997), 63–65, 76–78.

9. When the historians write their histories, they can and should analyze the matter of Montenegrin people and culture. That cannot be our preoccupation here, but we should be fair and not presume the worst. See Judah, *The Serbs*.

10. Mosa Pijade was a friend of Tito's. See Richard West, *Tito and the Rise and Fall of Yugoslavia* (New York: Carroll and Graff, 1995).

11. Interview with author, tape recording, January 1996, Bosnian Survivors Oral History Archives, Project on Genocide, Psychiatry and Witnessing, University of Illinois at Chicago.

12. Radovan Karadzic's poetry books are *Mad Spear* (Sarajevo: Svjetlost, 1968), *Remembrance of the Century* (Sarajevo: Svjetlost, 1971), and *Black Fairy Tale* (Sarajevo: Svjetlost, 1990). He also published a book of children's poetry. Tvrtko Kulenovic translated the Karadzic texts for me.

13. Ferida Durakovic, personal communication.

14. Tvrtko Kulenovic, personal communication.

15. Robert Jay Lifton, *The Protean Self: Human Resilience in an Age of Fragmentation* (New York: Basic Books, 1993), 161.

16. These insights on the fundamentalist mentality are discussed in Lifton's *The Protean Self*.

17. Karadzic, *Black Fairy Tale*, 9–12.

18. Karadzic, *Mad Spear*, 17.

19. Karadzic, *Remembrance*, 30.

20. See Bogdan Bogdanovic, "Murder of the City," *New York Review of Books*, 27 May 1993, 20.

21. Lifton, *Protean Self*, 162.

22. Karadzic, *Mad Spear*, 80–81.

23. See the text and endnotes of Chapter Four.
24. For more on Slobodan Milosevic see Aleksa Djilas, "A Profile of Slobodan Milosevic," *Foreign Affairs* 72, no. 3 (summer 1993), 81–96; also Judah, *The Serbs*.
25. Laura Silber and Allen Little, *Yugoslavia: Death of a Nation* (New York: TV Books, 1995), 205.
26. Norman Cigar, *Genocide in Bosnia* (College Station: Texas A&M University Press, 1995), 108.
27. Silber and Little, *Yugoslavia*, 218.
28. Cigar, *Genocide*, 37.
29. Silber and Little, *Yugoslavia*, 220.
30. Silber and Little, *Yugoslavia*, 232.
31. Cigar, *Genocide*, 52.
32. Interview with Peter Jennings, ABC Evening News, 4 February 1993.
33. In the Reuters Transcript Service, Interview Conducted 4 February 1993, New York.
34. In the Reuters Transcript Service, Interview Conducted 4 February 1993, New York.
35. Radovan Karadzic, interviewed on McNeil/Lehrer Newshour. Transcribed on the Reuter Washington Report, 8 February 1993.
36. Cigar, *Genocide*, 63.
37. Interview of Radovan Karadzic by Dmitry Yakushkin, *St. Petersburg Times*, 19 September 1993, 8d.
38. Robert Jay Lifton, *The Nazi Doctors: Medical Killing and the Psychology of Genocide* (New York: Basic Books, 1986), 15–16.
39. Another qualification has to do with a specific attitude that can be detected in Karadzic's public statements. I have described this attitude as an "ideology of conflict and division," but perhaps ideology is too strong a word to use, as Karadzic was no ideologue. It is more accurate to call it a "mentality of conflict and division." This may be thought of as a new strain of genocidal mentality. The mentality of conflict and division is a view perversely derived from Freudian psychodynamic principles in emphasizing the centrality of unconscious intrapsychic conflict in explaining human behavior. This worldview envisions tensions and clashes between different ethnic or national groups as roughly akin to unconscious intrapsychic conflict. It depicts ethnic or national conflicts as naturally exploding into extraordinary violence because at the essence of ethnic conflicts are unmitigated aggressive impulses stemming from unresolvable unconscious conflicts. In response, Karadzic, the genocidal leader, positions himself as a healer of this unconscious conflict writ large, and seeks a remedy through the division of opposed groups by expulsion or extermination.

    This mentality, which appears only intermittently, is the only trace I could find of Karadzic deploying something psychiatric in the service of genocide. Yet the very proposition of a psychiatrist as a genocidal leader is hard to let go of. So the speculations continue, and we hear questions like: Did Karadzic order mass rapes because he knew what psychological damage would result? These are questions that deserve answers, but questions that remain unanswered and that also reflect on how problematic it is for us to understand how leaders can persuade people to hate, to hurt, and to kill.

    Although Karadzic was not deploying himself as a psychiatrist, he was deploying himself as a professional. He brought to his work as a genocidal leader certain skills of communication, administration, and intellectual vision that are part of what it means to be a professional. Pulling off such an ambitious social project as genocide requires the participation of professionals, as discussed in Robert Jay Lifton and Eric Markusen, *The Genocidal Mentality: Nazi Holocaust and Nuclear Threat* (New York: Basic Books, 1990).
40. IFOR is the NATO military force in Bosnia-Herzegovina.

Chapter 6   *Psychiatric Apologists and the Denial of Genocide*

1. Predrag Kalicanin, Jovan Vukolic, Veronika Ispanovic-Radojkovic, and Dusica Lecic-Tosevksi, eds., *The Stresses of War* (Belgrade: Institute for Mental Health, 1993).
2. For discussions on related topics see Norman Cigar, *Genocide in Bosnia* (College Station: Texas A&M University Press, 1995); Ervin Staub, *The Roots of Evil: The Origins of Genocide and Other Group Violence* (Cambridge and New York: Cambridge University Press, 1989); and Robert Jay Lifton and Eric Markusen, *The Genocidal Mentality: Nazi Holocaust and Nuclear Threat* (New York: Basic Books, 1990).
3. An opportunity for indirect contact arose when the filmmaker Mandy Jacobson traveled to Belgrade. She visited the Serbian psychiatrists at their Institute and interviewed them for her film on Bosnian survivors of rape They told her how pleased they were that their work was attracting the interest of mental health professionals from the United States, and they spoke of some letters they had received. In person, they conveyed no new information nor any more moral sense than had been apparent in their letters and books (Mandy Jacobson, personal communication).
4. Unpublished letter by the author.
5. Several other American professionals have informed me that they also received such letters.
6. Ervin Staub, *The Roots of Evil: The Origins of Genocide and Other Group Violence* (Cambridge and New York: Cambridge University Press, 1989), 86–88.
7. Predrag Kalicanin, Dusica Lecic-Tosevksi, Jovan Bukelic, and Veronika Ispanovic-Radojkovic, eds., *The Stresses of War and Sanctions* (Belgrade: Institute for Mental Health, 1994).
8. Danilo Kis, *HomoPoeticus: Essays and Interviews* (New York: Farrar, Straus, and Giroux, 1995), 15.
9. Leo Kupfer, *Genocide: Its Political Uses in the Twentieth Century* (New Haven and London: Yale University Press, 1981) and *War Crimes in Bosnia-Herzegovina* (New York: Helsinki Watch, 1992) pp. 1–14.
10. Ironically, Robert Jay Lifton was one of the leaders of this group, which was awarded the Nobel Peace Prize.
11. Staub, *Roots of Evil*, 151–155, 184–187, 208–209, 227–230.
12. The Holocaust scholar Yehuda Bauer made this point concerning the distinction between genocidal potential and genocidal aggression in a lecture at the Yale Psychiatric Institute in October 1993.
13. Richard Lauer, "From Murderers to Heroes," *Franfurter Allgemeine Zeitung*, 6 March 1993, as quoted in *Sanctions*.
14. Eduard Klain, "Yugoslavia as a Group," *Croatian Medical Journal*, War Supplement 1, no. 3 (1991), 3–13.
15. Staub, *Roots of Evil*, 22–23.
16. See Tim Judah, *The Serbs: History, Myth & the Destruction of Yugoslavia* (New Haven and London: Yale University Press, 1997).
17. See Judah, *The Serbs*.
18. Anonymous, interview with author, tape recording, 1996, Bosnian Survivors Oral History Archives, Project on Genocide, Psychiatry and Witnessing, University of Illinois at Chicago.
19. It reads, "When well documented human rights abuses are denied or covered up by governments and other institutions, such denial is a further violation of human rights of the victims and is antithetical to the mental health of victims and their families." Policy Statement on the Denial of Human Rights Abuses, Board of Trustees, American Psychiatric Association, approved December 1993.
20. The American Psychiatric Association has not been silent on genocide in Bosnia; many APA members cared deeply about it. In 1993, at the urging of Herb Sacks, they passed a motion condemning Radovan Karadzic. Ray Freedbury, chair of the

APA's Committee for the International Abuse of Psychiatry and Psychiatrists, invited me to work with the committee on the issue of psychiatrists and genocide in Bosnia. But on the issue of apologist professionals we did not get beyond the review stage.

21. Robert Jay Lifton, *The Nazi Doctors: Medical Killing and the Psychology of Genocide* (New York: Basic Books, 1986).

22. Paul Chodoff, "Involuntary Hospitalization of Political Dissenters in the Soviet Union," *Psychiatric Opinion* 11 (1974), 5–19; Walter Reich, "The Case of General Grigorenko: A Psychiatric Reexamination of a Soviet Dissident," *Psychiatry* 43 (1980), 303–323.

23. Ironically, they claim that "the Institute was built to help the soldiers of World War Two to recover more easily from their psychic wounds" (*Stresses*, 19).

24. In the meantime, other professionals do not cease, but continue to work on behalf of war criminals, terrorists, and apologists from Serbia. One made some very ironic arguments. On March 13, 1996, the following appeared as a letter to the editor in the *New York Times* in response to an article on the war crimes tribunal by the legal scholar Theodore Meron. "You fail to disclose that Professor Meron has met and advised lawyers and prosecutors involved in activities of the International War Crimes Tribunal. As for the tribunal, it must create its own credibility. Resources must be allocated to the defense of the accused at the same level as funds allocated for salaries of judges, prosecutors and prosecution investigators." It was signed: "Nikola Kostich, Milwaukee; The writer, a lawyer, represents Dusko Tadic, a Bosnian Serb, before the War Crimes Tribunal."

The letter telling me to "cease and desist" also came from his hand. This Kostich was representing both the Bosnian Serbs accused of genocide and the psychiatrists from Serbia who wrote apologia for the genocide. An interesting connection.

25. Lawrence Wechsler, "Letter from Serbia: Aristotle in Belgrade," *The New Yorker*, 10 February 1997.

26. Nebojsa Popov, ed., *Serbian Side of the War* (Belgrade: Republica, 1996).

27. For more on Kosovo see *Open Wounds: Human Rights Abuses in Kosovo* (New York: Human Rights Watch/Helsinki, 1993); Hugh Poulton, *The Balkans: Minorities and States in Conflict* (London: Minority Rights Publications, 1993).

Part III   *Too Much History*

1. From Tina Rosenberg, *The Haunted Land: Facing Europe's Ghosts after Communism* (New York: Random House, 1995), xviii. Timothy Garton Ash deepens and extends the question by asking "whether to remember and treat the past at all, in any of the diverse available ways, or simply to try to forget it, and look to the future; when to address it, if it is to be addressed; who should do it; and finally how?" In Timothy Garton Ash, "Truth after Dictatorship," *New York Review of Books* 45, no. 3 (February 1998), 35–40. See also Timothy Garton Ash, "Central Europe: The Present Past," *New York Review of Books* 42, no. 12 (July 1995), 21–23, and his "Bosnia in Our Future," *New York Review of Books* 42, no. 20 (December 1995), 27–31.

2. Health statistics are provided in Arif Smajkic, ed., *Health and Social Consequences of the War in Bosnia-Herzegovina*, 4th edition (Sarajevo: Svjetlost and Institute of Public Health of Bosnia-Herzegovina, 1996).

3. Interview with author, tape recording, April 1997, Bosnian Survivors Oral History Archives, Project on Genocide, Psychiatry and Witnessing, University of Illinois at Chicago.

4. Interview with author, handwritten notes, January 1996, Bosnian Survivors Oral History Archives, Project on Genocide, Psychiatry and Witnessing, University of Illinois at Chicago.

5. Joseph Roth, *The Radetzky March* (Woodstock, N.Y.: Overlook Press, 1932) and *The Emperor's Tomb* (Woodstock, N.Y.: Overlook Press, 1950).

6. The memory work involved in recovery from collective traumatization is by no means linear or homogeneous. In his "Notes on Trauma and Community" (in *Trauma: Explorations in Memory*, ed. Cathy Caruth [Baltimore and London: The Johns Hopkins University Press, 1995], 183–199), Kai Erikson suggests that trauma "can surely be called pathological in the sense that it induces discomfort and pain, but the imagery that accompany the pain have a sense all their own"(p. 198). Erikson found that trauma can destroy but also create a communality, organized around trauma-induced "revised views of the world" (p. 198), and that "something of the sort can also happen to whole regions, whole countries" (p. 190).

7. Ash, "Truth after Dictatorship."

8. See Chris Hedges, "Never Again, Again: After the Peace, the War Against Memory," *New York Times*, 14 January 1996, Section 4, 1.

9. See Ash, "Truth after Dictatorship,"40.

Chapter 7   *Doing Testimony Psychotherapy with Survivors of Ethnic Cleansing*

1. H. [pseud.], interview with author, tape recording, March 1995, Bosnian Survivors Oral History Archives, Project on Genocide, Psychiatry and Witnessing, University of Illinois at Chicago.

2. Shoshana Felman and Dori Laub, *Testimony: Crises of Witnessing in Literature, Psychoanalysis and History* (New York and London: Routledge, 1992); Geoffrey Hartman, *The Longest Shadow: In the Aftermath of the Holocaust* (Bloomington: Indiana University Press, 1996); Lawrence Langer, *Holocaust Testimonies: The Ruins of Memory* (New Haven and London: Yale University Press, 1991); Terrence DePres, *The Survivor: An Anatomy of Life in the Death Camps* (Oxford: Oxford University Press, 1976).

3. Jean Amery, *At the Mind's Limits: Contemplations by a Survivor at Auschwitz and Its Realities* (Bloomington: Indiana University Press, 1980), as quoted in James E. Young, *The Texture of Memory: Holocaust Memorials and Meaning* (New Haven and London: Yale University Press, 1993), 1.

4. Young, *Texture*, as well as his *Writing and Rewriting the Holocaust* (Bloomington: Indiana University Press, 1988).

5. See Felman and Laub, *Testimony*; Langer, *Holocaust Testimonies*; and Hartman, *The Longest Shadow*.

6. Inger Agger and Soren Jensen, *Trauma and Recovery Under State Terrorism* (London: Zed Books, 1996).

7. See A. J. Cienfuegos and C. Monelli, "The Testimony of Political Repression as a Therapeutic Instrument," *American Journal of Orthopsychiatry* 53, no. 1 (1983), 43–51.

8. Agger and Jensen, *Trauma and Recovery*.

9. Inger Agger and Soren Jensen, "Testimony as Ritual and Evidence in Psychotherapy for Political Refugees," *Journal of Traumatic Stress* 3 (1990), 115–130.

10. Inger Agger, *The Blue Room: Trauma and Testimony among Refugee Women: A Psychosocial Exploration* (London: Zed Books, 1992).

11. Agger and Jensen, *Trauma and Recovery*, 228.

12. Alija Isakovic, *Rjecnik bosnakskog jezika (Karakteristicna leksika)* (Sarajevo: Bosanska knjiga, 1995), 304.

13. Bosnian survivor, personal communication.

14. "pricanje" means to tell a story. See Isakovic, *Rjecnik Bosnakskog*, 250.

15. A. [pseud.], interview with Alma Dzubur, tape recording, 1995, Bosnian Survivors Oral History Archives, Project on Genocide, Psychiatry and Witnessing, University of Illinois at Chicago.

16. Some leading activists in the United States were Steven Walker, Roy Gutman, Susan Sontag, and Catherine Mackinnon. See Susan Sontag, "Godot Comes to Sarajevo," *New York Review of Books*, 21 October 1993, 52–59; Stephen W. Walker, "Genocide: We are Responsible," *Tikkun* (November/December 1993), 19–22; and Steven A. Holmes, "State Department Balkan Aides Explain Why They Quit," *New York Times*, 26 August 1993, A12.

17. I strongly believe that these experiences also have to be documented as historical and legal evidence of war crimes for possible use in a truth commission or war crimes tribunal. See Theodore Meron, "The Case for War Crimes Tribunal in Yugoslavia," *Foreign Affairs* 72, no. 3 (summer 1993), 122–135.

18. I. [pseud.], interview with author, tape recording, 1997, Bosnian Survivors Oral History Archives, Project on Genocide, Psychiatry and Witnessing, University of Illinois at Chicago.

19. Carl Schmitt, *The Concept of the Political* (Chicago and London: University of Chicago Press, 1996).

20. Jonathan Shay, *Achilles in Vietnam: Combat Trauma and the Undoing of Character* (New York: Atheneum, 1994), 229 n. 13

21. See Agger and Jensen, *Trauma and Recovery*.

22. See Felman and Laub, *Testimony*; Geoffrey Hartman, *The Longest Shadow*; and Langer, *Holocaust Testimonies*.

23. Daniel Schaecter, *Searching for Memory: The Brain, the Mind, and the Past* (New York: Basic Books, 1996).

24. For a discussion of the shattering of trust after trauma, see Judith Herman, *Trauma and Recovery* (New York: Basic Books, 1992); Jennifer J. Freyd, *Betrayal Trauma: The Logic of Forgetting Childhood Abuse* (Cambridge and London: Harvard University Press, 1996); and Ronnie Janoff-Bulman, *Shattered Assumptions: Towards a New Psychology of Trauma* (New York: The Free Press, 1992).

25. Interviews and discussion at Sarajevo Seminar, October 1997, Bosnian Survivors Oral History Archives, Project on Genocide, Psychiatry and Witnessing, University of Illinois at Chicago.

26. Jonathan Shay, *Achilles in Vietnam: Combat Trauma and the Undoing of Character* (New York: Atheneum, 1994), 194.

27. See Claude Lévi-Strauss and Didier Eribon, *Conversations with Claude Lévi-Strauss* (Chicago and London: University of Chicago Press, 1991); and Leszek Kolakowski, *The Presence of Myth* (Chicago and London: University of Chicago Press, 1989).

28. *Unfinished Peace: Report of the International Commission on the Balkans* (Washington, D.C.: Carnegie Endowment for International Peace, 1996), 152.

29. Herbert Hirsch, *Genocide and the Politics of Memory: Studying Death to Preserve Life* (Chapel Hill and London: University of North Carolina Press, 1995), 178–180.

30. Dusan Kecmanovic, ed., *Psihijatrija* (Beograd i Zagreb: Medicinska knjiga, 1989).

31. For the army of international mental health consultants, it will also require a different mentality than is commonly expressed by trauma mental health professionals whose investment in the sense of their being a movement goes along with a belief that we possess a terrific body of knowledge that must be shared the world over.

32. See Arthur Kleinman and Joan Kleinman, eds., "Social Suffering," *Daedalus: Journal of the American Academy of Arts and Sciences* 125, no. 1 (winter 1996), special issue.

33. See Inger Agger and Soren Jensen, "Introduction: Mental Health and Human Rights," in Inger Agger, *Mixed Marriages: Voices from a Psycho-Social Workshop held in Zagreb, Croatia* (Brussels: European Community Humanitarian Office, 1996), 12–14.

34. Agger and Jensen, "Introduction."

35. Felman and Laub, *Testimony*, 74–75.

36. Robert Jay Lifton, lecture delivered at the 9th Annual Meeting of the International Society for Traumatic Stress Studies, 1993.

37. See Anthony Marsella, Matthew Friedman, Ellen Gerrity, and R. Scurfield, eds., *Ethnocultural Aspects of Posttraumatic Stress Disorder* (Washington, D.C.: American Psychological Association, 1996).
38. See Felman and Laub, *Testimony*, 75–76.
39. See Robert Jay Lifton, *Death in Life: Survivors of Hiroshima* (New York: Random House, 1967), 3–12; Felman and Laub, *Testimony*; also Phillip Hallie, "Skepticism, Narrative, and Holocaust Ethics," *Philosophical Forum* 16, nos. 1–2 (fall/winter 1984/5), 33–49.
40. See Alessandro Portelli, *The Death of Luigi Trastulli and Other Stories* (Albany: State University of New York Press, 1991), 29–58.
41. Joseph Roth, *The Radetzky March* (Woodstock, N.Y.: Overlook Press, 1932) and *The Emperor's Tomb* (Woodstock: Overlook Press, 1950), 164.

Chapter 8   *Artists Witnessing Ethnic Cleansing*

1. Danilo Kis, *HomoPoeticus: Essays and Interviews* (New York: Farrar, Straus, and Giroux, 1995).
2. The most widely read diary internationally is that of Zlata Filipovic, *Zlata's Diary: A Child's Life in Sarajevo* (New York: Viking, 1994).
3. Nadja Halilbegovic *Sarajevo's Childhood Wounded by War* (Ankara: Ministry of Culture, 1995).
4. Zlatko Dizdarevic, *Sarajevo: A War Journal* (New York: Fromm International, 1993).
5. Zlatko Dizdaveric, "Sarajevo's 700 Days," *The New York Times Magazine*, 10 April 1994, Section 6, 36.
6. Zlatko Dizdarevic, interview with author, tape recording, May 1994, Bosnian Survivors Oral History Archives, Project on Genocide, Psychiatry and Witnessing, University of Illinois at Chicago.
7. "Spy Photos Said to Indicate Mass Graves in Serb Held Town," *New York Times*, 10 August 1995, 1.
8. Tvrtko Kulenovic, lecture delivered at the conference sponsored by Villa Aurora on "Writing in a Time of War: Surviving in Sarajevo," Beverly Hills, California, 27 March 1996.
9. See Tim Judah, *The Serbs: History, Myth & the Destruction of Yugoslavia* (New Haven and London: Yale University Press, 1997).
10. Kemal Hadzic, personal communication.
11. Roland Barthes, *Camera Lucida: Reflections on Photography* (New York: Hill and Wang, 1991).
12. See Jamey Gambrell, "Sarajevo: Art in Extremis," *Art in America*, May 1994, 100–105; *Witnesses of Existence* catalogue (Sarajevo: The Obola Gallery, 1993).
13. On the other hand, it is both a product and an extension of the nonpolitical sensibility of living together in Bosnia-Herzegovina.
14. Tvrtko Kulenovic, personal communication.
15. Sanjin Jukic, interviews with author, tape recording, April 1994, Bosnian Survivors Oral History Archives, Project on Genocide, Psychiatry and Witnessing, University of Illinois at Chicago.
16. Carin Kuoni, *Joseph Beuys in America: Writings by and Interviews with the Artist* (New York: Four Walls Eight Windows), 141. On Joseph Beuys, see Donald Kuspit, "Joseph Beuys: The Body of the Artist," *Artforum* (summer 1991), 80–87; Caroline Tisdall, *Joseph Beuys* (New York: Solomon R. Guggenheim Museum, 1979).
17. See discussion on bystander in Ervin Staub, *The Roots of Evil: The Origins of Genocide and Other Group Violence* (Cambridge and New York: Cambridge University Press, 1989).
18. Dori Laub addresses the multiple layers of witnessing in Shoshana Felman and Dori

Laub, *Testimony: Crises of Witnessing in Literature, Psychoanalysis and History* (New York and London: Routledge, 1992), 75–76.

19. Tvrtko Kulenovic, "History of an Illness," *Stone Soup* 2 (1996), 38–49.
20. See the discussion of Alan Resnais's *Hiroshima mon amour* in Cathy Caruth, *Unclaimed Experience* (Baltimore: Johns Hopkins University Press, 1996), 25–56.
21. Damir Uzunovic, unpublished manuscript, presented at the Villa Aurora symposium on "Writing in a Time of War: Surviving in Sarajevo."
22. Tvrtko Kulenovic, interview with author, typewritten notes, September 1996, Bosnian Survivors Oral History Archives, Project on Genocide, Psychiatry and Witnessing, University of Illinois at Chicago.

Chapter 9   *The Bosnian Awakening*

1. The village of Sapna in Bosnia returned to life in January 1996, and two men were quoted, "We are trying, but we really need help so that people can return. What we most need are materials for roofs, doors, windows. . . . All of these children, none of them were here for the last four years. . . . But they know how to play soccer." In Raymond Bonner, "Muslims Resurrecting Their Village," *New York Times*, 19 January 1996, Section A, 7.
2. Bosnian students in Sarajevo, personal communications.
3. Kemal Bakarsic, interview with author, tape recording, January 1996, Bosnian Survivors Oral History Archives, Project on Genocide, Psychiatry and Witnessing, University of Illinois at Chicago.
4. *The Sarajevo Hagaddah* (Sarajevo: Svjetlost, 1988). See also Dr. Moric Levy, *Sefardi u Bosni* (Sarajevo: bosanska biblioteka, 1997).
5. Kemal Bakarsic, "Rare Books: The Story of the Sarajevo *Hagaddah*," *Judaica Librarianship* 9, nos. 1–2 (spring 1994–winter 1995), 135–143.
6. Claude Lanzman, "The Obscenity of Understanding: An Evening with Claude Lanzman," in Cathy Caruth, *Trauma: Explorations in Memory* (Baltimore: Johns Hopkins University Press, 1995), 202. See also Claude Lanzmann, *Shoah: An Oral History of the Holocaust* (New York: Pantheon, 1985).
7. Teacher, interview with author, handwritten notes, October 1997, Bosnian Survivors Oral History Archives, Project on Genocide, Psychiatry and Witnessing, University of Illinois at Chicago.
8. Mixed Marriage Association, interviews with author, tape recordings, October 1996 and October 1997, Bosnian Survivors Oral History Archives, Project on Genocide, Psychiatry and Witnessing, University of Illinois at Chicago.
9. Caritas is the name of the Catholic humanitarian aid organization.
10. Inger Agger, personal communication.
11. Inger Agger, "Mixed Marriage, Ethnic Cleansing, and Identity in Bosnia-Herzegovina," report for "Nordic Comparative Studies on the Reception of Refugees from a Repatriation Perspective," Institute of Anthropology, University of Copenhagen, 1996, 21–22.
12. The United States government shared these concerns, specifically about the Iranian presence. See Elaine Sciolino, "What's Iran Doing in Bosnia, Anyway?" *New York Times*, 10 December 1995, Section E, 4.
13. Imam Senad ef. Agic, "The Reality of the Genocide Against Bosnian Muslims," unpublished manuscript; and Imam Senad ef. Agic, interview with author, handwritten notes, March 1998, Bosnian Survivors Oral History Archives, Project on Genocide, Psychiatry and Witnessing, University of Illinois at Chicago.
14. B., interview with author, handwritten notes, November 1998, Bosnian Survivors Oral History Archives, Project on Genocide, Psychiatry and Witnessing, University of Illinois at Chicago

15. Timothy Garton Ash, "Truth after Dictatorship," *New York Review of Books* 45, no. 3 (February 1998), 35–40.
16. "The Islamic Declaration: A Program for the Islamicization of Moslems and Moslem Peoples," *South Slav Journal* 6, no. 1 (1983). Quoted and discussed in Noel Malcolm, *Bosnia: A Short History* (New York: New York University Press, 1994), 147–148.
17. Interviews with author in Bosnia-Herzegovina, tape recordings and handwritten notes, 1996 to 1998, Bosnian Survivors Oral History Archives, Project on Genocide, Psychiatry and Witnessing, University of Illinois at Chicago.
18. See note 17, this chapter.
19. Ibrahim Spahic, interviews with author, handwritten notes, 1996 to 1997, Bosnian Survivors Oral History Archives, Project on Genocide, Psychiatry and Witnessing, University of Illinois at Chicago.
20. John Fine, *The Bosnian Church: A New Interpretation. A Study of the Bosnian Church and Its Place in State and Society from the Thirteenth to the Fifteenth Centuries* (Boulder, Colo.: East European Quarterly, 1975). See also Malcolm, *Bosnia*, 27–42.
21. John Fine, "The Medieval and Ottoman Roots of Modern Bosnian Society," in Ivo Banac and Mark Pinson, eds., *The Muslims of Bosnia-Herzegovina* (Cambridge: Harvard University Press, 1994), 8.
22. See note 17, this chapter.
23. Ivan Pavkovic, my collaborator at the Project on Genocide, Psychiatry and Witnessing, has been pursuing reform of mental health policies in Croatia and Bosnia-Herzegovina. See Ivan Pavkovic and Boris Astrachan, "Reform and Ethics: An Epistolatory Exchange," *Medicus Journal* (Zagreb, 1998).
24. Tvrtko Kulenovic, personal communication.
25. See note 17, this chapter.
26. Rusmir Mahmutćhajic, personal communication.
27. Rusmir Mahmutćhajic, *Living Bosnia: Political Essays and Interviews* (Sarajevo: Oslobodenje, 1994), 203.
28. S. (anonymous), interviews with author, handwritten notes, April 1997, Bosnian Survivors Oral History Archives, Project on Genocide, Psychiatry and Witnessing, University of Illinois at Chicago.

Epilogue

1. There is perpetual controversy over the definitive *Ulysses* text. I refer to the one I used during a college literature course: James Joyce, *Ulysses* (New York: The Modern Library, 1914), 35. See also Stuart Gilbert, *James Joyce's Ulysses* (New York: Vintage Books, 1955).
2. I owe much to Timothy Garton Ash's interweaving of the personal and the historical in his magnificent book *The File: A Personal History* (New York: Random House, 1997).
3. Timothy Garton Ash, *The Magic Lantern: The Revolution of '89 Witnessed in Warsaw, Budapest, Berlin, and Prague* (New York: Random House, 1990).
4. Francis Fukayama, *The End of History and the Last Man* (New York: Avon, 1979).
5. Anselm Keifer is a leading contemporary German artist whose canvases explicitly confront the Nazi legacy. See Corinne Robins, "Your Gold Hair, Margarete," *Arts Magazine*, January 1989, 73–77.
6. *Unfinished Peace: Report of the International Commission on the Balkans* (Washington, D.C.: Carnegie Endowment for International Peace, 1996). Ironically, the Carnegie Endowment had also sponsored the first such commission in 1913. See their republication of their report, *The Other Balkan Wars* (Washington, D.C.: Carnegie Endowment for International Peace, 1993).
7. Even before the 1996 federal elections were held, commentators referred to them as

the war's last battle. They claimed that rather than building common democratic institutions, the elections were consolidating power in new governmental structures that only deepened the ethnic nationalistic divisions and furthered the partitioning of Bosnia. Yet the fact that elections were held at all is one step along the path toward democratization and stabilization.

8. "Memory, so far from being merely a passive receptacle or storage system, an image bank of the past, is rather an active, shaping force; that it is dynamic . . . that it is dialectically related to historical thought, rather than being some kind of negative other to it." Raphael Samuel, *Theatres of Memory* (London and New York: Verso, 1994), x.

9. There is a vast literature on the social, cultural, and psychological ravages of communism. See the recent contributions: Ash, *The File*; Tina Rosenberg, *The Haunted Land: Facing Europe's Ghosts after Communism* (New York: Random House); and Paul Berman, *A Tale of Two Utopias* (New York and London: W. W. Norton & Co., 1996). Also of interest are the classic text Czeslaw Milosz, *The Captive Mind* (New York: Vintage, 1993); Eugenia Semyanovna Ginzburg, *Journey into the Whirlwhind* (New York: Harcourt, Brace & World, 1970); Eva Hoffman, *Exit into History: A Journey Through the New Eastern Europe* (New York: Viking, 1993); and Milan Kundera, *The Book of Laughter and Forgetting* (New York: Penguin, 1981).

10. See Introduction to Part One, note 4.

11. On "outsideness," see chapter 5 in Caryl Emerson, *The First Hundred Years of Mikhail Bakhtin* (Princeton, N.J.: Princeton University Press, 1997), and of course Bakhtin's primary texts listed therein.

12. One clear priority is to tell the history of Serbs' suffering in World War II without succumbing to Serbian nationalism. Some interesting efforts at retelling history have come in the creative arts, such as Emir Kustarica's 1997 film *Underground*.

13. For example, see Zbigniew Brzezinski, "Never Again—Except for Bosnia," *New York Times*, OP-ED, 22 April 1993; John Danton, "Ever Again," *New York Times*, 25 April 1993, Section 4, 1.

14. Walter Benjamin, *Illuminations: Essays and Reflections* (New York: Schocken Books, 1968), 257–258. See also Carolyn Forche, *The Angel of History* (New York: Harper Perennial, 1994).

15. Note the allusion to the remarkable title story of Delmore Schwartz, *In Dreams Begin Responsibilities* (Norfolk, Conn.: New Direction, 1939).

16. Robert Coles, *Doing Documentary Work* (New York and Oxford: Oxford University Press, 1997).

Index

About the Author

Stevan M. Weine, M.D., is an associate professor of psychiatry and co-director of the Project on Genocide, Psychiatry, and Witnessing at the University of Illinois at Chicago.